Herbert Hoover and the Jews

The Origins of the "Jewish Vote" and Bipartisan Support for Israel

SONJA SCHOEPF WENTLING

&

RAFAEL MEDOFF

Copyright © 2012 Sonja Schoepf Wentling & Rafael Medoff
All rights reserved.

ISBN: 1469978423
ISBN 13: 9781469978420

The David S. Wyman Institute for Holocaust Studies

Editorial Board

Dr. Ari Babaknia, Chair

Prof. Ari Goldman

Rabbi Dr. Irving Yitz Greenberg

Yossi Klein Halevi

Prof. Marvin Kalb

Dr. Rafael Medoff

Cynthia Ozick

Prof. Thane Rosenbaum

1200 G St. NW, Suite 800
Washington, D.C. 20005
www.WymanInstitute.org / 202-434-8994

For Sophia and Ian, my two gifts
—Sonja Schoepf Wentling

For Tali, Yoni, Shira, Zev, and Elan, each one an inspiration
—Rafael Medoff

Table of Contents

Acknowledgments	ix
Foreword by Senators Rudy Boschwitz & Tom Daschle	xi
Chapter 1: The "Chief" and the *Shtadlanim*: Parameters of a Friendship	1
Chapter 2: Hoover, Relief, and Pogroms in Eastern Europe, 1919-1922	23
Chapter 3: Hoover, Zionism, and the Palestinian Arab Riots of 1929	41
Chapter 4: Hoover, Anne Frank, and the Problem of Immigration	63
Chapter 5: Hoover and the Holocaust	79
Chapter 6: Hoover and the Origins of the "Jewish Vote"	109
Chapter 7: Republicans, Democrats, and the Birth of Israel	141
Conclusion	161
Bibliography	167
Notes	185
Index	215

Acknowledgments

Herbert Hoover and the Jews was composed in a somewhat unorthodox manner. Each of us had, separately, researched and written about different portions of Hoover's life and career: Prof. Wentling on the pre-presidential and presidential years; Dr. Medoff on the post-presidential period. In the course of bringing the two halves of this book together, we reviewed, commented upon, and on occasion brought about changes in each other's sections. In the end, however, each segment to a great extent reflects the scholarly and literary style of its primary author. We feel confident readers will agree that this was an eminently successful collaboration.

Concordia College kindly provided Prof. Wentling with financial support to undertake research at the Hoover Institution Archives, the American Jewish Archives, and the Center for Jewish History. A Starkoff Fellowship from the American Jewish Archives facilitated Prof. Wentling's research there. The Herbert Hoover Presidential Library Association generously awarded fellowships to both Dr. Medoff (1988-1989) and Prof. Wentling (1997-1998) to facilitate the research that has been incorporated in this book. Special thanks to Nathan Moskowitz, Benyamin Korn, Mordechai Haller, and Elliot Zolin, who provided helpful suggestions at various junctures, and Prof. Rob Stolzer, who kindly assisted with the cover design.

We are also pleased to acknowledge, with deepest gratitude, the assistance provided by the staff of the Herbert Hoover Presidential Library; the Franklin D. Roosevelt Library; the Harry S. Truman Library; the Library of Congress; the American Jewish Historical Society; the American Jewish Archives; the American Friends Service Committee Archives; the Columbia University Library and Archives; the Yale University Library and Archives; the Special Collections Department of the University of North Dakota Library; the Kansas State Historical Society; the University of North Dakota Library; the Central Zionist Archives; the Jabotinsky Institute (Metzudat Ze'ev); the Weizmann Archives; the United Nations Archives; the YIVO Institute of Jewish Research; the Jewish National Library (at Hebrew University); the Public Record Office (London); the Temple Archives (Cleveland); the Hadassah Archives; the Menachem Begin Heritage Center, and the Hoover Institution Archives at Stanford University.

Sonja Schoepf Wentling

Rafael Medoff

April 1, 2012

Foreword

by Rudy Boschwitz and Tom Daschle

If someone had asked us, prior to reading this book, which post-World War I president of the United States had the least interaction with Jews or Jewish concerns, our guess might very well have been Herbert Hoover. After all, others occupied the Oval Office during the most pivotal moments in recent Jewish history. Franklin Roosevelt was president during the Holocaust. Harry Truman was president immediately prior to, and during, Israel's creation. Later presidents figured significantly in the evolution of America-Israel relations and the struggle for Soviet Jewry. Hoover, by contrast, would seem to belong with Calvin Coolidge and Warren Harding among the presidents who had minimal impact on, or interest in, matters of Jewish concern. *Herbert Hoover and the Jews* demonstrates that such assumptions are mistaken and that Hoover in fact had a profound and enduring impact on the Jews and their place in American political culture.

The story of Herbert Hoover and the Jews is, as the following pages reveal, a story of constant surprises. Hoover has long been characterized as heartless toward the common man because of his cautious response to the onset of the Great Depression. Yet we discover in these pages that it was precisely Hoover's heartfelt response to the suffering in World War One-era Europe that saved millions of innocents, including major Jewish communities, from starvation. He also pressed the Polish authorities to act against the pogroms that raged in the aftermath of the war. Hoover's humanitarian missions in Europe won him renown at home and helped catapult him to the White House.

An austere Quaker from the cornfields of Iowa, Hoover neatly fit the stereotype of the midwestern WASP who had nothing in common with Jews. Yet *Herbert Hoover and the Jews* shows that throughout most of his life, Hoover enjoyed the friendship and collaboration of a circle of devoted Jewish associates, including such distinguished public servants as Lewis Strauss, Bernard Baruch, Louis Marshall, and Felix Warburg. "Among all the men who came into my orbit of life," Hoover wrote Strauss in his final years, "you are the one who has my greatest affections..."

Naturally presidents are influenced by the experts and advisers around them. Yet we find Hoover choosing to embrace Zionism despite the fervent anti-Zionist sentiment that dominated his State Department. To what extent Hoover's position was the product of his affection for the biblical prophesies of the ingathering of the Jewish exiles, or his encounters with the devastated Jewish communities of Eastern Europe during World War I, or his admiration, as an engineer, for the Zionist pioneers who were making the desert bloom, is an intriguing question that Professors Wentling and Medoff explore in these pages.

Accounts of America's response to the Holocaust usually mention Hoover only in connection with the tightening of U.S. immigration restrictions by his administration, shortly before Hitler's rise to power. The rest of the story, as it unfolds in the pages to follow, finds the post-presidential Hoover defying expectations by urging admission of more Jewish refugees—particularly a group of 20,000 German Jewish children—to the United States and promoting other efforts to rescue Jews from the Nazis. Having devoted much of our own attention over the years to human rights causes, we know all too well that it is not always the politically popular stance to take.

Finally, and significantly, this book sheds new light on the remarkable origins of the "Jewish vote" in American politics and the emergence of bipartisan support for Israel, which is certainly an issue of utmost relevance today. Although Hoover himself never received significant Jewish electoral support, it was the result of his initiative that the major political parties first began to seriously court Jewish votes in the 1940s, that they both embraced the cause of creating a Jewish state, and that bipartisan backing for Israel ultimately became a permanent part of American political life. As lifelong participants in this bipartisan consensus, we take great pride in the fact that to this day, so many Americans, of all political leanings, continue to appreciate the essential justice of Israel's cause and the compelling moral principles, so similar to our own, that guide its mission as a nation.

The Hon. Rudy Boschwitz, a Republican, represented Minnesota in the United States Senate from 1978 to 1991, and subsequently served as U.S. Ambassador to the United Nations Commission on Human Rights, in Geneva.

The Hon. Tom Daschle, Democrat of South Dakota, served in the United States House of Representatives from 1978 to 1986 and the United States Senate from 1986 to 2004. He is the only U.S. Senator to serve twice as both the Minority and Majority Leader.

Chapter 1

The "Chief" and the *Shtadlanim*: Parameters of a Friendship

May 21, 1917.

The majestic New Willard Hotel must have been quite a sight to behold for the young Jewish traveling shoe salesman when he emerged from the horse-drawn carriage on that bright spring day. Hailed as Washington's first skyscraper when it was renovated in 1904 and located just two blocks from the White House, the Willard had welcomed its share of presidents and prime ministers over the years. Lewis Lichtenstein Strauss, Jr. probably felt a bit like a visitor from another planet on his very first visit to the nation's capital.

Strauss's life in Charleston, and later Richmond, Virginia, had not been without hardship. At the age of ten, he was attacked by a gang of rock-throwers and lost most of the vision in his right eye. During his high school years, he nearly died from typhoid fever. And he was forced to turn down a scholarship to the University of Virginia because his family needed him in its shoe business.[1]

Yet here he was, at age twenty-one, stepping into the ornate building, which because of its clientele of movers and shakers, Nathaniel Hawthorne once said "more justly could be called the center of Washington than either the Capitol or the White House or the State Department." And he was about to present himself, unannounced, to the head of one of the Wilson administration's most important wartime agencies. Fortunately for young Strauss, Herbert C. Hoover, chairman of the U.S. Food Administration and rising political star, was much more impressed by resolve than by resumés. When Strauss, at his mother's urging, told Hoover he had come to volunteer in the effort to feed war-torn Europe, the future president replied: "Hang up your coat."[2]

Hoover deeply admired young men such as Strauss, who were ready to volunteer their talents in times of crisis. Hoover embraced the same ethos. Even after accepting President Woodrow Wilson's call to head the Food Administration in 1917, he had continued leading his earlier relief effort for war-torn Belgium without financial compensation: "I believed the [new] position would carry more moral leadership if I were a volunteer alongside of my countrymen in war," he recalled.³

Lewis Strauss, right, with Herbert Hoover, left, circa 1919.

Reflecting years later on the spirit of volunteerism among young men such as Strauss, Hoover called their selfless service "a tribute to character and idealism."⁴ He attracted and was impressed by men who mirrored his values and commitment to service. A journalist friend once noted that Hoover liked to surround himself with young men who were full of potential and, who, like himself, had to struggle in order to "make it."⁵

Hoover's friendships with Strauss and other American Jews were forged in times of war and driven by a common belief in America's obligation to aid the suffering and to alleviate the chaos in Europe. The upheaval of the Great War would haunt Hoover for the rest of his life and lead him to conclude that America was not just different from Europe but that its uniqueness needed to be preserved.⁶ To Hoover, the American system was the "high tide of a thousand years of human struggle" and with it came responsibility.⁷ He was imbued with a sense of American exceptionalism that was not unlike that of his Jewish friends, who as Americans and as Jews, felt a special obligation toward their co-religionists on the continent. This sense of mission and obligation formed a basis for friendship.

Doing Rather than Talking

Hoover's own philosophy was deeply rooted in his Quaker upbringing and experience as an engineer. Born in 1874 in West Branch, Iowa, to practicing Quaker parents, young Herbert was thoroughly imbued with the values of their faith.⁸ He learned to accept the precepts of hard work, plain living, and earnest faith. He was also deeply influenced by the Quaker sense of harmony, unity, and voluntary community cooperation. A cooperative work ethic, with all the members of the community doing their best in their particular "callings" in life for the good of everyone, would stay with Hoover throughout his private and public careers.[9]

Orphaned at the age of nine, Hoover quickly learned self-reliance. In 1884, at age ten, young Herbert was sent to Newberg, Oregon, to live with his austere uncle and aunt, Henry and Laura Minthorn, where he continued to be raised in the Quaker traditions. His life as an orphan influenced Hoover's later philanthropic concern for underprivileged children and his own sensitivity about personal matters. It also reinforced his humility, quiet manner, and dislike of immodesty. And it honed his strong work ethic and sense of obligation toward family and friends. Hoover's education at Stanford University gave him a sense of community and helped him develop into a successful international mining engineer. By the age of forty he had built a business empire—mining zinc, lead, gold, and silver—that extended from Australia to Burma, Siberia, and California. No less than one hundred thousand men worked for Hoover and he had accumulated a growing fortune of at least one million dollars.[10]

Hoover was a man of public action and his involvement in both international business and humanitarian relief preceded his tenure as president by many years. As an engineer and entrepreneur overseeing his vast business empire, he traveled around the world five times before the advent of World War I.[11] In the six years leading up to 1914, Hoover spent significant time in many European countries, including Great Britain, France, Belgium, Italy, and Germany.

When the guns of August ushered in the Great War, he was sitting in his office in London, nervously vacillating between "small hope and great fear," as he "gaz[ed] out of the windows at the passing troops."[12] Hoover was just a few days shy of his fortieth birthday, but party celebrations were far from his mind. Concerned for his business and the many people it employed, he felt a more personal connection to the Old World than most officials in the Wilson administration. Hoover realized the onset of the war meant that "years of privation" lay ahead for the world and that he needed to do something about it.[13] President Wilson asked his countrymen to "remain neutral in thought and action," but Hoover could not avoid being caught up in the chaos of war. Panic gripped London and the European continent, banks shut down, and thousands of American tourists found themselves stranded. Relying on his ingenuity and connections with fellow engineers, Hoover, always the business manager, assembled a committee to assist American expatriates and greatly relieved the overworked American Consulate in London. They organized the safe return of some 120,000 Americans, from all across Europe, in just six weeks.[14]

The operation that brought Americans safely out of wartime Europe made Hoover very much aware of the deteriorating conditions on the continent, especially in German-occupied Belgium. It also compelled him to put his management skills to use yet again, this time for food relief efforts. Filled with a sense of duty to serve the public, which overcame his shy and reserved persona, Hoover worked tirelessly behind the scenes through influential public men and journalists. His humanitarian imperative was genuine, but he also saw the Belgian Relief enterprise as a testimony to American know-how and the notion that "business could be applied to philanthropy." A British government official characterized Hoover's relief organization as "a piratical state organized for benevolence," with its own flag, the authority to negotiate with the diplomats of the European powers, fix the price of its food rations, and a Chief in charge, who enjoyed virtual diplomatic immunity. The U.S. ambassador to Belgium, Hugh Gibson, was deeply impressed by Hoover's organizational skills: "Hoover is a wonder and has the faculty of getting big-calibre men about him," Gibson wrote in his diary. "We [the relief committee] were not in session more than an hour, but in that time we went over the needs of the Belgian civil population, the means of meeting immediate needs, the broader question of finding food from other parts of the world to continue the work, the problem of getting money from public and private sources to pay expenses, and finally the organisation to be set up in Belgium, England, America, and Holland to handle the work."[15]

As chairman of the Committee for the Relief of Belgium (CRB) and later as head of the U.S. Food Administration, Hoover knew that public relations was one of the keys to the success of such efforts. For example, he skillfully used the threat of news media exposure to persuade the German government to refrain from interfering in the Belgian relief operation. The result was that the people of Belgium were fed throughout all four long years of war. In a speech to a group of Rhodes scholars preparing to depart for Belgium in 1915, Hoover highlighted the significance of American humanitarianism: "When this war is over the thing that will stand out will not be the number of dead and wounded, but the record of those efforts which went to save life."[16]

As President Wilson's food administrator, Hoover managed to double U.S. food shipments to Europe between 1917 and 1918, without the American public having to endure any significant shortages or rationing. Hoover's success was due in no small measure to his use of publicity to encourage food conservation. Through pledge drives, posters, and other forms of advertising, by enlisting the movie industry, and by mobilizing local food conservation committees, Hoover not only managed the nation's food supply but made the idea of voluntary conservation a part of mainstream American culture.¹⁷

Hoover's focus on doing rather than talking permeated the American Relief Administration (ARA), the massive relief enterprise he ran from 51 Avenue Montaigne in Paris. In 1919, ARA headquarters had grown into a busy complex of fifty offices that resembled more a military operation than an aid organization devoted to alleviating human suffering. There were no pictures on the wall but a giant map that tracked all ARA shipping movements and multiple charts listing all the required foodstuffs for no less than twenty-five countries. Even Hoover himself recalled the place as rather "inhuman" and "mechanical" as he reflected upon the unparalleled extent of human disaster that had swept over Europe.¹⁸

Hugh Gibson, seated, in Belgium in 1918.

Americans, Hoover wrote in his memoirs, had never seen real famine, not even during the Civil War. "It is impossible for one who has never seen real famine to picture it—the pallid faces; the unsmiling eyes; the thin, anemic and bloated children; the dead palls over towns where the children no longer play on the streets; the empty shops; the dull, listless movements and dumb grief of the women; the sweep of contagious diseases and the unending procession of funerals."¹⁹

In writing his memoirs, Hoover poured over thousands of telegrams, "frayed papers from the working front," that gave testimony to the overwhelming task of relief and reconstruction. In public, Hoover was loathe to show his emotions, but in private such messages tore at his heart, even many years later. The telegrams still "throb[bed] with human emotion" as he was working on his memoirs in the early 1950s. He held in his hand "a dry Telegram from Harrington: this special train of food has encountered blown-up tracks and bridges. Will be delayed some days." To that message, Hoover appended this reflection: "That is all the record shows but I see that long delayed train en route to save a half million lives in Riga. I see Harrington, with two American sergeants, urging it along. I see the flat car which they were pushing ahead of the slow moving train for safety jumping the rails. I see Harrington and his men rushing for help to repair the track. I see them and their crew shove the pilot car over the embankment. I see them hurrying to gather carts from the villages and farms; passing through the actual fire of a raging battle. And I see Harrington in an empty box car slowly picking out with one finger by the light of a guttering candle that telegram—this very original—on his typewriter."[20]

In its nine months of operation, the American governmental relief operations moved some nineteen million tons of food, seed, clothing, medicine, and other miscellaneous supplies to twenty-two European nations. Two-thirds of the supplies came from the United States, and Americans provided 95 percent of the $3.5 billion cost through congressional appropriations and private donations. Between 1914 and 1919 alone, an estimated 83 million men, women, and children in more than twenty nations received food or other supplies. After governmental relief ceased with the signing of peace in June 1919, relief work was carried on under the leadership of American charitable agencies. By 1923, Hoover's relief efforts would extend to forty-five nations and several hundred million people. Hoover biographer George Nash calculates that "Herbert Hoover was responsible for saving more people than any other person in history."[21] In the eyes of Chicago philanthropist and Sears, Roebuck head Julius Rosenwald, Hoover stood "head and shoulders above any other human being in the preservation of human life."[22]

Friendships Forged by War

Hoover's remarkable success in feeding Europe during and after the war deeply impressed American Jews. They saw in him a man of determination and conviction who leaped into the fray and got things done. "May I as one of 110 million Americans thank you from the bottom of my heart for your great work on behalf of millions of the stricken in Europe," wrote Rabbi Stephen S. Wise, leader of the recently-established American Jewish Congress, in 1919. "I am thinking not only of...your devoted help {to the Jews] in Poland and elsewhere, but...your larger, inclusive service which has so greatly honored the name of our country in all European lands." Hundreds of thousands of Jews in Poland, the Ukraine, and Romania directly benefited from Hoover's humanitarian campaign and in many cases owed their lives to his efforts. In the words of his assistant Lewis Strauss, Hoover was the only one among the western leaders gathered in Paris at the time to "champion Jewish rights" in Poland. It was Hoover's protest that also carried the most weight, because he was, as Strauss explained, the "man from whom

Poland had discovered that she was to receive more, besides promises, than from any individual in Europe, [and] whose friendship she therefore feared to jeopardize and whose counsel she deeply respected..." Hence, it was thanks largely to Hoover's personal intervention that Jewish suffering in Poland was alleviated.²³

Hoover had much in common with a certain segment of the American Jewish leadership. German-born or descended American Jews were typically less attached than East European Jewish immigrants to the Old World lifestyle or religious observances. But they often immersed themselves deeply in the world of Jewish or general philanthropy. Those who were particularly successful in their professions—and there were more than a few—became powerful leaders in the philanthropic world. Strauss, Felix Warburg, Louis Marshall, James Becker and others were inspired by Hoover's record of accomplishment and collaborated with him in providing much needed relief to Europe during and after the war.

The war and its aftermath also had a profound personal effect on Hoover and his Jewish supporters. Hoover's wife, Lou Henry Hoover, acknowledged that these years of war, famine, and revolution took a "psychic toll" on her husband: "A certain definite, and very original, kind of joy of life was stamped out of him by those war years."²⁴

Likewise Lewis Strauss, when asked to tell of some of the experiences he had shared with Hoover in Europe, explained to a gathering of Jewish intellectuals in 1920 that only "some very sad and somber" memories came to mind. At the same time, those times of stress, when tens of thousands of Jews fell victim to murder, pillage, and destruction, highlighted to Strauss the significance of "being a Jew" and the necessity to do his part.²⁵ As for James Becker, his widow noted that "the man who had returned from so overpowering an experience in Europe was very different from the wealthy young Jewish boy from the Middle West..."²⁶

Felix Warburg

Felix Warburg, for his part, did not experience the tragedy of war-torn Europe first hand, but his life was nonetheless profoundly affected by it, because it catapulted him to the forefront of Jewish philanthropy and American Jewish leadership. The challenges associated with a massive humanitarian operation in the midst of war and famine forged a lasting bond between them and turned these American Jews into lifelong supporters and admirers of Hoover. They formed a loose inner circle of Jewish confidantes upon whose judgment Hoover often relied in Jewish matters.

Lewis Strauss had decided to volunteer in order "to bear his part as a man, an American, and a Jew."[27] He came to greatly admire Hoover, and looked at him as a man without prejudice. In an interview given over four decades after their initial encounter and reflecting upon Hoover's tolerance and compassion, Strauss insisted that Hoover did not care about differences with regard to race, politics, or religion, but that he foremost "appreciated talent." "He didn't care whether the man who had it was of his political persuasion. He was absolutely colorless as to race, and he didn't care anything about denomination. He knew that I was a Jew."[28]

Apparently the only instance in which the two discussed their differences occurred in a matter of translation of Scripture related to the meaning of the Lord's Prayer. As Strauss described it, Hoover appeared distressed and apparently "had been concerned since boyhood with the clause 'and lead us not into temptation,'" because it seemed incompatible with his idea of God. Strauss replied that the literal translation of the text was "do not put my faith to the test," a phrase which seemed to satisfy Hoover because it "had evidently bothered him a long time."[29]

There was an understanding and mutual respect between the two men. Strauss, whom Hoover affectionately called "my jewel of a secretary," never worked on Jewish High Holy Days and Hoover himself often took that time off as well, since without Lewis's presence, the operations of the office virtually shut down. Toward the end of his life, Hoover penned a letter to his friend and former secretary that was rare for its expression of emotion and warmth. "Among all the men who came into my orbit of life," Hoover wrote, "you are the one who has my greatest affections, and I will not try to specify the many reasons, evidences or occasions."[30]

Hoover was known to his workers and volunteers as "the Chief"—a term of reverence that stemmed from his days as an engineer in charge of mining operations. "It fit him," recalled Strauss. "No other adjectives were required to describe him." Hoover was a "man of decision," he explained, "he was a man who was never uncertain about what he intended to do—what he wanted to do—what was right to do." It was through doing that Hoover showed his "great human compassion." Strauss explained that Hoover "felt for people who were suffering," and that it was "not a mawkish feeling." The Chief "did not shed tears over the Belgian babies; he did something about it. Compassion led to action on his part, and not to haggling."[31]

After his tenure as Hoover's private secretary for two years, Strauss entered the investment banking firm of Kuhn, Loeb & Co., and also intensified his contribution to the world of philanthropy. His friendship with the Chief continued and led him to get actively involved in Hoover's presidential election campaigns. During Hoover's career as secretary of commerce, their communication was limited, but throughout the 1930s and beyond Strauss initiated contact with his former boss primarily on Jewish matters. It was Strauss who would solicit Hoover's support for the Jewish development of Palestine or advise him concerning Hitler's persecution of German Jewry.

Strauss's own political career did not take off until much later. As an early advocate of atomic energy he chaired the Atomic Energy Commission (AEC) during both the Truman and Eisenhower administrations. The vigorous Democratic opposition to Strauss's nomination as secretary of commerce under Eisenhower, reinforced Strauss's view that Hoover, too, had been mistreated by his opponents when they blamed him for the Great Depression. In responding to the economic crisis, the Chief "did not change his principles—he stuck to his guns," Strauss insisted. Others may have regarded Hoover's consistency as stubbornness, but to Strauss it was a virtue that Hoover was an "unmoved and immovable rock." In later years, when Hoover's reputation finally began to improve in the eyes of the public, Strauss was pleased to note that the American people "had finally come around to their senses."[32]

Felix Warburg, for his part, was not the embodiment of the Horatio Alger rags-to-riches story like Hoover or the epitome of the young idealistic volunteer like Strauss. As one of the sons of the famous Warburg banking family, Felix had grown up with privilege. Light-hearted and a lavish spender, he seemed the least likely candidate to increase the family's fortune and to leave a lasting imprint on American history. His brother Max was running the banking house in Germany, while his brother Paul, an early advocate of the Federal Reserve System, would serve on the first Federal Reserve Board. Yet with his marriage to Frieda Schiff, the only daughter of the German Jewish patriarch and banking magnate Jacob Schiff, Felix entered his father-in-law's investment firm Kuhn, Loeb, & Co. as a partner and would emerge as the leading American Jewish philanthropist after Schiff's death in 1920.[33]

Hoover and the Joint Distribution Committee

It was Warburg's work as chairman of the American Jewish Joint Distribution Committee (JDC, or "the Joint"), the largest Jewish organization for overseas philanthropy, that caught Hoover's eye. Impressed by the Joint's success in organizing relief efforts for Jews in war-torn Europe, Hoover, as head of the Food Administration, called on Warburg to conduct a census of food supplies in New York. It was this first meeting between the two that laid the foundation for a lifelong friendship. Warburg recalled in a radio speech in 1928 that at first he was reluctant to comply with Hoover's request because he was not personally acquainted with the head of the Food Administration. But he found Hoover's personality "irresistible," and he came to admire what he called "[Hoover's] straightforward actions and the strong dictates of his heart."[34]

Warburg, like Hoover, closely identified with American institutions and values, and often proved more the pragmatist than the ideologue. Strongly anti-Bolshevist, he supported the anti-Communist Russian Information Bureau and advocated U.S. military intervention in the Russian Civil War of 1918-1920. Ultimately, however, despite his strong opposition to Communism, Warburg was prepared to deal with the new Soviet regime, if necessary, to aid Russia's Jews. After new U.S. immigration restrictions closed the doors to all but a handful of East European Jews in the early 1920s, Warburg and the JDC negotiated an agreement with the USSR that enabled 125,000 Russian Jews to settle in agricultural colonies in Soviet Crimea. Not unlike Hoover during the Great War, the leaders of the Joint also undertook an aggressive publicity strategy that even tapped into new venues such as silent films. The first such cinematic effort, *Back to the Soil: A Story of Jewish Hope, Struggle and Achievement*, chronicled Warburg's 1927 visit to the Crimean colonies and emphasized the hopeful and healthy life there.[35]

James Becker, a young idealistic Jew from the wealthy German-Jewish elite of Chicago, joined the American Relief Administration in January 1919. He was "tickled to death" to be part of Hoover's operation and was assigned to report on the conditions of Jews in Poland. Just twenty-four years old, Becker considered Hoover all-powerful, like a "king," who "always gets what he wants." The power of the American Relief Administration, according to Becker, was "startling, makers and breakers of governments, because none of the governments of Central or Southeastern Europe can stand without being fed by the Commission." Becker subsequently went to work for the JDC because he wanted to "do more work on the Jewish problem and be where I could be of some value to the Jews. And I am not coming home until I have done something." He was the first JDC worker to cross into Ukraine in 1920, a land torn by civil strife and one of the worst famines in history, and millions of Jews in the crossfire of it all.[36]

Becker's work brought him into close contact with JDC chairman Felix Warburg. Their working relationship eventually grew into a deep and lasting friendship, "almost like father and son." And it was Warburg who invited Becker on a five-month trip around the world on the luxury liner *Resolute* in 1927. While this was quite an adventure in itself, the JDC chairman had also asked his young friend to come along in order to assess the progress of the Jewish settlements in British Mandatory Palestine as well as the Crimea. England had been granted the mandate over Palestine by the League of Nations, based on London's 1917 promise, in the document known as the Balfour Declaration, to "facilitate" the establishment of a "Jewish national home" there. Young East European immigrants, with backing from Diaspora sympathizers including the JDC, had begun the task of draining swamps and building new towns and kibbutzim. Although sympathetic to these efforts, Warburg, like most Reform Jews in the United States, did not favor establishment of a sovereign Jewish state there. He viewed Palestine and the Crimean colonies as equally legitimate havens for East European Jews in need.[37]

The Joint was one of the few private charities allowed to collaborate with ARA relief work in Europe. It was primarily due to Strauss's persistence that American Jewish relief workers gained access to Eastern Europe in the immediate postwar chaos. Boris Bogen, the JDC's chief of relief work in Europe, was able to enter Poland in February 1919 only thanks to the intercession of Strauss and as an unofficial member of the Hoover Food Mission.[38]

Once in Poland, though, Bogen soon realized that the previous logistical difficulties in arranging food shipments paled in comparison to the dangers he encountered as a Jew in Warsaw. There was an "intense feeling of anti-Semitism," he wrote, where "no Jew felt really safe on the streets after dark."[39]

With the World War I-era collapse of multiethnic empires throughout Europe and the formation of nation states such as Poland, Czechoslovakia, and Ukraine in their place, Jews increasingly were viewed by their countrymen as a national and often undesirable minority. Jews suffered doubly—not only did they share in the suffering caused by the breakdown of Europe's economic and social infrastructure, but they also found themselves repeatedly the targets of antisemitic rage. In 1918-1919 alone, more than sixty thousand Jews were murdered in pogroms in Poland and Ukraine. Bogen, who throughout his time as JDC representative in Europe maintained strong relations with officials in the ARA, praised Strauss for his role as facilitator between the ARA and the JDC, describing him as a "very earnest fellow," who was "exceedingly interested in doing the right thing for our people."[40]

Hoover's reputation as someone who could get things done—a "man of decision," as Strauss called him, an almost-omnipotent "king," as Becker admiringly described him—was not the only reason that inspired young Jews to work for the Chief. In many respects, Hoover's transnational endeavors of humanitarian relief reflected the confidence of an increasingly powerful United States, which felt a sense of moral responsibility to be engaged in world affairs. The zeitgeist of progressivism, with its agenda of reform at home and abroad, meshed well with both Hoover's Quaker social philosophy of voluntarism as well as American Jews' growing sense of responsibility toward their fellow Jews in war-torn Europe. Bogen spoke of a "subconscious sense of responsibility existing in the heart of every Jew for the conduct of his co-religionists." For Hoover, relief and reconstruction in Europe was not merely altruistic in character but also had a political objective—to thwart the spread of Bolshevism. For some American Jews, the collaboration between American and Jewish relief efforts symbolized a kind of blending of American and Jewish values in the pursuit of a more just world.[41]

German-born or descended Jews represented the most accomplished, affluent, and influential segment of American Jewry during the World War I era, although numerically they were a minority in the community, thanks to a recent large influx of Russian and other East European Jewish immigrants. Men such as Strauss and Warburg, while proudly identifying as Jews, were acutely sensitive to anything that could potentially undermine their acceptance by American society. They abhorred radicalism and Jewish nationalism, and tread carefully on hot button issues such as immigration and Zionism. They rejected the Zionist goal of a sovereign Jewish state in Palestine, fearing it would compromise their own status in the United States. They preferred what came to be known known as "non-Zionism"—building up Palestine as a haven for European Jewish refugees and as a Jewish cultural center, but short of sovereignty and not involving any expected immigration of American Jews. This enabled them to work for development of the Holy Land for those Jews who might need it, or without threatening their own status as Jews in the diaspora.[42]

Hoover's circle of Jewish acquaintances also included Louis Marshall, the most prominent American Jewish leader during the 1920s and a longtime Republican. Marshall, an attorney who came from humble beginnings like Hoover, was raised in a religiously observant home but joined New York City's most prominent Reform synagogue, Temple El-Emanuel. Like Hoover, he saw the world and his obligation to his fellow men through the prism of his faith. Marshall was a staunch defender of individual liberty, a strong advocate of human rights, and a conservative on social and constitutional issues. At the same time, he was a Wilsonian on the international stage and imbued with a sense of responsibility to help the poor and downtrodden masses of Europe. Marshall was also a leader of the American Jewish Committee (AJC), a prominent Jewish defense organization that favored discreet behind-the-scenes contacts with government officials, a method of engagement reminiscent of the old world *shtadlan* [court Jew] rather than the modern era. While the AJC was officially anti-Zionist until shortly before Israel's creation in 1948, a number of its most prominent members, including Marshall, were non-Zionist. It was Marshall, in fact, who would broker an important agreement with the Jewish Agency for Palestine in 1929, which significantly increased the role of non-Zionists in the development of the Holy Land.[43]

Marshall actively championed Jewish rights at the Paris Peace Conference following World War I. He and his colleagues strongly believed the solution for the persecuted people of Europe was to be found in Europe, not through mass immigration to the United States. The influx of large numbers of East European, Yiddish-speaking Jews to the U.S. during the years before World War I changed the demographic balance of American Jewry and threatened the dominant position of the Warburgs and the Marshalls in the U.S. Jewish leadership. They were not anxious for another such influx. When *American Hebrew* editor Reuben Fink publicly suggested in 1919 that two million Polish Jews be brought to the United States, he received an angry retort from Marshall, who warned that such a wave of immigration would "arouse the worst outbreaks of anti-Semitism in the United States that have ever occurred." He accused Fink of "endangering the peace and quiet of the Jews of America," and blasted the proposal as "the most shocking and perilous suggestion that has ever come to my attention." Not incidentally, Marshall was also perturbed by the fact that Fink had taken it upon himself to propose such an immigration scheme rather than working through proper channels and leaving it to the AJC to deal with such matters.[44]

Louis Marshall

There is some irony in the fact that at the very time Wilsonians such as Marshall were pushing for the president's new diplomacy overseas, the United States itself was entering a period of introspection and growing nativism. In the first six months of 1919 alone, while the Paris Peace Conference delegates were hashing out the terms of the postwar settlement, eleven bills endorsing stricter immigration laws were introduced in the House of Representatives and five were proposed in the Senate. The legislation primarily targeted immigrants from Eastern and Southern Europe that is, Jews, Slavs, and Italian Catholics. With the subsequent passage of the Immigration Acts of 1921 and 1924, the United States ushered in a new chapter in its history by establishing a system of restrictive immigration quotas based on national origin.[45]

Nativism, together with anti-Communism stoked by the rise of the Soviet Union, fueled antisemitism in the United States as well. American industrial icon Henry Ford launched a vicious and prolonged antisemitic attack by publishing the *Protocols of the Elders of Zion*, a forgery that alleged a Jewish world conspiracy to destroy Christianity and form a world government. Ford serialized the *Protocols* in his newspaper, *The Dearborn Independent*, and later reprinted them in a series of widely distributed booklets. Hoover was a member of the American Committee on the Rights of Religious Minorities, an anti-discrimination group headed by Rev. Arthur J. Brown. In December 1920, the committee circulated a petition expressing indignation at the spread of antisemitic propaganda nationwide. Although the petition did not make specific reference to Henry Ford, it did vigorously refute the anti-Jewish stereotypes Ford was trying to popularize.[46]

Strauss felt certain about Hoover's moral compass, whether the Chief spoke out against antisemitism or not. In Strauss's view Hoover had demonstrated both in Europe and in the United States that he was on the side of justice and tolerance. In an essay published in *The American Hebrew* titled, "Herbert C. Hoover and the Jews," he hailed Hoover as the only U.S. government official to effectively press Poland and its prime minister to act against the pogromists. Strauss was particularly impressed by the fact that Hoover stood up for the Jews when no one was really looking or listening. Just a few months after his return from Europe in the fall of 1919, Hoover addressed a convention of the Polish National Committee in Buffalo, New York, and reminded the audience there that "whatever the qualities of the Jewish people in Poland may be in the minds of their critics, it must be borne in mind that their present position is the doing of the Gentile and all the world has yet to pay for these accumulated centuries of injustice." Hoover hoped that the non-sectarian work of the Joint would place "the whole Jewish problem in Poland on a new footing to which I have every reason to look forward with confidence."⁴⁷ The persistence and intensification of antisemitism in Poland during the years to follow, however, would prove Hoover's optimism to be misplaced.

The Presidential Campaign of 1928

After returning to the United States that fall, a number of Hoover's "politically amateur friends," as he called them, urged him to run for president in 1920. Although a registered Republican, he had served in a Democratic administration and conceivably could have aligned himself with either party. Riding a surge of public popularity because of his achievements in Europe, Hoover unexpectedly won New Hampshire's Democratic primary while he was still trying to make up his mind whether to run at all. He also later won the Michigan Democratic primary, but by that time had decided to pursue the Republican nomination. However, despite the best efforts of "eager supporters from the ARA, the Food Administration, and the engineering societies," Hoover's campaign suffered a mortal blow when he was defeated in the primary in his home state of California. When the dust had settled, the new Republican president, Warren Harding, appointed Hoover Secretary of Commerce, a post in which he would continue in the administration of Calvin Coolidge. After eight years of peace and prosperity—during which he briefly flirted with the idea of running for president in 1924—Hoover emerged as the Republican frontrunner for 1928.⁴⁸

Hoover's Jewish friends strongly supported his 1928 campaign. Yet despite the large Jewish population in New York State and the possibility they could tip its crucial 45 electoral votes, neither Hoover nor his Jewish supporters made any effort to gain from his record on Jewish issues, such as his work with the Joint. (The only exception was the decision by the JDC's leaders to postpone the release of Hoover's endorsement of the Crimea project until after Labor Day in order to amplify its political value.) Two Hoover-for-President ads in *New Palestine* that autumn featured quotes from prominent Jews praising Hoover in general terms, without specifying either Hoover's aid to European Jewry or his support for Zionism. In the first, a quote from Marshall touted him as someone who "literally saved millions of lives...[and who] added justice to the good name of our country." A statement from Strauss emphasized that "together with the thousands of men and women who have worked with Mr. Hoover, I look back upon the years of my association with him as the most useful and inspiring period of my life." Herman Bernstein, a prominent Zionist journalist and activist, was cited as praising Hoover as the "only American who is accepted by the world as a representative of the best that is in the American nation." Bernstein called Hoover's declarations on religious liberty and denunciation of bigotry "direct and unmistakable," and argued that "Mr. Hoover's life-work has been one uninterrupted demonstration of deep human sympathy, of his big-heartedness and broadmindedness. His great relief work at home and abroad swept aside religious and racial frontiers and barriers." The second ad, signed by Marshall, Strauss, Bernstein, Julius Rosenwald, Felix Warburg, and several others asserted: "The proven qualities of Herbert Hoover make him preeminently the logical choice for the great office of President of the United States. His humanity, so well known to millions and particularly to Jews who suffered in an area where humanity seemed to vanish in the jaws of war and famine, needs no further mention."[49]

The notion that Hoover's aid to European Jewry, not to mention his support for Zionism, "needs no further mention" dovetailed with the German-American Jewish elite's rejection of the very idea of a candidate making narrow appeals for the votes of a specific ethnic group. They feared any suggestion that Jews voted as a bloc or cared only about Jewish concerns would separate American Jews from non-Jews and incite antisemitism. Distinctly Jewish political behavior would lead to the political segregation of the Jews, they believed. When the prominent Jewish author and playwright Israel Zangwill asserted, in a 1923 speech, that a "Jewish vote" would be advantageous, Marshall repudiated him immediately. Likewise when Strauss, during the 1928 race, inquired about soliciting Jewish votes for Hoover, Marshall rebuffed him: "I would consider it as a most serious error if any effort were made to create a Jewish Campaign Committee. Were such an attempt made I would attack it openly. It would, in my judgment, be an insult to the Jews, who are the most independent of voters."[50]

In the mid and late 1920s, the Democratic Party sought to attract the large urban vote by portraying itself as the party of immigrants, minorities, and the working class. The Democrats' choice in 1928 of New York Governor Al Smith, the first Catholic presidential nominee, strengthened this perception of the Democrats as the 'Party of the People.' Marshall noted that Smith "is popular with the Jews of [New York City's Lower] East Side, because he has always sympathized with them in their trouble and has exhibited strong friendship for them." He believed an election-eve Republican overture to Jewish voters would be seen as hypocritical since the GOP had not previously demonstrated any specific interest in Jewish issues. Marshall was convinced, moreover, that such appeals would be futile, given the fact that the Democrats had a more attractive record on specific

Jewish concerns such as immigration or Jewish appointments to public service positions.[51]

Warburg, too, rejected any last minute appeal to Jewish voters. The Chief was not like professional politicians who purposely catered to Jews in order to get their votes, he insisted. According to Warburg, Hoover was uncomfortable with the very idea of advertising his actions on behalf of the Jews. "Knowing Mr. Hoover as I do, I am convinced that these and other facts [Hoover's humanitarian record] can only be used in the campaign without his consent and therefore with great circumspection. He is extremely sensitive and would be embarrassed to find political capital manufactured from actions which he feels are personal, and only in the line of duty to his fellowmen." Moreover, Warburg contended, Hoover's sympathy for the Jews was based on principle and not trivial campaign rhetoric:

> His respect for the religious beliefs of others is a cardinal principle with him, not a campaign platitude. As a Jew, I look forward to his election; not because he is an especial friend of the Jews for I do not believe that his feelings toward Jews differ in the slightest degree from his attitude toward his other fellow citizens and he has not followed the practice of the professional politician, who flaunts friendship for Jews as a catch-vote. On the contrary, Hoover's love of toleration and fair-play, and his use of properly qualified assistants without regard to their faith are qualities which appeal to me as a self-respecting Jew.[52]

Hoover's speeches and radio broadcasts did not do justice to his "rare character," Warburg insisted. Hoover was not a typical candidate, "but a friend of human beings, unselfishly interested in the welfare and happiness of the citizens at large. That is why most of the people who have worked under him, and to whom he has sometimes given quite difficult tasks, admire him and, not only that but love him." Smith's narrow focus on repealing prohibition made him better suited for "a brewers' convention" than the "elite of the Democratic party," Warburg charged. Hoover, by contrast, was a visionary and could inspire people to good citizenship.[53]

The Democrats' nomination of the first Catholic candidate sparked a national debate over religious bigotry. Republicans and leading Protestant magazines hailed prohibition as a moral cause and made it their central criticism of Smith. Some extreme opponents of Smith, especially in the South, extended their anti-prohibition rhetoric into attacks on Smith's "Romanism," that is the suggestion that Smith, as a Catholic, would be secretly loyal to the Vatican.

The Democrats and many leading Catholic periodicals sought to focus attention on what they called the bigotry of the Republican party. The National Republican Committee insisted that anti-Catholic attacks were condoned neither by the party nor its candidate. Nonetheless, by the autumn of 1928, some Smith supporters not only were accusing the Republican Party of intolerance, but were also criticizing Hoover for not speaking out on the matter. Finally, on September 29, Hoover publicly expressed his "indignation" over a pro-Republican broadside which asserted that he and the GOP were counting on America's women to prevent the country from becoming "Romanized and rum-ridden."[54]

The debate intensified when Henry C. Hansbrough, a former Republican senator from North Dakota, twice wrote to Hoover, accusing the campaign of condoning religious bigotry. In an address in Minneapolis, Hansbrough went so far to demand Hoover's withdrawal from the race. Hansbrough was not exactly a disinterested party; he headed a group called the Smith Independent Organization. Still, Hansbrough's stature as a former senator and his previous affiliation with the GOP gave his attacks widespread attention in the news media and compelled the Hoover camp to respond vigorously.[55]

In addition to denying the substance of Hansbrough's charges, Hoover and his supporters strongly criticized the senator's own credentials. Senator Reed Smoot of Utah, for instance, characterized Hansbrough as a "disgruntled office-seeker" and a publicity hound, noting that Hansbrough's letters were made public before Hoover himself received them. Smoot, a member of the Mormon Church, not only fervently denied the charges that Hoover was intolerant, but turned the tables on the senator from North Dakota, saying Hansbrough himself was guilty of bigotry since he had attacked Smoot solely because of his Mormon faith.[56]

Hansbrough did not help his own cause by making wild allegations about Hoover supposedly holding large oil concessions in Colombia and Mexico, protecting British business, and endorsing imperialism. It was to be expected that Republican National Committee spokesman Henry J. Allen would call Hansbrough's attacks "a most malicious campaign of libel and slander." But even John J. Raskob, chairman of the Democratic National Committee, declared: "The country is in a sorry state when two men contending for highest office above reproach have got to be subjected to the indignities of slander, lies and charges of all kinds which have not even the slightest foundation in fact."[57]

Financier and political advisor Bernard Baruch, another member of Hoover's circle of Jewish acquaintances, was particularly irritated by Hansbrough's blasts. Hoover, as "the son of Quaker ancestors," certainly "knows what it means to be persecuted," Baruch declared. Baruch, who worked closely with Hoover when they both served in the Wilson administration (Baruch chaired the War Industries Board), recalled Hoover's stirring words in his acceptance speech at the Republican convention: "By blood and conviction I stand for religious tolerance both in act and spirit." Never, Baruch insisted, "has there been a more courageous declaration of the idea that there must be and shall be no exhibition of religious intolerance in this campaign."[58] In a letter of appreciation to Baruch, Hoover noted that he had tried his best to "keep this [the religious] issue out of national politics." The problem, however, was that "there is no controlling the extremists on either side. It is my impression that if we could stop discussion on the whole question of tolerance by speakers on both sides and thus discourage the engendering of further feeling on the subject, it would be infinitely better both for your side and for the future of the country."[59]

While some Jews spoke out in praise of Hoover's tolerance, others sought to rally Jewish support for the Republican nominee by emphasizing his humanitarian record. One New York City rabbi, Abraham Burstein, prepared a pamphlet in Yiddish and English touting Hoover's wartime service to European Jewry, calling him "The Modern Moses of War-Stricken Europe," who "led Israel out of the Slavery of Starvation and Despair." Several hundred thousand copies were distributed in the New York area. Herman Bernstein, editor of the New York *Jewish Tribune*, published a series of articles praising Hoover's humanitarian record and delivered lectures endorsing his candidacy. Chicago philanthropist and Sears, Roebuck head Julius Rosenwald likewise argued that Hoover stood "head and shoulders above any other human being in the preservation of human life."[60]

Bernard Baruch, left, with Al Smith.

In the end, neither the enthusiastic pronouncements of his Jewish friends nor memories of Hoover's relief efforts sufficed to win over many Jewish voters in 1928. Although polling data from 1928 is not as thorough as the data available in later years, studies of a number of cities offer some sense of how Jews voted in the Smith-Hoover race. After the election, Lewis Strauss commissioned New York Judge and Democratic Party activist Samuel Rosenman to analyze voting trends among ethnic minorities such as Jews, Italians, Irish, and African Americans in selected election districts of New York State. Comparing votes cast for president, governor, lieutenant governor, and assemblyman, Rosenman concluded that in districts with a large Jewish population, there was considerably stronger support for the Jewish candidates for governor and lieutenant governor. But when it came to the presidential race, the vote was more or less in conformity with the political complexion of the district. In the poor, congested, and predominantly Democratic districts in New York City and its environs—areas with a large concentration of Jewish residents—Smith carried the vote overwhelmingly. In the affluent and mostly Republican districts upstate—regions with few Jewish voters—Hoover received the average or better than average level of support for a GOP candidate. Overall, Rosenman concluded, Smith received about 72% of Jewish votes in New York City. Later analyses by political scientists of heavily-Jewish voting districts in other cities concluded that Smith received 61% of Jewish votes in Boston, 60-65% in Chicago, and 48% in Philadelphia. Based on these results, it seems Smith received about 67% of the Jewish vote nationwide. It would take many years, and sharply changed circumstances, before a significant number of Jewish voters would again back a Republican presidential candidate.[61]

There were no major issues of Jewish controversy at stake in the 1928 election, leaving Jewish voters to make their selection based on other factors. In the broadest sense, Jews naturally inclined to support the candidate and party that were most closely identified with minorities and the working class. The GOP was perceived by many as the party of WASP culture and privilege, whereas during the 1920s, the Democrats were increasingly regarded as the party that cared about the needs of the urban working man. Moreover, their nominee was a member of a religious minority; some Jews naturally assumed he would be more understanding of the needs of other religious minorities. There was also a more specific reason Jews would prefer Smith to Hoover. The grandson of European immigrants, and himself a resident of Manhattan's Lower East Side, Smith repeatedly used his position as a New York State Assemblyman (1903-1915) to champion the interests of the immigrant generation. Whether it was a relatively minor issue such as supporting legalization of playing baseball on Sundays, or his vice-chairmanship of the Factory Investigating Commission, which pressed for better working conditions in the wake of the Triangle Shirtwaist Company fire, Smith earned a reputation as someone who cared about ordinary working people. He continued promoting progressive labor legislation as governor of New York in 1918-1920 and 1922-1926. While Jewish voters in 1928 undoubtedly harbored a sense of appreciation for what Hoover did to aid their European coreligionists during and after World

War I, they were understandably more inclined to support a candidate who helped them and their families.⁶²

Hoover's Jewish friends did not spend much time wringing their hands over the failure of most Jewish voters to support their man; they had not expected the results to be much different. They rejoiced that, as Warburg put it, "our Chief is now the nation's chief" and eagerly looked forward to Hoover's administration. And American Jews such as Warburg, Baruch, Strauss, and Bernstein would continue to support Hoover for president in 1932, when the Chief himself conceded that he just "had to fight it out to the end." His Jewish friends did not abandon him just as he had not abandoned their brethren in one of the most trying years of Jewish history. In an essay titled, "What Hoover has Done for the Jews," Republican Jewish activist Edward Rosenblum emphasized the Chief's "humanitarian and personal interest" in the Jews. Writing in 1932, Rosenblum noted that Hoover counted prominent American Jews among his "very dear and intimate personal friends" because he had stood with them during the dark years of pogroms and famine in postwar Eastern Europe.⁶³

Chapter 2

Hoover, Relief, and Pogroms in Eastern Europe, 1919-1922

Friday, April 11, 1919 began much like any other day for Herbert Hoover, at his desk at 51 Avenue Montaigne in Paris, headquarters of the American Relief Administration, the vast postwar aid initiative he managed. Meetings, phone calls, and correspondence crowded every minute of the morning—until Lewis Strauss, pale and visibly shaken, burst into the room with an urgent telegram from Poland.

Recalling the episode some time later, Strauss described how Hoover's hand trembled as he read it, and his face, "smooth as a boy's when I knew him first, not quite three years ago, and now seamed with an infinite number of fine lines, the mark of vicarious suffering—seemed to grow suddenly older."[64] Not that Hoover was a stranger to receiving bad news. Since Hoover's arrival in Paris the previous December, the ARA had been constantly in crisis mode. Starvation, revolution, and disease were a daily reality. As Hoover put it, "The Third and Fourth Horsemen of the Apocalypse—famine and pestilence—were experienced and hard riders."[65]

But this telegram from Colonel William Grove, the ARA's chief representative in Poland, brought bad news of a different sort: Polish soldiers in Pinsk had shot and killed thirty-seven Jews. Moreover, Grove reported, there were indications that the killings had taken place at a gathering of Jews that had been called to "arrange proper distribution of [the U.S. aid ship] *Westward Ho's* cargo or American financial relief."[66] In addition to the obvious human tragedy of innocent lives lost, Hoover had to consider the broader danger that the episode would cause the American public to question the wisdom of getting mixed up in Europe's postwar turmoil altogether. Hoover's swift intervention would be necessary.

This was not the first time since the armistice that Poland's Jews had been ravaged by violence. In fact, although hostilities officially ceased on November 11,

1918, chaos prevailed in many regions for years to follow. Ethnic rivalries flared and starvation spread throughout central and eastern Europe against the backdrop of the disintegrating Austrian and Russian empires. In Poland, anti-Jewish pogroms erupted on the very day the guns of August fell silent, and reached a peak in the spring of 1919. Policymakers in Washington and across Europe, and especially the delegates to the Paris Peace Conference, viewed these developments with mounting alarm. Would these antisemitic outbursts undermine the negotiators' efforts to bring about the reorganization and reconstruction of postwar Europe?

Planning Poland's Future

The future of Poland, in particular, had emerged as one of the most intractable problems at the conference, and a special Commission on Polish Affairs had been established to sort out competing claims by Bolsheviks, White Russians, Ukrainians, Latvians, Estonians, and Baltic Germans with regard to Poland's eastern frontier.[67] The Allies aimed to achieve a postwar settlement that would both keep Germany in check and erect a *cordon sanitaire* of new nation states as a bulwark against the advance of Bolshevik Russia. Towards the end, most of the delegates were inclined to grant Poland favorable territorial terms and a wide degree of self-rule. They assumed that Jewish concerns could be adequately addressed by the Polish government and not require any outside interference. The pogroms challenged that assumption.[68]

In the small Polish industrial town of Kielce on November 11, 1918, mob assaults on Jewish residents left four dead and at least 250 wounded. Less than two weeks later in Lwow (Lemberg), Jews found themselves caught in the middle of the Polish-Ukrainian struggle for control of Eastern Galicia. Hundreds of Jewish civilians were victimized by both Polish and Ukrainian pogromists.[69] Col. Grove, surveying the situation in February 1919, saw a connection between the pogroms and Poland's shortage of food and basic supplies.[70] He warned his colleagues that unless the "Inter-allied Economic Council takes steps to relieve this situation by furnishing raw material, the ground is fertile for [even more] trouble."[71]

Leaders of the Joint Distribution Committee, in New York City, took a keen interest in the situation in Poland, but initially balked at Hoover's request to allocate $3 million in support of the ARA's relief efforts there. The JDC preferred to use the funds for long-term reconstruction rather than immediate relief, to be managed by its own supervisors. Hoover read the riot act to the JDC's European director, Boris Bogen: "Here are people actually starving and they are talking of constructive measures, of 'sending their own supervisors.' It's all tommy-rot." Lewis Strauss, deeply worried about the peril to Polish Jewry, was particularly anxious to mend fences between the ARA and the JDC and enable Bogen to take part in relief efforts there. "Unless the Jewish people had some representative to attend to their specific needs," they would not receive "their full share of assistance," he implored.[72] The JDC ultimately acceded to Hoover's request, and in fact went further, agreeing to cover a pledge made by the cash-strapped National Polish Relief Committee of Chicago. Having repaired relations with the ARA, Bogen was invited by Hoover to join his exploratory Food Mission to Poland in February 1919.[73] The purpose of the mission was to survey conditions in Poland in general, without specific reference to the Jews, but Strauss assigned ARA staff member James Becker to send Hoover private reports on the status of Polish Jewry. Strauss and Hoover may not have agreed with Becker's view that "there should be no relief rendered until there was established in any place demanding relief, a stable government which would insure absolute justice," but they appreciated the need for a first hand assessment of the situation.

Becker spent his first several weeks in Lwow, which he described as "by far the worst spot in Poland." There were no couriers or lines of communication that he could utilize and for several weeks he felt entirely cut off from the rest of the world.[74] Supervising general food distribution while simultaneously compiling his reports to Hoover, Becker ruffled more than a few feathers. The local Jewish Relief Committee fretted that Jews were not receiving their fair share of the food allotments, while Poles considered him "anti-Polish" because they suspected he favored the Jews. A weary Becker wrote, only half in jest, about the "fine prospects of being decorated in a long wood box."[75]

The JDC's Bogen, in his memoirs, wrote of the intense antisemitism he found in Poland during the mission: "[The] hunger of the Jew was a special problem, because the Jew was regarded as being apart, an inhabitant by sufferance of whom it would be well to be rid, an enemy of Poland."[76] When the ship *Westward Ho,* a joint venture of the JDC and the National Polish Relief Committee, arrived at Danzig, it could be simply handed over to the Polish government for distribution, Bogen noted with envy; but cargo assigned to Poland's Jews had to be supervised every step of the way to ensure it would find its way to the Jewish population.[77]

Bogen and Becker both realized that while the economic needs were immediate and real, long-term guarantees were necessary to ensure Jewish survival. "In America we had talked blandly of the economic rehabilitation of the Polish Jews,"

Bogen recalled. "We thought we need but enter and lift the Jew to his feet and set him joyously on his old way. But it was more than economic well-being of the Jew that had been destroyed; the spirit was in the dust and even the meaning of life had been forgotten, since life had not been seen these four years, but only existence."[78] Likewise, Becker concluded that economic aid alone would not protect the Jews and expressed to Strauss the hope that "America [will] demand in the strongest terms full freedom for the Jews of Poland." The leverage to do so, he proposed, would be a threat to withhold U.S. loans.[79] President Wilson himself had already intimated that something of that sort could be in the offing. Frustrated by the Polish government's tough negotiating stance in Paris and continued military operations against the Lithuanians and Ukrainians, Wilson had warned Polish Prime Minister Ignace Paderewski "if the Polish Government should not promptly and fully comply with the wishes of the [Allied Supreme] Council [to cease hostilities], I think that it could be made to comply by a declaration that all of the supplies now going and to go to it will be stopped." Wilson told colleagues at the Paris conference that if Poland were uncooperative, "we could, if necessary, threaten to stop the victualing."[80]

Support for an independent Poland had been one of the core principles of Wilsonian foreign policy and a new postwar order in Eastern Europe, but anti-Jewish atrocities in Poland could further erode American goodwill. The Wilson administration had already suggested a possible link between the treatment of Polish Jewry and the future of U.S.-Polish relations. After earlier reports of pogroms, Secretary of State Robert Lansing instructed the U.S. ambassador in France to warn Polish officials that "if these reports [about pogroms] are true, the sympathy of the American people for Polish aspirations will undoubtedly be affected."[81] The ambassador reported back that Polish nationalist leader Roman Dmowski dismissed the reports of massacres as exaggerations. Dmowski insisted that Poles were "blameless for such crimes," since Poland found itself in a state of anarchy, where German and Russian prisoners as well as Bolshevik revolutionaries were inciting disorder. Reports about pogroms had "little foundation in truth" and amounted to "organized propaganda" by Polish and Russian Jews."[82]

Responding to the Pogrom

The April 1919 pogrom in Pinsk brought matters to a head.[83] After reading the telegram about the killings, Hoover instructed Strauss to summon the Polish

Prime Minister to the ARA office for a frank one-on-one. Hoover's long association with Paderewski began when the Polish leader, an accomplished concert pianist, visited the West Coast in the early 1890s and Hoover, then a student at Stanford, arranged for him to perform on campus. They subsequently became more closely acquainted as a result of Hoover's wartime relief efforts in Eastern Europe. In his memoirs, Hoover recalled that Paderewski was a shrewd negotiator at the Paris Peace talks, but "was not particularly strong as an administrator" and required from the Americans a whole staff of expert advisers for his governmental departments of finance, railways, and food.[84]

Their meeting in April 1919 began with what Strauss characterized as a "crushing experience," when an American doughboy accidentally sat down on the Polish prime minister's silk top hat. Frantic aides secured a flat iron to straighten the hat, but its slightly wrinkled appearance matched the atmosphere of the tense meeting.[85]

The Polish leader was adamant that the victims in Pinsk were Bolshevists and traitors against the Polish state, who deserved their fate.[86] Hoover was not impressed. He insisted it was "impossible" and "unwise" to level such a "blanket accusation" against all Jews of Poland. He showed Paderewski the Warsaw telegram, which quoted representatives of the American Jewish Committee on the ground in Poland, reporting a massacre of unarmed Jewish civilians, not Bolshevist agents. Moreover, the killings took place during a gathering at a synagogue to receive American funds and relief supplies.[87] Stories of Jewish persecution in Poland were filling American newspapers, Hoover warned, and in the light of U.S. relief to Poland, the Pinsk attack "could develop into a most serious embarrassment to all of us."[88] More bad press about Polish behavior was undermining the country's position at the peace negotiations and as a recipient of Western aid. Paderewski needed to recognize the "extreme gravity" of the situation, Hoover insisted; the "most vigorous investigation should be made at once."[89]

While Paderewski was considering Hoover's warning, more trouble was brewing. The new U.S. envoy to Warsaw, Hugh S. Gibson, strolling through the city's Jewish Quarter on May 1, found the streets nearly empty; talk of another pogrom was in the air, he reported, and the Jews "were not taking any chances."[90]

On May 7, a Polish mob aroused by an anti-Jewish blood libel murdered eight Jews in the town of Kolbuszowa. On May 27, pogromists struck in Czestochowa, slaying five Jewish residents, including a doctor, who was set upon while trying to aid the other victims.[91] Reports of attacks by Polish soldiers on Jews in Vilna and Minsk soon followed.

The news horrified Americans. "Jews Massacred, Robbed by Poles," a front-page *New York Times* article announced. Protest meetings were staged from coast to coast, including a rally at Madison Square Garden in New York City on May 21 that attracted tens of thousands of participants.[92] "[I]f America stands for anything in her service of humanity, then let America speak now," declared keynote speaker Charles E. Hughes, the 1916 Republican presidential nominee.[93] He charged that American newspapers were "suppressing news of the persecution and slaughter of Jews in Poland because they were anxious to establish Poland as a strong and independent nation, and were unwilling to print news which would discredit her."[94] As political pressure mounted, the U.S. Senate adopted a resolution condemning the pogroms and urging President Wilson to raise the issue with Polish officials at the Paris peace talks. Louis Marshall called on the president to press the Poles for concrete steps to protect the Jews and punish the perpetrators of "these crimes against humanity."[95] Prime Minister Paderewski, recognizing the need to restore Poland's image in the eyes of American public opinion, belatedly heeded Hoover's advice and formally asked President Wilson to appoint a committee to investigate the Pinsk killings.[96] Hoping to quell "tendentious rumors" about Poland's intolerance and "to put and end to this unworthy activity [demonstrations against Poland]," the prime minister requested "a special mission to Poland, in order to investigate and report on the true state of things, thus dispelling the accusations, under which my country is laboring."[97] The request may have been layered in hubris, but the bottom line was clear.

Polish American organizations, fighting a rear guard action in defense of Poland's good name, vehemently denied any pogroms had occurred and asked the State Department to release all reports written by the American Ambassador in Warsaw, believing they would vindicate their claims. "Individual quarrels and outbreaks of looting, unavoidable in a half-starved and ravaged country, had been exaggerated and colored," W. O. Gorski of the Polish Information Bureau insisted. The Pinsk massacre was an execution of Bolshevists, he claimed, seconding the Polish authorities' position.[98] As the war of words escalated, rallies by Polish workers spilled over into street fights with Jewish protesters in New York City, Chicago, Milwaukee, and elsewhere.[99]

"The continuation of this agitation [by protesters in the United States] is likely to do the future of Poland in American estimation a great deal of harm," Hoover wrote President Wilson on June 2. "I do believe that regardless of the temporary obsession of the Polish Government for territorial aggrandizement, it must be a fundamental principle with us that we must support the Polish Republic."[100]

A quick resolution of the matter was not only in the best interest of the Polish republic but also Poland's Jews, Hoover emphasized. The Jews in Poland, he said, had not been especially supportive of the new Polish state and to some extent had even been receptive to Bolshevik influence. He urged Wilson to include on the investigative committee two prominent American Jews who might be able to convince Polish Jews that their best hope for a better life was a democratic Poland.[101] Hoover strongly believed that democracy and prosperity were the most effective barriers against the spread of Bolshevism. An independent democratic Polish republic was essential to guard against the spread of Bolshevism, help maintain stability in Eastern Europe and, in the process, protect the lives and liberty of the Jewish minority.[102] In the end, Wilson chose Henry Morgenthau, Sr., former U.S. ambassador to the Ottoman Empire, to serve on the committee. Some American Jewish leaders were unhappy at the selection of Morgenthau, fearing he might bend over backwards to demonstrate his impartiality. Jacob Schiff cabled a warning to Morgenthau not to be "misled by Poles" in assessing the facts; "the eyes of Jewry are upon you."[103] James Becker, in letters to his parents back in Chicago, likewise worried that the "vain" Morgenthau might "fall easy prey to the flattery of those oily, clever Poles." Only the League of Nations, not Jewish leaders or investigatory committees, could really make a difference when it came to minority protection, Becker wrote.[104]

Protection for Minorities

In June 1919, in the midst of the controversy over the Pinsk pogrom, Poland became the first country to sign the agreements fashioned at the Paris peace talks known as the Minority Treaties, pledging to safeguard the basic rights of religious, racial, and linguistic minority groups residing within its borders.[105] Louis Marshall, who chaired the *Comité des Delegations Juives*, the Jewish delegation to the Paris talks, and was influential in drafting the minority protection treaties, which he called "the most important contribution to human liberty in modern history."[106] The publicity over the pogroms played no small role in persuading Poland's leaders to sign the treaty, but their acquiescence did not change the fact that they regarded the treaty as a humiliation and a limitation on their nation's sovereignty.

Meanwhile, Polish newspapers heatedly accused Jews of being the prime movers behind such foreign interference in Poland's internal affairs. Some Polish editors attributed "every ungrateful influence or event to Jewish intrigue," Ambassador Gibson noted.[107] The daily *Rozwoj (Development)* insisted that Jews were not Polish citizens, but simply foreigners living in Poland who would be better off leaving the country altogether.[108] Since Jewish complaints had triggered the false pogrom charges against Poland, Poles were "entitled to consider all the Jews who live in Poland as traitors."[109] The Morgenthau committee was a "provocation" and far from impartial: "To place, however, at the head of a commission that has to examine the relations between Poles and Jews in Poland a well-known Jewish leader, is something more than tactlessness and even indecency, it is the gauntlet thrown to truth and to our national honor." Wilson was "throwing a blazing torch into accumulated powder."[110]

Ambassador Gibson himself, however, was not particularly sympathetic to the plight of the Jews. Even Strauss, who generally admired Gibson's "broadmindedness" and considered him a friend, admitted in a letter to Felix Warburg "that it would be only a matter of time before [Gibson] would be completely won over" to the Polish point of view concerning the Jews. Hence, Strauss concluded, Gibson could not be counted upon and would be "of little service" in ferreting out the truth about Polish Jewry. Weary of Gibson's reporting, Hoover's young secretary wanted nothing more than to jump into the Polish mayhem himself and sort out the truth, even if it meant leaving behind his important position at the ARA. "I should like nothing better than to cast all other interests to the winds, and devote my entire strength, and whatever judgment I have been blessed with, to personal service among Galician shambles," Strauss confided in a letter to Felix Warburg. Yet after consulting with Marshall and Harvard law professor Felix Frankfurter, Strauss conceded that he was right where he was supposed to be—at ARA headquarters, the linchpin between ARA operations and JDC relief efforts, and enjoying Hoover's ear and trust.[111]

The American ambassador may have been unfairly blamed for a comment by the U.S. Military Attaché in Paris for claiming that "no pogroms without our knowledge had taken place in Poland," but his stated views were not that much better. Gibson conceded that Polish Jews suffered from legal and social discrimination, not to mention sporadic violence, but insisted that the Polish authorities "did their best to stop all excesses." In his view, Poland's clashes with Russian Bolsheviks and the general disarray in the country at least explained, if not excused, such outbursts.[112]

On one occasion, Gibson accused American Jews of seeking to "weaken Poland in the interest of Germany who [*sic*] does not desire a formidable economic or political rival in the East." Gibson railed against the "Jewish propaganda machine" that was "devoted chiefly to polemics against the Poles and the Polish Government." Even the Polish Jews, Gibson claimed, resented the propaganda coming from mostly American, English, and German Jews and referred to it as "harmful meddling." "I am sure," he asserted, "that some of our American Jewish agitators would be surprised at the sort of welcome they would receive from their co-religionists if they were to come here." The American government was in a position to bring Poles and Jews together, but that work was being "delayed and hampered by the attempt of American Jews to hurt Poland in the eyes of the world." American Jews should focus on efforts "to help lift up Poland and lift their own people along with the country."[113]

Gibson was especially severe in his attitude towards the JDC. In a July 1919 letter to the American Mission in Paris, Gibson declared: "It is hard for an ordinary Christian to get in here but almost any Jew seems to be able to manage it and at risk of being called a Jew baiter I hereby proclaim my view that it's all wrong." Gibson claimed that JDC representatives had "abused the privileges accorded them" under the auspices of the American Relief Administration. The Polish government had been "very generous" with JDC representatives by granting them "unusual freedom of movement" in time of war and recognizing them as having virtual "governmental sanction." Gibson accused JDC officials Jacob Billikopf and Harriet Lowenstein (Felix Warburg's secretary) of spreading "foolish propaganda" about the dreadful treatment of Jews. According to Gibson, there were only one or two American Jews who had done good rather than harm; most notably Dr. Boris Bogen, head of the JDC in Europe. "But as a rule," he concluded, "these people seem to devote their efforts to knifing Poland."[114]

Gibson went so far as to accuse the JDC of undermining American foreign policy. "This [JDC activity] seems to me to be perilously close to coming under the Revised Statutes [of the U.S. Criminal Code] which have some remark about people who mix into affairs of foreign policy against the views of their Government," he asserted. To guard against future embarrassments, Gibson urged the State Department to designate someone "to go over the applicants for passports and cull out the names of pronounced Zionists and other troublemakers." Gibson, still smarting from a dressing-down given him by American Zionist leaders, Felix Frankfurter, and Louis Brandeis in a private meeting in Paris in June, tried to convince the State Department to block Frankfurter from visiting Poland during the Morgenthau committee's mission. "After seeing some of Frankfurter's general attitude on this question, I feel that this [Frankfurter's visit] would be deplorable and that he should not be given a passport," he wrote. His pleas, however, were denied.[115]

Several years later, when new pogroms erupted in Poland, Gibson found more inventive reasons to argue that U.S. intervention "will harm our national interests." Within a few years at most, Gibson contended, "the question [of whether to aid the Jews] will probably arise in a greatly aggravated and magnified form in connection with Russia, and whatever steps we take now will establish a precedent which will either help or hinder us at that time." In Gibson's view, there was evidence that, in fact, "the Soviet regime is in the hands of the Jews, and that their oppression is Jewish oppression." When "the present restraints are removed," he predicted, "there will be a massacre of Jews on a scale unprecedented in modern times. If we begin intervening in Poland at this time, even in a mild way, we shall have established a precedent which will enable the Jewish leaders to bring pressure to bear upon the [State] Department and upon Congress to go into Russia even more energetically and actively for the protection of the Jews." Such intervention would "probably be ineffectual," but in any event, "in view of the chaos which will exist in Russia for many years, such interference might well jeopardize our national interests without any accompanying advantage to the Jews." Hence, Gibson concluded, the U.S. government should not "lend its influence in behalf of any native element in a foreign country" except in a case of "gross injustice and cruelty, as in the case of Armenian massacres and the like."[116]

The Committee Arrives

Morgenthau, together with renowned engineer Maj.-Gen. Edgar Jadwin, attorney Homer Johnson, and a staff of twelve, arrived in Warsaw on July 13, 1919. Gibson, eager to make a good impression, took them to the opera and an array of lavish dinner receptions hosted by Polish aristocrats. Captain Arthur L. Goodheart, counsel to the commission, described in his memoirs the vigorous effort by Morgenthau and his colleagues to convince the Polish leadership that concrete steps against the pogroms would be in their best national interest. At a press conference with Polish reporters, Morgenthau noted with dismay that Poland, not content with having secured its freedom after long years of arduous struggle, was now complaining about its "Jewish problem."

Morgenthau said the situation reminded him of a pessimistic lady he knew. After giving birth to a healthy boy, she was asked whether she was happy now.

The lady, however, replied "No," because she had a toothache.[117] General Jadwin then offered the press a metaphor of his own: in America, he said, "we have a cake called a doughnut, which has a hole in the middle. We call someone an optimist, who sees the cake, and someone a pessimist, who only sees the hole." He advised the Poles to stop focusing on the hole.[118] Shortly after the commission's visit ended, Hoover decided to have a first-hand look at the situation in Poland. Although much of the Polish press had been less than kind to President Wilson's role in shaping the future of postwar Poland, the chairman of the American Relief Administration was treated as a hero. In accordance with national custom, the entire Polish cabinet lined up to greet Hoover upon his arrival and present him with a loaf of bread and salt. Years later, Hoover recalled with amusement how the bread, which was a foot and a half in diameter and presented on a heavy wooden platter, nearly caused a major faux pas. When it was handed to Hoover, he was still holding his silk top hat in his right hand, so the Chief quickly passed it to the nearest aide in order to avoid having it fall to the ground and create a spectacle. Yet the weight of the loaf and platter proved too much for the aide as well, so he handed it to the next fellow over. The considerable load of this Polish gift made one American dignitary after the other pass on loaf and platter until it reached the last American doughboy.[119] The Polish cabinet ministers, thinking the peculiar spectacle was some sort of American custom, applauded enthusiastically.[120]

For Hoover, the "profoundly touching" part of the ceremony was being greeted by masses of children—over 30,000, by Gibson's count—who, his Polish interlocutors told him, had been brought straight from the soup kitchens around the country where they received their only daily nourishment, thanks to Hoover's efforts. The children marched before Hoover and his team, waving paper banners with the American and Polish national colors. "If it had not been for what Hoover had done there would be mighty few of those children alive," Gibson noted in his diary. The amused ambassador observed that the children threw so many flowers in Hoover's path, that "they might just as well have been strewing banana peels for he nearly broke his neck two or three times." The procession was briefly interrupted when a wild rabbit unexpectedly hopped through the lines, setting off considerable commotion among the youngsters.[121]

Hoover's upbeat visit gave the Polish authorities, and Ambassador Gibson, a respite from the tensions surrounding the Morgenthau mission. Paderewski had implored President Wilson to visit Poland as a sign of America's unwavering support for the Polish Republic. But since Wilson was busy at home, promoting his idea to create a League of Nations, he asked Hoover to go in his place.

The Chief arranged a special train from the Swiss frontier to Warsaw, and accompanied by several Generals and Admirals, the intent was to impress the Poles, show American support, and give advice on the country's economic situation.[122] Hoover's whirlwind visit to Warsaw and Cracow only lasted a few days, but following on the heels of the Morgenthau mission, it greatly assured the Poles of U.S. support. Gibson thoroughly grasped the significance of Hoover's visit, when he noted in his diary that the Chief should have stayed for ten days or two weeks because there were "a lot of things that he can do better than anybody else." On the other hand, the American ambassador conceded that the intensity of Hoover's visit left him utterly exhausted, similar to having a "hang-over."[123]

The Morgenthau mission ended after three weeks with no agreement among the commissioners. "[We] had no end of arguments in trying to agree on a joint report,"[124] Morgenthau wrote Gibson. Morgenthau, on the one hand, and Jadwin and Johnson, on the other hand, could not see eye to eye on the nature, severity, or causes of anti-Jewish persecution in Poland.[125] They could not even agree on using the term "pogrom;" Jadwin and Johnson, doubting the violence was government-supported, preferred "excess." (Gibson too eschewed the word "pogrom." He complained in one dispatch to the State Department that "if a Jew is injured it is called a pogrom. If a Christian is mobbed, it is called a food riot."[126]) In the end, they decided to submit two separate reports.

The principal difference between the two reports lay in their evaluation of the causes of antisemitism in Poland. Morgenthau stressed the turmoil set off by Poland's new independence and ongoing random violence as major contributing factors. Jadwin and Johnson blamed the Jews' separatist religious and social lifestyle, dating back to the Middle Ages, for Polish hostility. According to Morgenthau, it was up to a democratic Polish government to restore peace and order and to treat all its citizens equally. Invoking Abraham Lincoln's famous words, he encouraged the Polish government to create a united rather than a divided house because "a house divided against itself can not stand."[127] Jadwin and Johnson, on the other hand, insisted that "this process of restoration is not solely dependent on the good will and exertions of the Poles themselves." On the contrary, their investigation revealed that the ball was in the Jews' court. After all, it was "the history and the attitude of the Jews, complicated by abnormal economic and political conditions produced by the war [that] have fed the flame of anti-Semitism at a critical moment."[128] For Jadwin and Johnson, it was up to the Jews to prove they supported an independent Polish republic and opposed Bolshevism.

Morgenthau had high hopes that the minorities protection treaty with Poland would guarantee the civil liberties of minorities and secure the protection of Polish Jews. Jadwin and Johnson, by contrast, rejected the treaty, opposing provisions in it that endorsed such things as the public funding of Jewish private schools. In their view, it was not religious differences that had kept Poles and Jews apart, but the history and attitude of the Jews.[129]

The two reports were submitted to the Senate in January 1920, but the lawmakers took no action. As violence in Eastern Europe subsided in late 1919 and early 1920, congressional interest in intervention in Europe faded. At the same time, public support for U.S. involvement in the League of Nations and postwar settlement decreased. Both the League and the minorities treaties came into effect without American participation, and the League failed to create any mechanism to handle its responsibilities under the minority treaty.

Hoover and Strauss looked back at the Pinsk episode as an example of an appropriate American response to the postwar European turmoil. Strauss hailed Hoover as the rescuer of Poland's Jews.[130] Hoover, speaking at the 1921 annual dinner of the Greater New York Jewish War Relief Fund, said his quick intervention on behalf of the Jews of Pinsk was necessary because Americans "knew no race and no creed," were sympathetic to the interests of the Jews, and could not tolerate "prejudiced action by an irresponsible government."[131]

Later that year, a brief dust-up over the issue added an unpleasant footnote to the story. An attendee at a private dinner between Hoover and Jewish leaders in Pittsburgh claimed Hoover had blamed the Zionist movement in Poland, and certain clauses of the minorities treaties, for causing tensions between Poles and Jews.[132] Louis Marshall, catching wind of the accusation, sent a letter of protest to Hoover. Zionism was "one of the fifty-seven varieties of excuses that the Poles have offered for their unfriendly attitude," he wrote. He recalled that Prime Minister Paderewski had once remarked to Marshall that he knew the Jews hoped to establish their own state in Poland because, he erroneously claimed, the Hebrew words for "Poland" and "Palestine" were one and the same.[133] Marshall need not have exercised himself so; Hoover replied, plausibly, that he had been misunderstood—he had been explaining the Polish authorities' view, not his own. "I did not for a moment intend to convey that it had my support and I have often expressed myself to the contrary in many of its particulars," he assured Marshall, who immediately backpedaled.[134]

Collaboration between the ARA and the JDC

Public controversy over Pinsk and other pogroms overshadowed the quiet but extensive collaboration between Hoover's ARA and the JDC elsewhere in Eastern Europe. Despite the protests and investigations, shipments of food, clothing, and medicine from the JDC continued to arrive in Poland and other East European countries, and were distributed on the basis of "need not creed," as the JDC put it. The JDC's collaboration with the ARA extended to Germany, Austria, Romania, the Baltic states, Ukraine, and Russia and contributed food, clothing, and medicine to Europeans devastated by war. Between 1914 and 1923, the JDC extended relief in the amount of almost $60-million, generously provided by American Jewish communities who were part of an ethnic minority that was composed of less than five hundred thousand families. Hoover was impressed by the dimensions of the JDC's effort, calling it a "magnificent demonstration of human compassion" that was of "critical necessity" to the relief of Europe.[135]

In the most trying postwar years of 1919 and 1920, Poland received by far the largest share of JDC's aid to Eastern Europe.[136] The JDC avoided the Polish government's onerous restrictions on Jewish organizations' contributions by routing its aid through Hoover's agency. The ARA was also helpful in addressing specific Jewish needs, such as requests for shipments of provisions for the baking of Passover matzos in the spring of 1919.[137]

Once the pogroms and the sense of immediate crisis in Poland subsided in late 1919, the ARA and JDC began shifting their attention eastward. Ukraine, like Poland, had to wrestle with the consequences of the disintegration of the Russian and Austrian Empires. While Poland regained its independence and sought to expand into the territories of Lithuania and Ukraine, while simultaneously defending itself against the Bolshevik armies, the Ukrainians found themselves caught in the middle of both Poland's and Russia's wars. More than one million inhabitants of Ukraine died between 1918 and 1920 as a result of these and other conflicts, including tens of thousands of Jews murdered in pogroms.[138] (An estimated four million Jews lived in the western Ukraine region that had been known under Imperial Russia as the Pale of Settlement.)

While the Allies endorsed and facilitated the restoration of Polish national sovereignty, however, they did not support Ukrainian independence. Instead, they viewed Ukraine's as more or less an extension of the Russian civil war between the Bolsheviks and the nationalist White Army.[139] Amidst a welter of competing ideologies and territorial claims, two Ukrainian republics, one proclaimed in Lwow, the other in Kiev, rose and fell. Violence, famine, and typhus were rampant, with Ukraine's Jews caught in the crossfire.

U.S officials tried, not always successfully, to keep track of the constantly-changing political and military situation and chart a course for American foreign policy in the region. Maj.-Gen. Edgar Jadwin, formerly a member of Morgenthau's investigative commission to Poland, who served as an American observer in Ukraine, held meetings with both Ukrainian nationalist leader Petliura and Russian White Army General Denikin to discuss the country's future. An "official" Ukrainian mission took up residence in Paris to advocate national independence, but was not recognized by the western powers; U.S. officials dismissed its appeals as "propaganda." In the State Department's view, the Ukrainian separatist movement was "largely the result of Austrian and German propaganda seeking the disruption of Russia" rather than a genuine reflection of popular sentiment. The Ukrainian separatists, according to Secretary Lansing, were "unable to perceive an adequate ethnical basis for erecting a separate state… [The U.S.] is not convinced that there is real popular demand for anything more than such greater measure of local autonomy as will naturally result from the establishment in Russia of a modern democratic government…" The State Department sought to "sustain the principle of essential Russian unity rather than encourage separatism."[140]

All sources indicated that Jews in Ukraine were suffering badly. Jadwin's committee reported to Washington that the Jewish situation in Ukraine was "deplorable." Boris Bogen of the JDC called conditions in Ukraine "indescribably bad." JDC representatives Judge Fischer and Max Pine offered a similar description of the situation in Kiev, which had endured sixteen changes of government in short order, destruction caused by retreating armies, and additional hardships brought on by the influx of tens of thousands of refugees from pogroms in other cities. Fischer and Pine recommended that no government should be recognized unless it punished those who had committed pogroms.[141]

With the signing of the peace treaty by Germany and the minority treaties by Poland, Romania, and others in the summer of 1919, the ARA mandate had run its course and the official American relief operation was terminated. Yet Europe's political and economic situation remained far from stable, and Hoover worked feverishly to obtain an extension of government relief aid. Hoover's appeals for even a modest U.S. allocation fell on deaf ears. President Wilson suffered a massive stroke in September 1919 which incapacitated him for the remainder of his administration, and none of his cabinet members saw continued U.S. government support of the ARA relief as particularly desirable. On the contrary, many in the administration feared that continued American involvement in Europe's reconstruction would open the door to the British and the French to renegotiate their war debts. Congress was equally reluctant to approve any open-ended commitment to restore Europe's economy. Mrs. Lou Hoover, an energetic advocate for programs to feed European children, complained bitterly that the Allies seemed "inclined to let the populations of Poland, Austria, and Armenia starve" while debating "the question of who is really responsible for feeding them."[142]

A new ARA publicity campaign featuring the movie *Starvation* did not have the desired effect. Despite the film's graphic scenes of suffering in Europe, some in the news media preferred to emphasize the positive. The *New York Tribune*, for example, headlined its review "Scenes Show How American Food Has Saved Europe." This implied the crisis had subsided, thus undermining the film's fundraising potential.[143]

Hoover now had little choice but to rely primarily on private donations to provide the ARA's budget. With his overwhelmed and much-reduced staff working for little or no pay, Hoover hit the road in late 1920 for a hectic speaking and fundraising tour. Winning the "love and gratitude of millions of [European] children offered greater protection to the United States than any battleship," he contended in his appeals.[144] He managed to raise $15-million in those early months, enough to keep the ARA going, but in sharply reduced fashion.[145]

Aid to Russia—with a Purpose

Hoover initially favored providing relief to areas of Russia torn by civil war, but he had in mind aid with a political purpose. Relief to the Russian Bolsheviks, he argued, could bring about a change of government or "at least a period of rest along the frontiers of Europe" and "some hope of stabilization." "This plan [of relief], if successful," Hoover explained to Wilson at the end of March 1919, "would save an immensity of helpless human life and would save our country from further entanglements which today threaten to pull us from our National ideals." Yet the continued aggression of Bolshevik armies as well as Communist successes in Germany and Hungary somewhat soured the Chief on the idea and led to his initial reluctance to respond to an urgent appeal for aid by famous Russian writer Maxim Gorky. In the summer of 1921, Gorky pleaded for immediate help from the Western powers and especially the ARA in order to stave off famine and its catastrophic consequences.[146]

The severity of the situation eventually compelled Hoover to reach the conclusion that American aid might be useful as a means of discrediting Russia's new Communist regime. In 1921, Hoover brokered a deal, known as the Riga Agreement, between Moscow and the ARA. The ARA pledged political neutrality in exchange for the Communists' promise of non-interference in the ARA's relief work. By this time, Hoover had accepted the post of secretary of commerce in the new administration of Warren G. Harding. The task of running the European relief efforts was given to Hoover's friend and fellow-engineer Walter Lyman Brown, with Colonel William N. Haskell in charge of operations on Russian soil. The Chief used his political clout and authority to sell relief to the American people and finally convinced Congressional leaders to secure appropriations for the purchase of the country's agricultural surplus. House Republicans initially agreed to allocate $10 million. Congress, however, doubled the appropriation after a dramatic appeal by Hoover to convert their surplus into humanitarian aid rather than let it go unused and spoil. This American relief effort focused on feeding children. At the peak of the campaign, in August 1922, ARA stations were providing at least one meal daily for more than four million Russian children.[147]

The importance of ARA-JDC collaboration increased after the privatization of American relief, although tensions occasionally flared between the two over administrative control and antisemitism.[148] JDC officials periodically fended off charges of favoritism toward Jews, reassuring their ARA colleagues that "the principle of need without regard to creed is the guiding principle of [the JDC's] work."[149] The ARA, for its part, had to contend from time to time with charges in the Jewish press that it was discriminating against Jewish children.[150] In the summer of 1922, for example, some New York Jewish newspapers accused the ARA of adhering to an Austrian law that barred food rations for foreign-born children. If true, it would have constituted a significant problem, given the large number of Jewish children in Austria who were of Polish origin. In fact, however, protests from the ARA had persuaded Austria's parliament to remove that clause from the nation's Child Feeding Law.[151] With Jews comprising a significant portion of its donor base and the JDC's help playing a crucial role in its operations, the ARA was anxious to maintain a positive reputation in the Jewish community. To that end, the ARA in early 1921 hired A.M. Goldberg of the International Jewish Press Bureau to monitor Jewish press coverage of its work. Goldberg was soon able to report, much to the delight of the ARA leadership, that its work was receiving sympathetic attention throughout the Jewish newspapers in both the United States and in Europe. "The attitude of the Jewish press in Europe is wholly sympathetic," Goldberg wrote, "and there is no doubt that Mr. Hoover's name is no less popular in any Jewish community in Europe than in any community in America."[152]

Based on his observations, Goldberg asserted that the coverage of the ARA-JDC work in the Yiddish-language press was likely responsible for a significant portion of donations from the American Jewish community. One extreme-left publication, *Die Naye Velt*, had criticized Hoover's work as "a diabolical plan aimed against the only workers' republic in the world," but such attacks, Goldberg assured the ARA leaders, emanated from "the smallest part of the Jewish press, whose readers comprise only 2% of the Jewish reading public"—and that newspaper, while "opposed to the ARA in principle," still opened its columns to "news of [the ARA's] actual accomplishment[s].[153] A rare attack on Hoover and the ARA, in the socialist Yiddish daily *Forverts* in June 1922, provoked an angry letter to the editor from an ARA spokesman accusing the newspaper of "incredible ingratitude." "Every Russian and every Jew," George C. Baker wrote, "was under a debt of gratitude to Mr. Hoover infinitely greater than ever can be paid." If they would study the facts, Baker added, "your people could devote their time to defending him from such attacks instead of fostering them."[154]

The ARA left Russia in 1923, but the JDC's work continued there for some time afterwards. Hoover bent the rules and authorized JDC representatives such as Joseph Rosen (its director in Russia) and Bogen to keep their ARA identity cards in order to facilitate their ongoing dealings with the Soviet authorities. Gestures such as this further endeared the Chief to the American Jews who worked with him during those tumultuous years. James Rosenberg credited Hoover with "saving millions of lives," not to mention "render[ing] an incalculable service to our country" by building up a huge reservoir of goodwill towards America among countless millions of ordinary Europeans. Even many American Jews who would later take issue with Hoover's policies as president appreciated his remarkable efforts to relieve Jewish suffering in Europe. "When we remember what Hoover has done in Russia," the socialist *Forverts* later editorialized, we are willing to forget many of his sins in America."[155]

Chapter 3

Hoover, Zionism, and the Palestinian Arab Riots of 1929

> *"Jews are never satisfied to be treated exactly like other American citizens. They want special privileges of all kinds...All the Hebrews in the country are still telegraphing about their friends and relations in Palestine...{This} makes me dislike them as a race more than ever."*[156]

These harsh sentiments were expressed not by some extreme fringe element, but by Assistant Secretary of State William R. Castle, an important figure in U.S. foreign policymaking and confidante of President Hoover, at the height of the 1929 Arab riots in Palestine. As Arab mobs slew more than one hundred Jews, including eight Jewish Americans, Castle's ire seemed to be focused more on the victims than the victimizers. President Hoover, grappling with his first major foreign policy crisis, found himself under intense pressure from anti-Zionist—and sometimes even antisemitic—officials in his own administration who hoped to turn him against the Zionist cause. Navigating between the conflicting pressures of the State Department, the British government, and the American Jewish community would prove no mean feat for the president.[157]

William R. Castle

Hoover was enjoying a pleasant weekend getaway in Virginia's Blue Ridge Mountains in late August, 1929, when Lewis Strauss brought word of trouble in the Holy Land. The bucolic serenity of the Rapidan campgrounds, which Hoover had purchased privately and then donated to the American public, gave way to a series of anxious consultations with advisers over the news of the Palestine turmoil.[158]

Hoover and his aides were hardly the only ones to be caught by surprise by the turn of events. Although in retrospect the signs of impending violence may have seemed obvious, at the time there were not many outside Palestine who predicted what lay ahead. Jewish development of the country in the years since the British ouster of the Ottoman Turks in 1918 had generally proceeded peacefully, and in fact, produced sufficient prosperity in the Holy Land to attract Arab immigration from neighboring lands. Brief anti-Jewish outbursts by Arabs in Jerusalem in 1920 and Jaffa in 1921 were dismissed by Zionist leaders as aberrations, the mischief of a handful of agitators who did not reflect the general sentiment of the local Arab population.

Tensions began to boil over at the time of the High Holy Days in 1928, when officials of the Muslim *Wakf*, which governed Jerusalem's Western Wall, objected to Jews blowing the *shofar* [ram's horn] during religious services at the site and employing a partition to separate male and female worshippers—practices that had been allowed under Ottoman law. Muslim preachers stoked the fires by claiming these Jewish practices were part of a conspiracy to take over the holy site and destroy the mosques situated on the adjacent Temple Mount plateau.[159] The British police made the already tense situation worse by forcibly removing the partition, setting off scuffles with Jewish worshippers in the middle of Yom Kippur services. British Constable Douglas Duff was hailed by Arabs as a hero.[160]

Haj Amin al-Husseini, the Grand Mufti, or senior Muslim religious authority, in Jerusalem, seized upon the episode to incite his followers against Palestine's Jews and assert his leadership role in the Arab community. It also provided him a welcome opportunity to divert attention from his Arab rivals' accusations of corruption. In the months to follow, Husseini's fiery speeches about a Jewish threat to take over not only the mosques in Jerusalem but the entire country inspired a wave of anti-Jewish agitation.[161] Stirred by the Mufti's fire-and-brimstone sermon at Friday afternoon prayers on August 16, 1929, hundreds of enraged Arabs brandishing knives and clubs streamed out of the mosques, attacked residents of the Jewish Quarter, and burned Jewish prayer books at the Western Wall. One Jewish youth was stabbed to death. The following Friday, Jerusalem's Arab rioters, joined by thousands more from neighboring villages, launched a fresh wave of attacks. Seventeen Jews were murdered in and around the city. There were attacks elsewhere throughout the country, including Safed, where at least 18 Jews were killed, and in Hebron, where Arab mobs massacred 59 Jewish residents. The fact that most of Hebron's Jews were members of the 800 year-old Sephardic Jewish community, which had no connection to the Zionist movement, made no difference to the attackers.

The British authorities were ill-equipped to deal with a crisis of this magnitude. A number of high-ranking officials had escaped the smoldering Middle Eastern summer to enjoy cooler European weather. The high commissioner of Palestine, Sir John Chancellor, for example, was in London at the time of the outbreaks. The commandant of police, Arthur Mavrogordato, was in England on leave, and several police chiefs and district commissioners were also out of the country. To make matters worse, budget cutting in recent years had reduced the Palestine Police force to just 2,100 men, and on the day the pogroms began, only 1,500 British policemen were on duty throughout the country, just 72 of them in Jerusalem. There was no military reserve, infantry, or even semi-military support on hand to back up the meager police force.[162]

A Consul General with an Agenda

In a series of cables to the State Department during the days to follow, the American consul in Jerusalem, Paul Knabenshue, described the mounting violence and the inability of the British authorities to cope with the crisis. He also reported that eight of the Hebron yeshiva students slain in the attacks were American citizens, a point that would figure prominently in subsequent discussions of how the United States should respond to the pogroms. Knabenshue's initial fear and concern for the safety of American citizens gave way to outright annoyance just a few days later. Thirty-three Jewish residents of Jerusalem who held U.S. citizenship had sought shelter in the American consulate building and made what Knabenshue called the "most ridiculously impossible demands" for protection from the pogromists. Vincent Sheean, a reporter for the North American Newspaper Alliance, felt sorry for the overwhelmed U.S. consul and came to the conclusion that such Jewish behavior could only be explained as a "pogrom complex." "It was a state of mind," Sheean explained, "that the moment the Jews felt themselves under attack, their lives in danger and their future insecure, they assumed that the world was in league against them."[163]

Like many of his colleagues in the State Department, Knabenshue was a harsh critic of Zionism, and he automatically blamed the Jews for "provoking" the Arab violence. To back up his preconceived notions, Knabenshue dispatched the fiercely anti-Zionist, and sometimes antisemitic, Sheean to survey events around the country. Sheean first visited Palestine in June 1929 and almost immediately underwent a dramatic conversion to the Arab cause. According to his account, he arrived with an "exaggerated admiration for the Jewish people" and an "antisemitism turned wrong side out" that made him gravitate toward everything Jewish—food, traditions, theater, and many Jewish friends, some of whom had encouraged him to visit the Holy Land. Yet, according to Sheean, within days of his arrival, he was struck by what he saw as the ancient Arab character of the country. Jerusalem, he decided, was "as Arab as Cairo or Baghdad, and the Zionist Jews (that is, the modern Jews) were as foreign to it as I was myself." Traveling the country in the aftermath of the riots, Sheean deplored the Arab violence but placed the onus on the Zionists for trying to claim a land that was "tiny" and "already inhabited." "Why couldn't the Zionists leave it alone?," Sheean lamented. "It would never hold enough Jews to make even a beginning toward the solution of the Jewish problem; it would always be prey to such ghastly horrors...The Holy Land seemed as near as an approximation of hell on earth as I had ever seen."[164] Sheean returned from his survey with a series of breathless "exposés" about Jewish "fascists" plotting to stir up trouble. He even claimed one Jewish provocateur confided to him that the Jews had deliberately incited the Arabs and were even hoping for some Jewish casualties, in order to advance some Zionist political aims. Knabenshue's subsequent dispatches to Washington about "Zionist fanatics" echoed the Sheean line.[165]

Although Knabenshue vehemently opposed any intervention by the Hoover administration to aid the Jewish victims of the pogroms, his alarm-laced reports may have inadvertently advanced that possibility, at least a bit. Haunted by memories of the slow French response to the Lebanese Druze rebellion of 1925 that he had witnessed as a consul in Beirut, Knabenshue told his superiors in detail of the spiraling Palestinian Arab violence and the British authorities' faltering response, especially their inability to properly protect foreign consulates such as his.[166] There were even indications that Transjordanian tribes, "incited by Jewish colonization," might soon invade the Holy Land to join the strife, he claimed. Without swift military action, the crisis could become unmanageable and turn into a drawn out conflict, Knabenshue warned.[167]

One result was that Secretary of State Henry Stimson took the somewhat unusual step of bringing U.S. concerns over the Palestine situation directly to the attention of Foreign Secretary Alan Henderson in London. The British press took note of Stimson's decision to bypass the U.S. consulate in Jerusalem and the Colonial Office administration, and instead go straight to the Foreign Office to express his "earnest hope that immediate and comprehensive steps may be taken for the restoration of order and for the protection of lives and property of American citizens." According to the *London Times*, this direct resort to the Home Government rather than to its representatives on the scene in Palestine was "rather unusual," although the Foreign Office tried to spin it as a positive sign of "U.S. confidence in the readiness and ability of the British authorities to cope with the situation." Several days later, in response to pleas from American Jews, Stimson also instructed the American ambassador in London as late as August 28 to "urgently bring to the attention of the Foreign Office that "in spite of reiterated requests" no special protection had been provided for the American consulate in Jerusalem.[168]

News reports about Arab violence reached the American Jewish community quickly via the Jewish Telegraphic Agency, and the secretary of state's desk was soon piled high with anguished protests from around the country.[169] New York Congressmen Emanuel Celler and Samuel Dickstein were among the earliest and most insistent voices pressing the State Department to remind London of its responsibility to safeguard Palestine Jewry and build up the Jewish national home, as required by the Balfour Declaration and the terms of the mandate.[170] Other protesters, including *Brooklyn Jewish Examiner* publisher Rabbi Louis Gross, cited the 1924 Anglo-American Convention on Palestine as the basis for U.S. intervention. That treaty, although created primarily to protect U.S. commercial interests in the Holy Land, included a provision requiring the British to refrain from modifying the terms of the mandate without American agreement, and a preamble endorsing the Balfour Declaration. The fact that American lives and property were harmed by the Arab attackers, gave the United States additional justification to get involved, the protestors insisted.[171] (An internal State Department inquiry on this point, however, concluded that the preamble was not binding, and U.S. intervention would be legitimate only if the British modified the mandate in such a way as to encroach upon the rights of American citizens.)[172]

Even if U.S. intervention was legally or morally justified it was not clear what form it should take. Jewish leaders argued, in a general way, that American pressure on London might result in a more conscientious effort by the British to stamp out violence. A more specific proposal, put forward by Congressman Celler and echoed by others, was that the Hoover administration should dispatch an American warship to the coast of Palestine.[173] "Jews are never satisfied to be treated exactly like other American citizens," Assistant Secretary of State Castle

Emanuel Celler

complained in his diary. "They want special privileges of all kinds. Now they want a battleship sent to Palestine, I suppose, to blow up both Arabs and British."[174] Proponents of sending a ship in fact were not proposing that it initiate military action, but rather saw it as a symbolic gesture, also known as "gunboat diplomacy," a show of strength to intimidate the rioters, bolster the morale of the victims, and provide a potential safe haven for American citizens in peril.

The State Department was entirely unsympathetic to Zionism and objected to using a navy cruiser as a demonstration of support for Palestine Jewry under any circumstances, but its opposition was especially vigorous at that time because delicate negotiations were underway between the United States and Great Britain precisely on the issue of naval reductions. As part of the ongoing post-World War I effort by the United States to advance the cause of international disarmament, Washington and London were struggling to find a mutually acceptable ratio of cruisers for both governments.[175] The State Department feared that sending a naval vessel to the shore of Palestine, a traditional sphere of British influence, would be regarded in London as a declaration of no-confidence in England's ability to maintain order. The last thing Foggy Bottom wanted was for the Palestine controversy to turn into a sustained diplomatic row that would undermine naval talks, as one *New York Times* report predicted might happen.[176] At an August 26 press conference, Secretary of State Stimson emphasized that Palestine was Britain's responsibility alone and any American involvement would be inappropriate. Referring to the suggestions to dispatch a U.S. ship, Stimson alluded to the unfavorable reaction in the United States when a British warship was sent to Nicaragua in 1927, a traditional American sphere of influence, in order to protect British citizens there.[177]

Ambassador Dawes, alarmed by Knabenshue's reports about Transjordanian Arabs organizing to invade Palestine, advised Stimson to at least consider moving an American cruiser closer to Palestine as a precautionary measure.[178] The secretary refused because it "might give offense to the British authorities, who have apparently acted with energy and vigor." He would not consider dispatching an American vessel unless the British "strongly desired one to be sent."[179] British

Prime Minister Ramsay MacDonald certainly did not want one. Hoping to conclude the naval reduction negotiations with the U.S. despite pressure from "big navy" conservatives at home, MacDonald would not countenance an American cruiser, or any other sign, however symbolic, of U.S. interference in Palestine. Foreign Office officials, responding to the American ambassador's inquiry, argued none too subtly that "from the point of view of protecting American interests in Palestine it was fortunate that the [British] Government had fast cruisers at Malta to send."[180] The Hoover administration's rejection of requests to send a cruiser was noted at the Foreign Office as evidence that the "American government has gone out of its way to show its friendly disposition."[181] The *London Times* likewise noted with satisfaction that the U.S. apparently recognized that "it might be less than courteous" to take naval action with regard to Palestine.[182]

An Appeal to the White House

Street rallies, such as a march by 15,000 Jews down Broadway to the British Consulate on August 26, gave the grassroots an opportunity to express their anguish. But that was no substitute for an official word from the highest authority in the land. On August 28, a delegation from the Zionist Organization of America traveled to Washington to meet with the British ambassador, congressional leaders, Secretary of State Stimson, and President Hoover.[183]

There was ample precedent, going all the way back to John Adams, for a presidential statement supporting the Zionist cause. Ex-president Adams, in 1819, wrote, "I really wish the Jews again in Judea an independent nation." John Quincy Adams spoke similarly. Abraham Lincoln, in 1863, wrote that "restoring [the Jews] to their national home in Palestine" was "a noble dream and one shared by many Americans." Theodore Roosevelt said it was "entirely proper to start a Zionist State around Jerusalem and the Jews be given control of Palestine." Woodrow Wilson endorsed the Balfour Declaration. The Senate and the House of Representatives, in 1922, unanimously adopted the Lodge-Fish resolution putting the United States officially on record in support of Balfour and the goal of a Jewish national home in Palestine. In a remarkable display of bipartisanship, isolationist Republicans, including lead sponsors Sen. Henry Cabot Lodge (of Massachusetts) and Rep. Hamilton Fish (of New York), joined hands with their political rivals for this common cause. Some of its supporters may have hoped to reap modest political gain; indeed, the *New York Times*, which opposed the resolution, charged that its backers were motivated by a desire to attract "the Jewish vote." Most of those who voted in favor, however, did not hail from states with significant numbers of Jewish votes nor did they have reason to expect their support would result in Jewish campaign donations. They were motivated by Christian religious affection for restoring the Jews to their Holy Land, sympathy for the plight of pogrom victims in Eastern Europe, admiration for the achievements of the Zionist pioneers in Palestine, or some combination thereof.[184]

Prior to the 1929 riots, Hoover had on several occasions expressed himself on the subject of Palestine's future. In 1922, he called for developing in Palestine "an asylum for the less fortunate masses of Jewish people and as a restoration of religious shrines." In 1928, he expressed admiration for the "unexampled perseverance, sacrifice and hard work" by Jewish pioneers. "The Holy Land, desolate and neglected for centuries, is being rebuilt not only as an inspiring spiritual center but also as a habitable and peaceful land that will in the near future harbor a large population with increased opportunities for prosperity among the farmers, the industrialists, the laborers and the scholars," he asserted. Hoover undoubtedly appreciated the echoes in Palestine of America's own westward pioneering endeavors, with which he was intimately familiar, in the remarkable achievements of the Jewish pioneers as they breathed new life into Palestine's ancient soil. In May 1929, Hoover received Nahum Sokolow, president of the World Zionist Executive, at the White House. According to *New Palestine*'s account, they reminisced about their first meeting at the Paris Peace Conference, and Sokolow briefed Hoover on the "developments in afforestation, sanitation, drainage and colonization" in Palestine, which Hoover, ever the engineer at heart, found particularly interesting. At the conclusion of the meeting, Hoover "expressed the hope that the program for reconstruction work in Palestine which is now being followed would be continually expanded." He also "reiterated his sympathy with the ideal of rebuilding Palestine as the Jewish National Homeland."[185]

No transcript exists of the ZOA delegation's brief August 1929 meeting with the president. We know only that Hoover assured them of his sympathy for the pogrom victims as well as his confidence in the ability of the British to restore order. The meeting with Stimson was much longer and concluded on an acrimonious note, with the secretary of state refusing to send the delegation's letter of protest to the British ambassador unless the language was softened.[186] On August 29, more than 25,000 protesters jammed Madison Square Garden to reiterate Jewish outrage over the Arab attacks. The first speaker was Herman Bernstein, the journalist, veteran Zionist activist and longtime friend and supporter of Herbert Hoover. He read a message of sympathy from the president. Hoover expressed his conviction that "out of these tragic events will come greater security and greater safeguard for the future under which the steady rehabilitation of Palestine as a true homeland [for the Jewish people] will be even more assured."[187]

Bernstein reported to Hoover that the presidential message set just the right tone for the rally, "thus preventing any reckless and inflammatory denunciation of Great Britain." Moreover, Bernstein had intervened with the outspoken Samuel Untermeyer to ensure that "several paragraphs which contained an unwarranted, fierce attack on the British Government" were omitted from his speech.[188] "What will [Great Britain] do?," Untermeyer asked in his address. "First of all, it will crush the outbreak before it has gone further with its orgy of destruction; and then it will adopt effective measures to carry out its plighted word to the Jewish people and the civilized world." A resolution adopted at the rally declared that American Jews "place implicit confidence in the good will of the MacDonald administration, and we rely upon the sense of fair play of the British people to support whole-heartedly the efforts to restore peace and order in the Holy Land." Speakers at other Jewish protests over the riots likewise typically refrained from criticizing the MacDonald administration in London, instead focusing on the failings of the colonial administration in Palestine.[189]

In a conversation with Bernstein on August 28, President Hoover reiterated that he was "strongly averse" to U.S. intervention in Palestine and believed that the request for a naval vessel would "unduly embarrass the British government."[190] According to Bernstein's reports to leaders of the American Jewish Committee, the president "earnestly advised" that "all inflammatory utterances criticizing the British government be strictly avoided."[191] Lewis Strauss privately conveyed a similar message to his associates in the Jewish leadership.[192] There was no evidence at the rallies of Jewish dissatisfaction over Hoover's response to the crisis. It seems to have been understood in the Jewish community that in view of the public's isolationist mood and the administration's reluctance to upset naval negotiations with London, the president would not consider intervening in Palestine.

Support for the proposal to send a warship ebbed quickly. World Zionist Organization president Chaim Weizmann made clear to American Jewish leaders that he remained confident the British would stand by the Balfour Declaration and therefore there was no reason for the United States to become involved. Felix Warburg, leader of the American non-Zionists, pondered the matter as he sailed back from the World Zionist Congress in Zurich, where Zionists and non-Zionists reached a landmark agreement enlarging the Jewish Agency, Palestine Jewry's governing body, to give non-Zionists a greater role. Warburg finally decided that he, "as an American," "had better keep my hands off," and telegrammed his AJCommittee friends accordingly; they then formally withdrew their support for the idea of sending a U.S. cruiser.[193]

Hoover's sympathy for those harmed in the attacks and his expressed solidarity with Jewish efforts in Palestine was featured, alongside the president's photo, on the front page of *The New Palestine*, the leading American Zionist periodical.[194] Jewish appreciation of Hoover's words may have been reinforced by the criticism he received from Arab sources. The Syro-Palestinian Congress, in Egypt, denounced the president's endorsement of Jewish aspirations in Palestine as "dangerous and illogical." The American consul in Damascus reported that a local newspaper published the president's telegram to the Madison Square rally under the headline "Hoover Deceived by Zionists."[195]

Meanwhile, reports of Consul-General Knabenshue's inhospitable treatment of those seeking refuge in the consulate began trickling back to the American Jewish community. A barrage of complaints to Washington ensued.[196] Assistant Secretary Castle was incensed at the Jewish outcry. "All the Hebrews in the country are still telegraphing about their friends and relations in Palestine," he wrote in his diary, "and now they are all beginning to countermand the requests they made at first and to curse the poor consul in Jerusalem for all the things he has been physically unable to accomplish. A performance of this kind makes me dislike them as a race more than ever."[197]

After the arrival of three cruisers, airplanes, and additional British reinforcements from Egypt and Transjordan, the rioting petered out by the beginning of September. With the help of French forces, the British thwarted a possible invasion by Bedouin tribes across the northern frontier into Palestine. The internal report by the Colonial Office expressed genuine relief after these tense days of murder, pillage, and destruction. The threat of a more widespread conflict had been very definite. Thousands of Arabs were poised to join the Palestine riots. This growing sense of Pan-Arabism did not escape the American consul John Randolph in Baghdad, Iraq. After monitoring anti-Zionist demonstrations in Baghdad and Iraqi sympathy for slain Muslim rioters in Palestine, Randolph surmised that "this Arab tendency to act as a unit seems destined to grow stronger rapidly and to offer to the British and other European and American powers a new problem."[198]

A Breakthrough in the Naval Talks

Meanwhile, September brought the long-awaited breakthrough in the bilateral naval negotiations between the United States and Great Britain. President Hoover and Prime Minister MacDonald agreed that the substantive gaps had been sufficiently bridged to schedule a meeting between them in early October.[199] Charles Dawes, the U.S. ambassador and a key figure in the negotiations, confidently noted in his diary that "a failure in conference to settle as between us this small remaining difference is unthinkable, even if it is not settled before the conference when MacDonald visits America next month." In both Washington and London, the Palestine disturbances appeared to be nothing more than a minor distraction that would not interfere with the bigger issue.[200]

American Jewish leaders nonetheless viewed the impending MacDonald visit as an opportunity to press their concerns about Palestine. Chaim Weizmann, meeting with MacDonald's private secretary shortly before the prime minister's departure, secured an appointment for Jewish leaders to speak with MacDonald in New York City. Felix Warburg, filling the leadership vacuum left by the unexpected death of Louis Marshall on September 11, would head the delegation. Weizmann urged Warburg to maintain a positive tone in the meeting. Weizmann advised him to express confidence in the British administration, while at the same time steering MacDonald away from pleasant generalities and securing practical commitments. "[Un]til the visit of MacDonald is consummated, and these delicate negotiations have reached a definite point, nothing should be done on our side to make the Prime Minister's stay in America unpleasant," Weizmann wrote Warburg. "The press—particularly the Jewish press—should abstain from attacks; but knowing of these conversations, should rely on the good faith of the Prime Minister, on his sympathy with our Movement, and on his own idealistic point of view; and should express the hope that the Prime Minister will see that the Mandate is carried out in spirit and letter, and that the safety in Palestine will be established beyond the shadow of a doubt."[201]

The British had in the meantime agreed to a request from the Jewish Agency to establish a commission of inquiry to examine the Arab riots. While preparing for the meeting with MacDonald, Warburg sought inclusion of a Jewish representative, or an American official sympathetic to Jewish Palestine, in the work of the commission. Warburg's representative, Jonah Goldstein, raised the idea with Consul Knabenshue, who coldly instructed him to direct his request to the Colonial Office. Knabenshue advised the State Department that while satisfying

Warburg's request "would probably allay much Jewish-American criticism here and in the United States against what they might claim to be our Government's indifference," it would also undoubtedly create resentment against us here and in other Moslem countries."[202] Knabenshue left no doubt as to which group he preferred to disappoint. Knabenshue also fed stereotypes of Jewish financial manipulating by claiming, in a report to Secretary of State Stimson, that Goldstein was probably planning to bribe Arabs. Goldstein undoubtedly thought this would "prove successful as do many other Jews," he wrote.[203]

Just a few days earlier, on October 4, Prime Minister MacDonald arrived in New York City to considerable fanfare. The visit was unprecedented. "[N]o British Prime Minister...ever considered that the United States was of sufficient importance to his policy to justify the expenditure of time which a voyage to this country would necessitate," the *Philadelphia Public Ledger* noted in a tone of enthusiasm typical of American press reaction to MacDonald's arrival.[204] The prime minister was greeted with a ticker-tape parade in Manhattan. Then it was off to the Rapidan retreat for several days of talks with President Hoover. The president, who had recently confided to aides his fear that the meeting could degenerate into a "huckster's quibble," sought to establish a general atmosphere of trust and goodwill rather than settle the small final details concerning naval parity.[205] In that respect, the meeting was a success, concluding with a joint statement affirming Anglo-American friendship, announcing agreement on the major issues of naval disarmament, and pledging to conclude remaining issues at their forthcoming London Naval Conference.[206] "It is my belief, after watching events in Washington last week as closely as a journalist could watch them," wrote Walter Lippmann, editor of the *New York World*, "that Mr. MacDonald and Mr. Hoover have really done what they said they were trying to do; they have given a new direction to the public mind in dealing with Anglo-American affairs."[207]

MacDonald received the Jewish delegation headed by Warburg on October 11 in Washington.[208] Warburg began by reading a prepared statement describing Jewish efforts in Palestine in general terms and stressing the need for Jewish-British cooperation.[209] Afraid that the Zionists' "barking in the same old tune of national home stuff" would alienate potential friends (not to mention the Palestinian Arabs), Warburg had deleted nine of the first draft's ten references to the Jewish national home, although the final text did insist on unfettered Jewish immigration to the Holy Land. MacDonald acknowledged the beneficial impact of Jewish development, promised that the commission of inquiry would be impartial, and asked the Jewish leaders to refrain from saying anything publicly

Prime Minister Ramsay MacDonald, left, with President Hoover, at the White House in 1929.

that might prejudice its findings.[210] In Warburg's view, the meeting with the British premier "passed off most pleasantly" and MacDonald's attitude was "very heartening."[211]

Consul Knabenshue, meanwhile, continued peppering the State Department with anti-Zionist reports. He observed with fascination the uproar in the Jewish world over a declaration by Hebrew University president (and old Warburg friend) Judah Magnes, calling for a binational Jewish-Arab Palestine instead of a Jewish national homeland.[212] The Jews "are divided into several rival groups and are developing bitter enmity among them," he remarked in one report to Washington. "The amount of scheming and plotting and planning that is being carried out is astounding." There were some Jews (evidently he meant Magnes) who were making an "earnest effort to bring about a peaceful and reasonable solution," but they usually were met with "a great deal of opposition from some of their brethren of the other factions."[213] The running theme of Knabenshue's reports was his "firm conviction" that the Jewish behavior was the "immediate cause" of the Arab riots, claiming that a pro-Zionist rally in Tel Aviv in August was one of the three main reasons for the Arab violence.[214] "Jews generally bring their troubles upon themselves," he reported. Knabenshue even cited the Kishinev pogrom in Russia in 1903 as an example of Jews supposedly provoking their attackers.[215] The only real solution for Palestine, he insisted, was to scrap the Balfour Declaration and the entire idea of a Jewish state. Citing continued Arab attacks on Jewish outposts, general strikes initiated by the Arab Executive, a "growing spirit of organized action among Palestinian Arabs," and the staging of anti-Zionist conferences, Knabenshue insisted that there was "extremely tense feeling of Moslems throughout the country." The Jews were sorely mistaken if they believed that the Arabs would welcome them in Palestine, he wrote; "more serious and widespread disturbances" were inevitable.[216]

Jewish leaders, by contrast, painted an optimistic picture of the long-term prospects for Jewish-Arab relations in Palestine. In a major address in November, Supreme Court Justice and veteran Zionist leader Louis Brandeis compared the Zionist settlers in Palestine to the pioneers who developed California and insisted that Palestinian Arab opposition to the Jews had been "grossly exaggerated."[217]

The commission of inquiry under Sir Walter Shaw concluded otherwise; its final report directly challenged some of the key aspects of the Zionist enterprise. After three months of hearings, the commission in March 1930 decided that Jewish immigration and land purchases provoked the pogroms.[218] It also contended that during World War I, the British made contradictory promises to the Jews and the Arabs concerning the future of Palestine, further complicating the situation. The Shaw Commission urged the MacDonald administration to clarify its intentions in Palestine; prevent "excessive immigration" by Jews; assure the Arabs that the Zionists did not "share in any degree in the government of Palestine;" and undertake a study of Palestine's cultivation methods in order to be able to regulate future Jewish land purchases.[219]

Not surprisingly, Consul Knabenshue was elated by the Shaw Commission report, which he saw as a vindication of his own stance. The question of Britain's conflicting promises cut straight to the heart of the problem, Knabenshue explained to his State Department colleagues. There was no logical reason that the British promise to the Jews should be considered any more binding than their promise to the Arabs, he insisted. The only reason the Balfour Declaration was taken more seriously was Jewish financial power: "The Jews possibly used their money and influence to aid the Allied cause, but aside from one important Jewish battalion, they did not sacrifice their lives, and risk their future in case of defeat, as did the Arab."[220]

While Knabenshue saw his own opinions confirmed by the Shaw report, the State Department's internal confidential exchanges did "express concern" that Shaw's recommendations signaled a change in the terms of the mandate that could cause possible embarrassment to the department. After all, in 1924 an Anglo-American convention on Palestine was concluded that gave the United States the same rights as any member of the League of Nations. The agreement included the Balfour Declaration in its preamble and the articles of the Palestine mandate. As a result, many American Zionists insisted, the United States had become party to the British mandate by making sure that Great Britain lived up to its obligation to help establish a Jewish national home. Even though officials in the State Department never publicly acknowledged such U.S. responsibility and consistently proclaimed a policy of noninterference in the Palestine matter, the Near Eastern Division was worried and continued to solicit Knabenshue's expertise. The consul reassured his colleagues in Washington that he was in constant contact with British colonial officials to make sure that the mandate terms did not change and the U.S. would not get drawn into the Palestine controversy.[221]

The State Department's internal inquiry concluded that the inclusion of the Balfour Declaration in the preamble to the Anglo-American Convention did not obligate the U.S. to endorse creation of a Jewish national home; and that only an actual modification in the mandate that encroached upon the rights of American citizens or the equality of economic opportunity constituted cause to intervene. In any event, Knabenshue reassured his colleagues, in case of a pro-Arab shift in British policy, the words of the mandate and the Balfour Declaration could be manipulated in such a way that no changes in the mandate were even necessary to justify the new policy.[222]

Jews on both sides of the Atlantic were disappointed in the findings of the Shaw Commission, but Weizmann, speaking at a meeting of the Administrative Committee of the Jewish Agency in Berlin, reassured his audience that he had had the opportunity to discuss the Shaw report with government officials prior to its publication and found that the British government was not completely behind its findings.[223] Nonetheless, the leader of the Jewish Agency realized that the question of a Jewish national home in Palestine had become a matter of public opinion and Zionists as well as non-Zionists alike had to await the final word from the British government, which was to be the result of yet another investigation.[224] While Jews were growing impatient with the duration of British inquiries into the Palestine riots, the Naval Disarmament Conference opened in London amid great ceremonial fanfare in January 1930. Attended by delegates from Great Britain, the United States, France, Japan, and Italy, the conference continued for three months. France and Italy ultimately dropped out, and the U.S., England, and Japan signed a three-power agreement on April 22.[225] President Hoover's attempt to secure Senate ratification, however, did not proceed smoothly. A number of admirals testified that the terms too severely restricted the U.S. naval program.[226] New York Congressman Hamilton Fish, an outspoken supporter of Zionism, chose that very moment, when Congress appeared to be delaying ratification of the naval treaty, to raise the issue of British failings in Palestine. Fish implored London to unambiguously uphold the Balfour Declaration and permit unrestricted Jewish immigration to Palestine. Although he was "not one of those who delighted in twisting the lion's tail simply to hear him roar," Fish insisted, American public opinion would not tolerate a British betrayal of its pledge to the Jewish people.[227] The congressman did not threaten to tie British mandatory policy in Palestine to congressional ratification of the naval treaty, but his impassioned speech on the floor of the Senate in opposition to the Shaw findings and recommendations undoubtedly left an impression on Hoover and across the Atlantic.

Two days after Congressman Fish questioned Britain's ability or willingness to meet its obligations under the mandate, Hoover asked the State Department for an update on developments in Palestine.[228] State reported MacDonald's statement before the House of Commons in April that the government would adhere to the terms of the mandate. Moreover, rather than adopt the Shaw Commission's recommendations, MacDonald had decided to send a second commission, under the auspices of Sir John Hope Simpson, to examine the problem further.[229] The delay in ratification of the treaty, combined with Fish's speech, set off rumors among British officials that American Jews were pressuring the Hoover administration to oppose the naval agreement. Similarly, Consul Knabenshue later reported to the State Department that the British High Commissioner for Palestine, Sir John Chancellor, told him U.S. Jews were threatening to lobby against the treaty if England did not pursue a pro-Zionist policy in Palestine. Prime Minister MacDonald asked Weizmann about possible American Jewish opposition to the treaty. Weizmann dismissed the rumor, as did Warburg.[230] There was, in fact, no evidence of any Jewish attempt to link Palestine to the naval treaty debate, and the treaty was ratified by the Senate in July.[231] But the Palestine matter did not go away any time soon and took center stage by October 1930.

Uproar Over the Hope-Simpson Report

From the start, Weizmann assured his American Jewish colleagues that officials of the MacDonald administration did not necessarily support the Shaw Commission's findings. He expected Hope-Simpson's report to rectify the situation. In October, however, the Hope-Simpson commission recommended that Jewish immigration be halted altogether. It proposed that future immigration schedules should be determined according to Palestine's unemployment rate, and government land should only be sold to landless Arabs. These recommendations were then incorporated into government policy as the Passfield White Paper.[232]

American Jews, Zionists and non-Zionists alike, erupted in protest. Weizmann and Warburg resigned as cochairmen of the Jewish Agency in protest over the "viciously antagonistic" report. Weizmann, Warburg noted with concern, was "broken in health and courage." Angry letters poured into the State Department and the White House, protesting "the unconscionable acts of Great Britain." A petition by an ad hoc group of doctors, nurses, teachers, rabbis, and students urged the president to appeal to the British to safeguard the terms of the Balfour Declaration. Wallace Murray, head of the Near Eastern Division, prepared what he called "a stock reply to the ordinary run of American Jews" which declined to comment on Britain's Palestine policy on the grounds that the official text of the report had not yet been received. Knabenshue urged his colleagues to resist "Jewish pressure to interfere." Murray warned Secretary Stimson that he would "soon be subjected to a concerted pressure by American Jewry demanding that you 'do something about it.'" Murray offered a novel argument for American non-intervention: "In view of our recent policy of tightening up still more on immigration into the United States, we could hardly be expected to stultify ourselves in the eyes of the British by arguing a contrary policy in the case of Palestine."[233]

While the Near Eastern Division within the State Department consistently argued for a U.S. policy of non-interference in Palestine, President Hoover was not so certain that such a policy course was legally and morally the right one to chart. After he received a memorandum from "a very able source in New York" (most likely his friend Lewis Strauss), which not only stated that "America was deeply interested" in the Palestine situation, but also implied that the United States had the right to intervene if Great Britain changed its policy toward the mandate, Hoover asked for Stimson's "advice." What might have evoked Hoover's interest in particular was the claim that Great Britain's reduction of the Balfour Declaration to a "scrap of paper" was a "violation of international law" and might have implications for any other agreement that resulted from the Paris Peace Conference affecting the rights and lives of Jews. Hoover, who regarded the minorities treaties concluded in 1919 as a viable part of the postwar structure of peace and stability in Eastern Europe, found the arguments in the memorandum to be of "considerable importance" and brought it to the attention of the secretary of state.[234]

After receiving Hoover's inquiry, Stimson spent the entire afternoon reading up on the Palestine problem and deliberating with his colleagues Wallace Murray and John Cotton of the Near Eastern Division. It was "a pretty ticklish question," the secretary conceded. On the one hand, as he noted in his diary, there was nothing in the 1924 Anglo-American convention that required U.S. intervention; on the other hand, "we cannot say to the Jews that they have no claim at all to the intervention of their government on the subject."[235] After his conference with Murray and Cotton, Stimson went to have a short talk with the president. Hoover, the secretary found, shared his sentiment, calling it "a difficult question" but seemingly not worth souring relations with the British. A consultation with Justice Brandeis did little to clarify matters. Brandeis's comparison of the Zionists to America's colonial settlers left Stimson cold; the justice was "a good deal like a red Indian toward a white baby so far as the Arabs were concerned," he decided.[236]

A President Under Pressure

Despite pressure from anti-Zionists in his State Department, Hoover remained steadfast in his support for the upbuilding of Jewish Palestine, but declined to publicly criticize the MacDonald government at the height of the controversy. In June 1930, he had sent a message to the annual convention of the Zionist Organization of America, declaring his hope that the "discouragements of the moment" would not prevent "advancing Jewish aspirations" in Palestine.[237] He later sent a similar message to the founding convention of the ZOA's Christian Zionist affiliate, the Pro-Palestine Committee. American Zionist spokesmen exulted that the president was "deeply concerned with the grave problems which confront the ideal of Zionism today."[238] While Stimson and Murray were unable to shake Hoover's core sympathy for the Zionist endeavor, they did manage to convince him to refrain from publicly criticizing the Passfield White Paper or sending a message to a Zionist protest rally in New York. ZOA lobbyist Max Rhoade would nonetheless conclude that overall, the Hoover administration had been "friendly" to Zionism.[239]

On Sunday, November 2, 1930, the thirteenth anniversary of the Balfour Declaration, Jews throughout America organized mass meetings to protest the White Paper and stress the fact that the Jews' coming to Palestine was not to the detriment of the Arabs but rather furthered their civilization and development. Before a crowd of forty thousand at Madison Square Garden, Felix Frankfurter insisted that Arab-Jewish relations could not be furthered by "concessions to false suspicion" but had to be based on the "truth about the advantages derived by the Arab from Jewish endeavor." Frankfurter went on to say that he refused to believe that the White Paper expressed the policy of His Majesty's Government. "The most charitable view to take of the ill-starred White Paper," he contended, "is that oblivion will be its fate." Other prominent speakers included Senators William

Borah and Robert Wagner, Rep. Hamilton Fish, Senator, New York City mayor Jimmy Walker, and philanthropists Julius Rosenwald and Felix Warburg.[240]

It was in the midst of this firestorm over Britain's White Paper that the rumor about a specific Jewish threat to lobby against the administration's pro-British policy was resurrected. None other than Consul Knabenshue sent a memo of concern to the chief of the Near Eastern Division, imploring him not to give in to Jewish pressure. This was not the first time, the consul warned, that American Jews had tried to influence the U.S. government. The British high commissioner himself had told him, he reported, that American Jews had threatened Prime Minister MacDonald that they would lobby against ratification of the naval treaty if the British government did not pursue a pro-Zionist policy. That alone, Knabenshue explained, was sufficient evidence that American Jews had tried repeatedly to exert their influence on the government and that the State Department had a "very trying time" in its efforts to "handle the Jews and prevent our Government from becoming involved." The U.S. government, the consul insisted, had to maintain its policy of noninterference because the British policy as spelled out in the White Paper was the "only possible solution of the problem."[241]

Several weeks later, when President Hoover received a request to send a message to a gathering of Zionists in New York, the State Department strongly discouraged him from doing so. After several exchanges within the Division of Near Eastern Affairs, Assistant Secretary of State J.P. Cotton advised Hoover that "it is pretty hard to make any statement now of any kind which would not be hopelessly cold and non-committal or else capable of great misinterpretation—one evil is about as bad as the other. Therefore I do suggest you do not send any message." In spite of the fact that the meeting did not have the character of a protest or demonstration, Wallace Murray warned, the occasion could be used to attack the recent British statement of policy. While from a "domestic point of view," Hoover might consider it "desirable" to make such a statement (in view of upcoming congressional elections), Murray warned that "from the viewpoint of our international relations it would be best for the President to avoid becoming involved in a demonstration of this character."[242]

Given the domestic turmoil that was increasingly consuming Hoover's attention, American Jewish leaders probably could not have expected much more from the president. In the wake of the Stock Market crash of October 1929 and the onset of the Great Depression, the president naturally shifted his focus almost entirely to the economic situation. Remote Middle Eastern conflicts, especially one such as Palestine where an American ally seemed to have steady control of the situation, fell to the bottom of the president's agenda. Hoover did, however, send a pro-Zionist message to be read aloud at the founding conference, in January 1932, of a new Christian Zionist group, the American Palestine Committee. Vice President Charles Curtis and Supreme Court Justice Harlan Stone were among those in attendance. "I am interested to learn that a group of distinguished men and women is to be formed to spread knowledge and appreciation of the rehabilitation which is going forward in Palestine under Jewish auspices," Hoover wrote, "and to add my expression to the sentiment among our people in favor of the realization of the age-old aspirations of the Jewish people for the restoration of their national homeland." Despite the Palestine turmoil of 1929-1930, Hoover's bedrock pro-Zionist sentiment was unshaken.[243]

London's Reversal

The British Foreign Office interpreted Hoover's silence on the Passfield White Paper to mean that the U.S. government was "evidently most unwilling to intervene in any way" on the Palestine question. British officials were further cheered by indications that the American press in general was "critical of the extreme Zionist viewpoint," however that was defined. Americans understood that the British government was doing its best and that in any case the Palestine conflict was "none of America's business," the Foreign Office believed.[244]

Nonetheless, the Jewish protests against the White Paper, combined with criticism in the House of Commons, had a significant impact on England's Palestine policy. Weizmann's resignation led to a series of negotiations with the British government that concluded, in February 1931, with a letter from Prime Minister MacDonald to Weizmann that effectively rescinded the most severe aspects of the Passfield White Paper and reaffirmed the British commitment to fulfilling the existing terms of the mandate.

The Campaign of 1932

When it came to the Palestine question, the Jews in Hoover's inner circle were naturally a source of considerable influence on the Chief. Technically, men such as Strauss, Marshall, and Warburg were non-Zionists rather than Zionists, meaning they were keenly interested in the development of the Holy Land as a Jewish cultural center and a haven for refugees, but not a "national home" or sovereign state. They feared the existence of a Jewish state would endanger their own American citizenship. In the 1920s and 1930s, however, the distinction between Zionism and non-Zionism was largely academic.[245] Jews were at most one-fourth of Palestine's population at that time, so the possibility of statehood was far from imminent. Even a prominent American Zionist leader such as Julian Mack could tell Strauss, in 1920, that "there is no use today in talking about Jewish nationalism and a Jewish nation...[T]he task on which all Jews should unite, is to build up that land [in order to secure] a refuge for East European Jewry."[246] That is why the Zionists and non-Zionists were able to conclude their 1929 unity agreement. Hoover's sympathy for Jewish Palestine was, to a significant extent, sympathy for the practical campaign of building towns and draining swamps, exactly the kinds of projects that appealed to the heart of an engineer and a progressive.

Under other circumstances, Hoover's sympathy for Palestine and memories of his World War I-era humanitarian campaigns might have sufficed to win him one-fourth to one-third of Jewish votes in 1932, even if he made no additional effort to attract Jewish support, as was the case in 1928. But this time around, the deepening Depression placed the incumbent president at a great disadvantage.

Desperate to find additional votes wherever possible, Hoover dropped his previous opposition to the narrow pursuit of ethnic votes, and authorized his aides to seek support in the Jewish community. The Republican National Committee publicized a list of the president's Jewish appointees. Jewish communal activist Maurice Bisgyer (who later served as executive director of B'nai B'rith for nearly three decades) volunteered to prepare pamphlets in Yiddish and Hebrew, featuring statements from the president's prominent Jewish friends. Felix Warburg made speeches to Jewish audiences, hailing Hoover's personal work ethic and his "open heart...to the opinions, beliefs, and creeds of other men." At Strauss's urging, Hoover preempted the Democratic nominee, New York Governor Franklin D. Roosevelt, by sending a message to the annual ZOA convention, reiterating American support for the Balfour Declaration and its promise of a Jewish national home. FDR's message was almost identical, but Strauss was pleased that at least Hoover's arrived first.[247]

Palestine was never an issue for Jewish voters in 1932. Like most Americans, the overwhelming majority of Jews faulted Hoover's response to the Depression as inadequate. His reputation as a humanitarian and problem-solver, which had played such a significant role in his political rise, was severely eroded, and his close collaboration with Jewish relief agencies, which had boosted his popularity in the Jewish community, was largely forgotten. On Election Day, an estimated 85% of American Jews cast their ballots for Roosevelt.

Chapter 4

Hoover, Anne Frank, and the Problem of Immigration

May 24, 1939.
A typical Washington dinner party. Government officials, diplomats, newspaper editors, and spouses rubbed elbows and made small talk. Occasionally the chatter turned to current controversy, and there was nothing more controversial at that moment than the battle on Capitol Hill over the Wagner-Rogers bill, which proposed to admit 20,000 German Jewish refugee children outside the quota system. Jay Pierrepont Moffat, chief of the State Department's Western European Division, found himself seated next to Laura Delano Houghteling, cousin of President Roosevelt and wife of the U.S. Commissioner of Immigration. Moffat, a staunch opponent of increased immigration, appreciated Mrs. Houghteling's view of the legislation and jotted it down in his diary: "[H]er principal reserve on the bill was that 20,000 charming children would all too soon grow up into 20,000 ugly adults."[248]

That same week, nearly four thousand miles away, two charming little girls were having photographs taken for their passports. Mrs. Edith Frank, a German Jewish housewife living in Amsterdam, was updating the passports of her daughters Margot, age 13, and Anne, age 10, because she was desperately hoping to receive permission to immigrate to the United States. If Wagner-Rogers had passed, Margot and Anne theoretically could have been among the fortunate thousands who would be able to escape the Nazis.

For bigots and nativists such as Mrs. Houghteling, the immigration laws enacted in 1921 and 1924 were crucial to safeguarding America from an influx of undesirables. In their view, the edict issued by President Hoover in 1930 to tighten immigration restrictions was a vital asset in keeping out the unwashed hordes, and Wagner-Rogers was a diabolical maneuver to evade the will of the people and their government. Undoubtedly much to Mrs. Houghteling's dismay, one of the most important supporters of Wagner-Rogers was the very man who had made it harder for refugees such as Anne Frank to reach America: Herbert Hoover.

FDR's Response to German Antisemitism

Adolf Hitler became chancellor of Germany on January 30, 1933. Anti-Jewish measures followed almost immediately. In addition to sporadic outbursts of antisemitic violence, early steps undertaken by the Nazi regime included the exclusion of Jews from government jobs, restrictions on Jewish doctors and lawyers, the imposition of tight quotas on Jews admitted to schools and universities, and a one-day national boycott of Jewish businesses. With Berlin's encouragement, local governments enacted additional discriminatory laws, such as prohibiting the kosher slaughter of animals.

The Roosevelt administration hoped to maintain friendly diplomatic and economic relations with Germany, and therefore refrained from publicly criticizing what it considered to be Germany's internal affairs. The administration's position posed a dilemma for Rabbi Stephen S. Wise. As leader of the American Jewish Congress, the World Jewish Congress, and the American Zionist movement, Wise was arguably American Jewry's most influential figure, and as a staunch supporter of Roosevelt and the New Deal, he enjoyed greater access to the White House than other Jewish organizational leaders. Privately, Wise was deeply troubled by Roosevelt's hands-off attitude regarding German Jewry, but he was reluctant to publicly take issue with a president whose other policies he so fervently supported.

In early March 1933, shortly before Hoover left office, Jewish leaders asked Lewis Strauss to seek a joint statement of some kind from Hoover and Roosevelt, protesting the mistreatment of German Jews. FDR declined. Hoover, for his part, was concerned a public statement might "embarrass" his successor and, in any event, he had already decided to stay out of the public limelight for at least the first few months of the new administration. He did, however, agree to send a behind-the-scenes message to the American ambassador in Germany, Frederic Sackett, instructing him "to exert every influence of our government" on the Hitler regime to halt the persecutions. By contrast, when William E. Dodd was chosen by Roosevelt later that year to replace Sackett, FDR informed Dodd that the persecution of German Jewry was "not a [U.S.] governmental affair" and

Rabbi Stephen S. Wise

therefore he should employ only "unofficial and personal influence," except with regard to the handful of American citizens in Germany.[249]

Rabbi Wise was disappointed by FDR's lack of cooperation, but chose to hold his tongue because, as he explained to a colleague, he "hesitate[d] to use up any of Roosevelt's limited time and to add to his terrible cares." That was in March. Another month passed, and still "the president has not by a single word or act intimated the faintest interest in what is going on" regarding the Jews in Germany, Wise confided to a friend. Three months later, nothing had changed: "FDR has not lifted a finger on behalf of the Jews of Germany," Wise wrote to a colleague in July. "We have had nothing but indifference and unconcern up to this time."[250] Wise kept his concerns private. He told 1,000 delegates at a conference of Jewish groups in New York City they should be satisfied "that no American ambassador has been sent to Berlin." It was small consolation, and short-lived, at that; the delay in sending a new envoy was not a protest against Germany's policies, and, in any event, six weeks later, Roosevelt chose his new ambassador.[251]

Other Jews of prominence were no more successful than Wise in getting anything out of Roosevelt regarding German Jewry. Longtime FDR friend and soon-to-be cabinet member Henry Morgenthau Jr. and New York judge Irving Lehman visited the White House in September 1933 to request a statement about the plight of Germany's Jews. FDR told them he preferred to make a statement about human rights abuses in Germany in general, without focusing on the Jews. Ultimately, however, he made no such statement. In the eighty-two press conferences FDR held in 1933, the subject of the persecution of the Jews arose just once, and not at Roosevelt's initiative. It would be five years, and another 348 presidential press conferences, before anything about the Nazi persecutions would be mentioned again. Although personally discomfited by Hitler's treatment of the Jews, Roosevelt was unwilling to strain American-German relations by publicly complaining about such human rights abuses.[252]

Nor was Roosevelt prepared to admit larger numbers of German Jewish immigrants to the United States. The quota for Germany theoretically permitted a maximum of 25,957 German citizens to immigrate each year. However, the harsh administration of the criteria for awarding a visa, including Hoover's 1930 edict tightening the "likely to become a public charge" clause, reduced the actual number of immigrants to a small fraction of the maximum allowed. In 1933, only 1,324 (5.3%) of the German quota places were filled. Hoover's action was taken in response to the onset of the Great Depression, at a time when there was no significant body of foreign nationals clamoring for haven from religious or ethnic persecution. Roosevelt, as president, declined to rescind the 1930 edict despite the changed international situation. As the plight of German Jewry worsened in the years to follow, he did permit a slight loosening of the administration of the quotas, but the German quota remained largely unfilled. In 1934, 3,515 German nationals immigrated to the United States (13.7% of the quota); in 1935, 4,891 (20.2%); in 1936, 6,073 (24.3%); in 1937, 11,127 (42.1%). Out of a total of 129,785 German nationals who could have been admitted during the first five years of the Hitler regime, only 26,930 (21% of the total) actually entered the United States. If the president so desired, nearly 83,000 additional German Jews could have been granted haven from Nazism without a contentious battle with Congress over the immigration system. All he had to was instruct the State Department to liberalize the way in which it administered the existing quotas.[253]

The Roosevelt administration strongly opposed congressional initiatives to increase Jewish refugee immigration, such as a 1933 bill proposed by Rep. Samuel Dickstein (D-New York) to loosen the visa requirements for "children and aged and infirm relatives of naturalized United States citizens" (it would have affected immigrants from any country, not just Germany, although Dickstein made clear his immediate concern was German Jewry). Some major American Jewish organizations, fearful they would be accused of flooding the country with refugees, also opposed Dickstein's bill and helped convince him to drop it.[254]

Hoover and Immigration

Hoover and the GOP did not take issue with Roosevelt's immigration policy. The overwhelming majority of the public likewise opposed increasing immigration. The 1917 Soviet revolution in Russia sparked anxiety about Communism and fears that European radicals would import it to America. The changing face of American society as a result of the influx of European immigrants provoked fears of foreigners in general, especially Catholics and Jews. Prominent anthropologists contributed to the public's growing racism and paranoia by promoting theories that non-Caucasian races were corrupting Anglo-Saxon society. These sentiments, combined with racial tensions related to the post-World War I movement of many African-Americans from the south to northern urban areas, contributed to an upsurge in support for the Ku Klux Klan, which at its peak, in the early 1920s, boasted a membership of more than four million. The onset of the Depression intensified these anxieties and fears throughout the 1930s.

Opposition to immigration sometimes was also motivated by antisemitism, which reached unprecedented levels during this period. By 1940, more than one hundred antisemitic organizations were active throughout the United States. The antisemitic Catholic priest Father Charles Coughlin published a weekly tabloid, *Social Justice*, to which more than 200,000 Americans subscribed, and his Sunday radio broadcasts were heard regularly by 3.5 million listeners, along with an additional ten million who tuned in at least once each month. Polls found over half of the U.S. population perceived Jews as greedy and dishonest, and about one-third considered them overly aggressive. Surveys between 1938 and 1941 showed that between one-third and one-half of the public believed that Jews had "too much power in the United States." Approximately 15% of those surveyed in the late 1930s or early 1940s said they would support "a widespread campaign against the Jews in this country," and another 20-25% would have sympathized with such a movement; only about 30% indicated they would have actively opposed it. Such sentiments lent a particularly ferocious tone to some of the opposition to immigration. In the face of this public mood, few Republicans—or Democrats, for that matter—were prepared to challenge the administration's restrictive policies on immigration.[255]

Hoover's name did surface, however, as a candidate for the newly-created position of League of Nations High Commissioner for Refugees Coming from Germany. The initiative for the commission came from refugee advocates associated with the Foreign Policy Association, chaired by James G. McDonald, and the American Jewish Committee. AJC vice president Morris Waldman included Hoover's name on his list of potential leaders for the new commission. McDonald supported Hoover's candidacy and during his travels through Europe in the autumn of 1933 canvassed a number of League supporters and delegates concerning Hoover. British legal scholar and diplomat Norman Bentwich favored the former president for the post, as did several others with whom McDonald spoke. But Spain's delegate to the League, Salvador de Madariaga, objected on grounds that Hoover had been insufficiently supportive of the League as president and therefore should not be given "an opportunity for service that would help him to recoup his prestige." French politician and diplomat Henri Berenger opposed Hoover's candidacy because he "has been defeated [in the presidential election] only recently." American diplomat Hugh Wilson poured additional cold water on the idea by telling McDonald "there was no chance at all of Hoover's acceptance." That may be so, in view of Hoover's declared intention to stay out of the public limelight during the early months of the Roosevelt administration. In any event, it seems likely that given the chilly relations between Roosevelt and Hoover, the White House would not have wanted to see Hoover offered a job that might help pave the way for his political comeback.[256]

To further complicate matters, the possibility of Hoover being chosen was leaked to reporters, spoiling McDonald's plan to keep the discussions behind the scenes until a strong consensus had formed around one candidate. Once it was clear to McDonald that there was no consensus supporting Hoover, the former president's name was dropped from the list of contenders. In the end, McDonald himself accepted the post of commissioner, only to resign two years later in protest against the international community's failure to take a serious interest in finding havens for German Jews fleeing Hitler.[257]

Visiting Nazi Germany

A substantial number of Americans visited Nazi Germany during the 1930s. Tourists who had spent time in Germany prior to 1933 wanted to see for themselves how things had changed under Hitler. Businessmen hoped to take advantage of new opportunities created by the improvements in the German economy. Students and academics still looked to Germany as a world center of scholarship, literature, music, and art. Political figures, including Herbert Hoover, sought to assess, first-hand, Germany's new leadership, the prospects for American-German relations, and the likelihood of war in Europe.

The Germans encouraged visitors, in the hope of improving the Reich's image abroad. Indeed, the luxurious zeppelin *Hindenburg* was designed for the specific purpose of facilitating tourism so as to impress foreigners and distract attention from Hitler's aggressive actions. Many Americans who visited Germany returned with glowing reports about its clean streets and efficient transportation. This was particularly the case during the summer 1936 Olympic Games in Berlin, when the Nazis made an extra effort to put their best face forward and hide evidence of the less pleasant side of life in Germany. American University chancellor Joseph Gray, for example, spoke highly of the "New Germany" when he returned from a visit in August 1936. German cities were "amazingly clean" and "everybody is working," he proclaimed. In "We Went to Germany," a *Vasser Review* feature about four students who spent the year 1934 at German universities, the girls praised the Nazis' accomplishments, denied American press reports about "militarism, terrorism, and bloodshed" in the Reich, called Americans' criticism of Germany "cruel," and defended what they called Nazi Germany's "right to work out her own destiny in her own way."[258]

Even President Roosevelt was to a certain extent taken in by these Nazi propaganda efforts. In October 1936, he told Rabbi Wise, "I have just seen two people who have toured Germany. They tell me that they saw that the Synagogues were crowded and apparently there is nothing very wrong in the situation at present." Wise, horrified, tried to explain how the Nazis deceived tourists. "He listened carefully," Wise reported to Justice Brandeis, "but I could see that the tourists (whoever they were, the Lord bless them not) had made an impression upon him."[259]

Some journalists strengthened these perceptions by filing news reports and features that cast Hitler in a positive light. Anne O'Hare McCormick's fawning interview with the Fuhrer for the *New York Times* in July 1933 helped set the tone for some of the early American press coverage of the Nazis. McCormick's dispatch, which appeared on the front page, began, "There is at least one official voice in Europe that expresses understanding of the methods and motives of President Roosevelt. This voice is that of Germany, as represented by Chancellor Adolf Hitler." Not only was the Nazi leader pro-American, he was humble, too: "Above [his office] is a small, simple apartment in which he chooses to live rather than in the spacious house next door that was once occupied by Prince Bismarck." Moreover, Hitler "has the sensitive hand of the artist," "smiles frequently," has a voice "as quiet as his black tie," and "his eyes are almost the color of the blue larkspur in a vase behind him, curiously childlike and candid..."[260]

Five years later, despite the alarming developments of the intervening years— among them the promulgation of the Nuremberg Laws, the militarization of the Rhineland in contravention of the Versailles Treaty, and the annexation of Austria—some *Times* reporters were still finding nice things to say about Hitler. In a September 1938 feature, Berlin correspondent Guido Enderis offered a pleasant portrait of a nature-loving Hitler relaxing in his humble "highland chalet."

The Fuhrer's home "is simple in its appointments and commands a magnificent highland panorama...Herr Hitler in principle detests the big cities, where 'the houses are thick and the sewers annoy the air.' He craves moderate altitudes and highland breezes."[261]

Hoover, too, visited Nazi Germany, but he utilized the occasion to cast the Hitler regime in a negative light. The genesis of the encounter was an invitation, in late 1937, from the government of Belgium, which wanted to honor the former president for his humanitarian efforts in World War I. Hoover ultimately decided to turn the visit into a broad survey of the situation on the continent, in February and March 1938. Germany was on the itinerary but Hoover had no plans to meet senior government officials there. Upon his arrival in Berlin on March 7, however, Hoover was informed by the U.S. ambassador, Hugh Wilson, that Hitler wanted to see him the next day. Hoover demurred but Wilson strongly pressed him to accept, and in the end the ex-president reluctantly assented. Wilson was the only other American permitted to attend the March 8 meeting at the Reich Chancellory. The one-hour conversation, in which Hitler did most of the talking, focused on employment, agriculture, housing, and other German domestic issues. Hoover acknowledged what he called the "hopeful, live atmosphere" in the country and the government's achievements. Hitler, appealing to one of Hoover's chief concerns, spoke at length about the threat that Communism posed to Germany and the rest of Europe. Hitler's justification of his totalitarian actions prompted Hoover to reply with a defense of "spiritual and intellectual freedom" and criticism of Germany's imposition of "restrictive measures."

Afterwards, Hoover apparently leaked details of the conversation, with a strong emphasis on the totalitarianism-versus-democracy angle, to Paul Smith of the *San Francisco Chronicle*. Smith was accompanying the former president on his trip to Europe, but the Nazis barred him from the Hoover-Hitler meeting because the *Chronicle* had been critical of Hitler. Smith relayed the account Hoover gave him to other American reporters in Berlin. The story appeared on the front page of the next day's *New York Times* under the headline "Hoover Blunt to Hitler on Nazism; Says Progress Demands Liberty." "Former President Herbert Hoover appears to have given Chancellor Adolf Hitler at noon today the unusual experience of hearing doubt cast on the fundamental ideas of National Socialism and on the likelihood that it will be a successful system of government," the *Times* report began. "Mr. Hoover is reported to have told the Fuehrer that in any case National Socialism is built on principles of government that it would be wholly impossible for the American people to tolerate in their own country." Whether or not the actual tone and content of the exchange were as contentious as the *Times* indicated is impossible to ascertain, but Hoover evidently hoped he would be seen as having been blunt, even confrontational, with the German leader. That he would take this approach is interesting in view of the fact that Hoover hoped to capture the 1940 Republican presidential nomination, and the party was dominated by isolationists who would not be impressed by the former president clashing with Germany's chancellor.[262]

The same afternoon he met with Hoover, Hitler was finalizing plans for the *Anschluss*, Germany's absorption of Austria. The day after Hoover left Germany, the Nazis bullied Austria's leaders into resigning, and shortly afterwards German troops marched into Vienna. The brutalization of Austria's Jews which accompanied the *Anschluss* cast a fresh international spotlight on Nazi barbarism. Accounts in the American press described the spiraling rate of suicide among Jews in Vienna and harrowing scenes of storm troopers forcing Austrian Jews to scrub the streets with toothbrushes. "Overnight," the *New York Times* reported, Vienna's Jews "were made free game for mobs, despoiled of their property, deprived of police protection, ejected from employment and barred from sources of relief."[263]

Approaches to Isolationism

Hoover delivered his first comments on the Anschluss and the broader European situation in an address to the Council on Foreign Relations, in New York City, on March 31, shortly after his return to the United States. The Hitler regime's economic and technological achievements could not mask its brutality and abuses, he declared. Perhaps in the realm of "material things," the German people were "today better off than five years ago," Hoover said. "Yet to a lover of human liberty there is another side to even this picture." Under the Nazis, life in Germany was characterized by "suppression of all criticism and free expression"; "drilling children and youth, stage by stage, to a governmentally prescribed mental attitude"; "a controlled press and organized propaganda"; the control or elimination of "every form of independent association from trade unions to universities"; the establishment of "concentration camps"; and "its darkest picture...the heart-breaking persecution of helpless Jews." At the same time, Hoover urged the U.S. to do its utmost to "keep out of other people's wars." President Roosevelt's October 1937 proposal to "quarantine" totalitarian regimes through economic pressure would mean "the building up of a war between government faiths or ideologies," reminiscent of "old religious wars." Hoover feared dormant European totalitarian impulses, reborn in the ideologies of fascism and communism, might drag America into conflicts that were "not our business."[264]

As Europe's conflicts multiplied in the mid and late 1930s, American public sentiment was becoming more firmly isolationist. A poll in 1937 found 71% of Americans thought the United States was wrong to have entered World War I; many believed the U.S. had been tricked into the conflict by greedy weapons manufacturers. The hardships of the Great Depression further intensified the view that domestic concerns required America's full attention and that the country could not spare any resources for overseas matters. While most Americans found Hitler's totalitarian ways distasteful, only about one-tenth were willing to go to war for any reason other than to fend off an invasion of America's shores. Extreme isolationists, whose best known spokesman was aviation hero Charles Lindbergh, coalesced around the America First movement. Even after the Germans ignited World War II in September 1939, the isolationists opposed all U.S. military aid to Great Britain and accused American Jewry of trying to drag America into the war with Germany. Hoover repudiated America First and advocated a more moderate approach, which he called "positive neutrality," based on the principle that "neither isolation nor intervention [are] possible or wis[e]." By 1941, he supported giving the British "the tools, and even warships" to fend off the Germans, although he opposed using American convoys to escort the delivery of those weapons.[265]

Nonetheless, some prominent Jewish supporters of FDR, such as Rabbi Wise, tended to view all of President Roosevelt's conservative critics, including Hoover, as part of a single bloc of extremists and reactionaries. Wise, who backed the administration's approach of aid to the allies short of war, spoke at an anti-isolationist rally in Madison Square Garden in April 1938, a few days after Hoover's speech to the Council on Foreign Relations. In his address, Wise in one breath denounced the Archbishop of Vienna, Theodor Innitzer, for supporting the Anschluss; the New York Catholic prelate Patrick Cardinal Hayes, for supporting Franco in the Spanish Civil War; and Hoover, for opposing American intervention in "wars of old world ideologies." Wise lumped the three men and their positions together, asserting that "any American who considers the war in Spain and the invasion of Austria wars of old world ideologies has ceased to be an American."

Ironically, however, Wise's own positions regarding U.S. policy towards Europe did not differ significantly from Hoover's. From the mid-1920s until the late 1930s, Wise was a self-described pacifist. He rooted for the anti-fascist Spanish Republican forces, as did many American liberals, but he never advocated

American action to help them. After years of regarding the Soviet Union as more a force for good than for evil, Wise finally decided, in the wake of the Soviet and German invasions of Poland in September 1939, that "they are both equally the enemies of democracy"—eighteen months after Hoover made exactly that point in the Council on Foreign Relations speech that Wise attacked. And it was not until well into 1941 that Wise completely abandoned his pacifism and endorsed U.S. military intervention against Hitler. Thus Wise's attack on Hoover in April 1938, like his attitude toward Hoover throughout the Roosevelt era, was shaped less by the particulars of Hoover's actual positions, than by Wise's worldview, in which most Republicans and conservatives were the enemy. Wise saw himself and the Roosevelt administration as allies in a struggle by progressives to aid Britain despite the opposition of Republican reactionaries and isolationists. Ironically, however, some officials in the administration itself seized precisely on Jewish leaders' support for England as a pretext for private antisemitic utterances. Assistant Secretary of State Adolf Berle, for example, wrote in his diary in 1940 that American Jewish support of Britain was evidence of "one phase of the Nazi propaganda justifying itself a little. The Jewish group, wherever you find it, is not only pro-English, but will sacrifice American interests to English interests..." As Wise would gradually discover, presumed friends, and presumed enemies, sometimes turned out to be something else entirely.[266]

The Search for Havens

As a result of the *Anschluss*, there were new calls from some members of Congress, as well as influential newspaper columnists such as Dorothy Thompson, for U.S. action to aid the Jews. The Roosevelt administration continued to resist engaging in what Undersecretary of State Sumner Welles called "polemics or recrimination over internal policies of other nations, regarding which we have no rightful concern." At the same time, State Department officials, fearing that such criticism would become "exceedingly strong and prolonged," decided it would be politically prudent to "get out in front and attempt to guide" the pro-refugee pressure before it got out of hand. Welles proposed to President Roosevelt the idea of holding an intergovernmental conference, in Evian, France, to discuss the refugee problem. FDR assented, while making clear in his March 24 announcement of the gathering that "no nation would be expected or asked to receive a greater number of emigrants than is permitted by its existing legislation."[267]

The Evian conference, which was held from July 6 to July 15, 1938, fell far short of refugee advocates' hopes. One speaker after another reaffirmed their countries' unwillingness to accept more Jews. The Australian delegate announced that "as we have no real racial problem, we are not desirous of importing one." The British refused even to discuss Palestine as a possible haven. One critic pointed out that "Evian" was "Naive" spelled backwards. The problem, however, was not naiveté so much as it was calculated indifference.[268]

While countries with vast amounts of unpopulated territory remained intransigent at Evian, the tiny Dominican Republic announced it would take up to 100,000 Jewish refugees. In the end, however, less than 1,000 arrived before the project was stalled, primarily due to pressure from State Department officials on the Dominican government to refrain from admitting refugees lest they turn out to be Nazi spies. In an episode that exemplified the administration's mindset, FBI agents in 1941 believed they discovered refugees-turned-Nazi spies sending shore-to-sea signals from the Dominican beach front to German submarines in the Caribbean. The lights that were seen turned out to be from the flashlights of refugee settlers doing chores near the beach. The fact that not a single Jewish refugee, whether in North America or South, was ever found to have become a spy for the Nazis did not dissuade the Roosevelt administration from insisting that immigration needed to be severely restricted because of the danger of such spies.[269]

Evian produced next to nothing, but the search for havens intensified during the months to follow. Roosevelt exhibited a kind of amateur geographer's fascination with the idea of moving large masses of people around and creating new countries or societies, although his interest in these matters tended to wax and wane. In the spring of 1938, FDR established a President's Advisory Committee on Political Refugees, and at Evian, an Intergovernmental Committee on Refugees was set up to implement a resettlement scheme if one ever materialized. From 1938 to 1941, the two committees examined dozens of proposals for settling Jewish refugees in far-flung corners of the globe. Roosevelt at one point hired the anthropologist Henry Field to carry out the so-called "M Project"—an assessment of 666 possible sites for settling refugees. Incredibly, not one of those sites ever passed muster in Washington's eyes. In some cases, local conditions were presumed to be too grueling for urban Europeans. In other instances, the first signs of local opposition qualified as an insurmountable obstacle. The Roosevelt administration at times seemed interested in persuading Latin American countries to absorb refugees, but at other times it regarded those areas as too close to the United States, given the imagined danger of Nazi spies slipping in among the newcomers. Typically, the U.S. opposed setting up havens in territories controlled by, or in close proximity to, its shores, while the British opposed creating havens in their colonies. Secretary of the Interior Harold Ickes urged opening the doors of the Virgin Islands, a U.S. territory, but the State Department persuaded the president that "all kinds of undesirables and spies" would enter the Islands disguised as refugees, and from there proceed to the United States. "I have sympathy," FDR told Ickes. "I cannot, however, do anything which would conceivably hurt the future of present American citizens." Underpopulated Alaska was not subject to the regular immigration quotas since it was not yet a state, but Ickes's promotion of Alaska as a possible haven fared no better. FDR said he would support only a plan in which no more than 10% of the newcomers would be Jews, so as "to avoid the undoubted criticism that we would be subjected to if there were an undue proportion of Jews." The State Department and nativist groups strongly opposed allowing any use of Alaska for refugee resettlement, and Roosevelt soon dropped the whole idea.[270]

Hoover took an active interest in one particular proposed haven: Central Africa. In mid-1938, Bernard Baruch, the financier and sometime presidential adviser—whom Hoover knew from their service on the Wilson administration's War Council—came to the conclusion that the Central African uplands, consisting of parts of Rhodesia, Tanganyika, Kenya, and Congo, should be developed into a "United States of Africa" for European Jewish and non-Jewish refugees. In correspondence with potential supporters, including Lewis Strauss, Baruch proposed that "Great engineers like Herbert Hoover should study the country for drainage, power, cultivation, mining minerals, and oil."[271]

The Africa scheme appealed both to Hoover's engineering instincts and his humanitarian impulses. He quickly became a leading member of Baruch's small working group to promote the plan. "[I]t does seem to have the soil, climate and resources upon which ten to twenty millions of white civilization could be builded," Hoover wrote in a statement of endorsement that Baruch circulated. The plan envisioned a self-imposed tax on world Jewry to raise the $500 million needed to establish the new country.[272]

In 1939, Hoover dispatched Lewis Strauss to England to sound out British leaders on the feasibility of the Central Africa proposal. "London seethes with schemes," a disappointed Strauss reported back to Hoover. Someone had offered "a plantation in Brazil which would take thousands [of Jews]—only Brazil will not admit them." A fellow associated with the Duke of Windsor was circulating a plan to settle "millions of refugees in the 'Suds'," which, Strauss discovered, "turn out to be swamps of the Upper Nile of the Sudan where no human life, white or black, exists." The British had offered one of their Western hemisphere possessions, the Caribbean nation of Guiana, and even offered to foot half the bill, but the Roosevelt administration was balking. As for Central Africa, Colonial Secretary Malcolm MacDonald trotted out studies claiming the area was too primitive to sustain a large settlement. Strauss insisted the studies were flawed and urged MacDonald to reexamine the idea, but to no avail.[273]

Finding a haven became a matter of greater urgency when the persecution of Jews in Germany intensified suddenly and dramatically in the autumn of 1938. On the night of November 9-10, the Nazis dispatched mobs of storm troopers to carry out nationwide pogroms which came to be known as Kristallnacht ("Night of the Glass"—a reference to the vast amount of plate glass shattered in attacks on Jewish property.) About 100 Jews were murdered and 30,000 more were sent to concentration camps. Nearly 200 synagogues were burned down, and more than 7,000 Jewish-owned businesses were destroyed. President Roosevelt condemned the pogrom and took two small symbolic actions: he recalled the U.S. ambassador from Germany for "consultations," but did not suspend diplomatic or trade relations; and he extended the visas of the 12,000-15,000 German Jewish refugees who were then in the United States as visitors, while emphasizing to reporters that liberalization of America's immigration procedures was "not in contemplation." The administration did, however, permit the German and Austrian quotas to be filled in the months to follow, the only time during the entire Hitler period that all of the quota places were utilized. The respite was brief. By 1940 and every year thereafter, the quotas were again severely underfilled.[274]

Hoover denounced Kristallnacht as "an outbreak of brutal intolerance," one he found particularly shocking coming as it did from "a race whose kindly fable of Santa Claus we tell to our children, whose magnificent music delights our people, whose literature and poetry our youngsters study, whose philosophy engages our scholars." The violence inflicted by the Nazis not only "grieves every decent American," he said, but "makes us fearful for the whole progress of civilization..." Hoover, Ickes, and 1936 Republican presidential nominee Alf Landon took part in a bipartisan radio denunciation of the anti-Jewish persecution, although President Roosevelt insisted beforehand that the Interior Secretary remove any explicit mentions of Hitler and Mussolini from his remarks.[275]

Hoover did not confine his response to verbal condemnation. When, in the wake of Kristallnacht, refugee advocates proposed a bold new measure to aid German Jewry, Hoover rallied to their side. The new proposal, crafted by Senator

Robert Wagner (D-New York) and Rep. Edith Rogers (R-Massachusetts) was legislation to admit 20,000 German refugee children outside the quota system. Supporters of the bill included clergymen, labor leaders, university presidents, actors (among them Henry Fonda and Helen Hayes), and political figures such as Alf Landon and his running mate, Frank Knox, and former First Lady Grace Coolidge, who announced that she and her friends in Northampton, Massachusetts would personally care for twenty-five of the children. Arguably the most prominent, and unexpected, political figure to back Wagner-Rogers was Hoover. His statement of support was read aloud at the congressional hearings on the legislation. In view of his earlier close association with restrictions on immigration, Hoover's endorsement of a bill allowing greater immigration surprised political observers, made the front page of the *New York Times*, and constituted a significant boost for the legislation. Hoover also assisted the sponsors of the bill behind the scenes, by pressuring wavering members of the House Immigration Committee to support the measure.[276]

Hoover's stance was especially noteworthy because it ran counter to his political interests. In the years following his defeat by Roosevelt, Hoover harbored ambitions of returning to the White House. In 1936, he hoped to be offered the Republican nomination, and as the 1940 election drew closer, he again dreamed of a deadlocked convention turning to him. To champion the influx of more immigrants in mid-1939, at a time when most of the Republican Party, like most of the general public, still was so strongly against immigration, could only harm his chances of a political comeback.

Some refugee advocates hoped to involve Hoover more actively in the Wagner-Rogers campaign, but Rabbi Wise and the State Department objected. At a meeting of the President's Advisory Committee on Political Refugees, chairman James McDonald proposed "that Mr. Herbert Hoover might assume leadership in raising funds and in administering the work of placing the children in suitable homes." Rabbi Wise, a member of the committee, objected, insisting that "no member of the Committee should make this suggestion to Mr. Hoover until it had been determined in advance that the President and the Department of State approved of the plan." There was little chance of the administration approving, given the icy relations between FDR and Hoover personally, and the possibility that Hoover conceivably could be the Republican candidate against Roosevelt in 1940. The committee members nonetheless agreed with Wise. As a result, instead of approaching Hoover, McDonald first broached the suggestion with State Department official Theodore Achilles, who strongly opposed it, effectively burying the idea.[277]

Numerous patriotic and anti-foreigner groups, including the American Legion and the Daughters of the American Revolution, mobilized against Wagner-Rogers. They shared the sentiment expressed in the aforementioned remark by the president's cousin, Laura Delano Houghteling, about "20,000 charming children" growing up into "20,000 ugly adults." The president himself took no position. When the First Lady asked him to support the bill, he declined, while saying he would not object if she endorsed it. (She did not do so, however.) An inquiry by a congresswoman as to the president's position was returned to Roosevelt's secretary marked "File No action FDR." Roosevelt was mindful of polls showing most Americans opposed to more immigration, and so he chose to—as Winston Churchill once described one of FDR's traits—"follow public opinion rather than to form it and lead it."[278]

In April 1939, a joint Senate-House committee held four days of hearings on Wagner-Rogers. Sympathetic witnesses offered moving humanitarian pleas. They also stressed that the children would not compete with American citizens for jobs. Nativist opponents presented standard anti-immigration claims as well as innovative assertions such as the claim that the wording of the bill could enable 20,000 Nazi children to come to the U.S., and therefore the effect of the bill would be to tear German families apart. The two subcommittees voted unanimously in favor of Wagner-Rogers. Opponents, however, then mounted a feverish behind-the-scenes counter-attack, which, together with the absence of White House support, resulted in a House Immigration Committee vote that in effect killed the Wagner-Rogers bill, by adding an amendment requiring the 20,000 child immigrants to be charged against the existing German quota. The amendment had the effect of nullifying the entire original purpose of the legislation. A year later, *Pets Magazine* launched a campaign to have Americans take in purebred British puppies so they would not be harmed by German bombing raids. The magazine received several thousand offers of haven for the dogs.[279]

Chapter 5

Hoover and the Holocaust

August 22, 1939.

A typical blazing-hot summer afternoon on the Tel Aviv beachfront. Swimmers frolicked in the surf, sunbathers sprawled on their cabanas, children built sandcastles, ice cream vendors peddled frozen treats. Suddenly, out of nowhere, an extraordinary sight began to take shape over the horizon: a ramshackle, 563-ton former cattle transport ship, flying a huge, homemade Zionist flag. And it was heading straight for the beach.

For the past two years, Zionist activists in Europe had been smuggling boatloads of desperate Jewish refugees to Palestine, in defiance of England's severe immigration restrictions. But they always arrived in the middle of the night. And they always landed far up the coast, at obscure destinations where British patrols were unlikely to find them. The S.S. *Parita*, overloaded to the bursting point with more than 800 refugees, had appeared in broad daylight and was making a beeline for the most crowded strip of beach in the eastern Mediterranean.

More than a month earlier, the *Parita*'s uneventful six-day voyage from Rumania ran into trouble when the landing ship that was supposed to meet it at Cyprus and take its passengers to Palestine, was intercepted by the British. Running dangerously low on food, the *Parita* docked temporarily at the Greek island of Rhodes, where a pair of kindly American ladies from a luxury cruise ship staved off calamity by sending over a small boat filled with cases of beer and oranges. Finally the *Parita* limped into the Turkish port of Izmir, where four days of bluffs, bluster, and bribery by Zionist activist Eliahu Ben-Horin convinced Turkish officials to let the *Parita* refuel and continue its voyage. This time, knowing the British were watching, Ben-Horin and his comrades decided the ship might as well do what the authorities least expected. And so as the Tel Aviv shore came into view on the afternoon of August 22, the *Parita*'s engines were cranked to full speed. The vessel shook wildly as it crashed across the surf, sending frantic beachgoers scattering in all directions.

On deck, a crew member with a makeshift bullhorn announced to the startled passengers: "We are sailing at the fastest possible speed for Tel Aviv!" "Toward Tel Aviv?" a bewildered refugee shot back. "But Tel Aviv has docks!" "Never mind," the crewman retorted. "We are sailing into Tel Aviv. We will probably be shot at by British warships, but we will go straight on, bullets or shells or not!" A chorus of cheers broke out. "Better we die in battle, than like hunted, exhausted animals!," a girl yelled. A rabbi—described by fellow-passengers as "tall and emaciated"—climbed atop a high pile of ropes and began calling out biblical verses prophesying the ingathering of the Jewish exiles. The Panamanian flag that had been used to disguise the *Parita* was taken down and a hand-sewn blue-and-white flag of Zion was hoisted. Hundreds of voices sang "Hatikvah," the unofficial anthem of the Zionist movement, over and over, until, with a heave and a loud crunching sound, the ship ran aground on the beach. Amazed onlookers rushed to the ship's side, embracing the passengers, weeping with joy, and hustling them off into the nearby marketplace where they could melt into the noisy, colorful embrace of Tel Aviv and avoid detection by the bewildered British police squads that would soon converge on the area.[280]

Late that night, in far-off Izmir, Eliahu Ben-Horin smiled with satisfaction at the news of the boat's crash landing and the escape of many of its passengers. Ben-Horin, 38, grew up in Russia but immigrated to Palestine in the 1920s as a teenager, spending seven backbreaking years with a Zionist labor brigade that helped build some of the country's earliest Jewish towns. In subsequent years, he became something of an international daredevil, bribing his way across the Rumanian-Soviet border in order to smuggle his relatives out of the USSR, then running guns from Germany to Palestine for the Labor Zionist militia, the Haganah, just before Hitler's rise to power. Dissatisfied with the cautious policy of the Labor Zionist leaders who dominated Palestine Jewry, Ben-Horin in the 1930s joined the more militant Revisionist Zionist movement, led by Vladimir Ze'ev Jabotinsky. In the spring of 1940, Ben-Horin accompanied Jabotinsky to the United States to raise funds and political support for the rescue of European Jewish refugees and creation of a Jewish state.

Ben-Horin was as different from Lewis Strauss, Felix Warburg, and Louis Marshall as night is from day. Like many of their generation, the wealthy, assimilated German-born (or descended) Jews associated with Hoover in earlier years kept their distance from Zionism, Yiddish culture, Jewish religious traditions, and other manifestations of Jewish separateness. Ben-Horin, by contrast, was

Eliahu Ben-Horin

the epitome of interwar East European Jewry—and of the new generation of East European immigrants who now dominated American Jewry: fluent in Yiddish (and Russian), fervently Zionist, and deeply attached to the Jewish world now facing acute peril in Europe. The desperate voyage of the *Parita* from Europe to the Promised Land epitomized the dangers and hopes of those Jewish masses on the eve of World War II. Strauss, Warburg, and Marshall represented a segment of American Jewry that was now rapidly dwindling. Ben-Horin represented the new majority. Within just a few years of the crash-landing of the *Parita* and his days of bribery and derring-do, Eliahu Ben-Horin and his comrades would be crafting relationships with Hoover and other leading Republicans that would have a significant impact on American politics.

The Food Blockade

On September 1, 1939, the Germans invaded Poland and World War II began. Polish Jewry, numbering more than three million, was the largest Jewish community in Europe. In the weeks following the German attack, information about the suffering of Polish Jews began reaching the American Jewish press. In addition to the expected news of Jewish communities hit by German bombardments or other war-related damage, there were soon reports of atrocities targeting Jewish civilians. One news report circulated by the New York-based Jewish Telegraphic Agency (JTA) described how "Nazis entered the Polish town of Ostrovie near Warsaw, forced all the Jewish men to dig a large pit and then lined them up before the ditch and shot them down from behind with machine-guns so that their bodies fell into the newly-dug grave." A week later, the JTA reported that "400 Jews had been massacred in the Polish town of Lukov and several hundred in Kalushin." Some reports of this nature made their way into the general press. Hoover, who was spending most of his time at his Palo Alto residence, may well have seen the November 3 article in the *San Francisco Chronicle* headlined "Thousands of Jews in a New Exodus from Vienna to Poland." It reported that "no one seems to know" what would happen to them, but since they were not permitted to take any belongings with them, if they could not find employment, they were "expected to starve."[281]

Soon after the German invasion, Americans concerned about the plight of European war refugees established a Committee for Polish Relief, and Hoover agreed in principle to lead its campaign to provide clothing and 200,000 meals daily to the Nazis' victims. But the American and British governments refused to permit the entry of any provisions into Axis-occupied territory. Appeals by American Jewish organizations to permit food shipments to starving European Jews were likewise rejected. In 1940, Hoover established his own Committee to Feed the Small Democracies, aiming to bring relief to the array of countries that had fallen before Hitler's onslaught. Hoover met with Secretary of State Cordell Hull in early 1941 to personally request permission to send food to occupied Europe, but was rebuffed. Neither a resolution cosponsored by 37 senators nor pleas by numerous church groups and newspaper editors made any difference. Hull insisted nothing could be done to end starvation in Europe except to win the war. "History will never justify the Government of the United States aiding with the starvation of these millions," he wrote bitterly to Hull, to no avail. Ironically, Hull's claim that defeat of the Nazis was the only solution was the same argument he and other Roosevelt administration officials would later make when asked to take steps to rescue Jewish refugees. In 1941, the Allies did agree to supply food for the population of German-occupied Greece, but insisted it was a one-time exception to their blockade.[282]

Random atrocities, followed by forced ghettoization, characterized the German treatment of Polish Jewry during 1939-1941. The arena and scope of anti-Jewish persecution expanded dramatically when the Germans invaded the Soviet Union in June 1941. Mobile execution squads, known as *Einsatzgruppen*, accompanied the German army as it moved eastward. In town after town, they took hundreds, sometimes thousands, of Jews into nearby forests or ravines, compelled them to dig mass graves, and then machine-gunned them into the pits. Ultimately between one million and two million Jews were murdered in this fashion. As early as July, there were sporadic reports in the U.S. Jewish press about enormous massacres in Nazi occupied western Russia.[283] Hoover may not have seen those reports, but it is unlikely he missed the *New York Times* article on October 26, 1941 describing some of the summer's mass killings in considerable detail. "Reliable sources," quoting "letters reaching Hungary from Galicia" and "eye-witness accounts of Hungarian officers" returning from the front, described "massacres of thousands of Jews deported from Hungary to Galicia and the machine-gunning of more thousands of Galician Jews" in August. There were between 10,000 and 15,000 victims, some of whom were "machine-gunned as they prayed in their synagogues," according to the *Times*. "The deaths are reported to have been so numerous that bodies floated down the Dniester with little attempt made to retrieve and bury them."[284]

Throughout 1942, increasingly shocking reports continued to reach the Western press. In March, a European representative of the American Jewish Joint Distribution Committee reported that in the Russian city of Borisov, "the Nazis had ordered Jews to dig a communal grave, into which 7,000 men, women and children—some shot to death, others only wounded—were thrown and covered with earth," and because of "the living breath of those interred," the field was "heaving like the sea." In June, Polish Jewish exiles in London released a report, based on information smuggled out of Poland, which concluded the Germans had "embarked on the physical extermination of the Jewish population on Polish soil," and had already murdered an estimated 700,000 Polish Jews. The report provided the names of many towns where the *Einsatzgruppen* had carried out mass killings in Poland and the Ukraine, as well as the dates of the slaughter and estimates of the casualty tolls. It also contained the first information about the use of poison gas to kill the Jews, describing the mobile death vans that were employed by the Nazis in the Chelmno camp, in Poland, in late 1941 and early 1942, before they had perfected the gas chamber technique.[285]

In August 1942, a telegram from the World Jewish Congress representative in Switzerland, Gerhart Riegner, to Jewish leaders in London and New York unveiled a shocking new development: "In Fuhrer's headquarters plan discussed and under consideration according to which all Jews in countries occupied or controlled Germany numbering 3 1/2 - 4 millions should after deportation and concentration in East be exterminated at one blow...the action reported planned for autumn methods under discussion including prussic acid." In fact, the plan was no longer under consideration but had already been adopted and was well underway.[286]

Undersecretary of State Sumner Welles was not convinced. He told Rabbi Stephen Wise, one of the recipients of the telegram, that "the real purpose of the Nazi government" in rounding up and deporting Jews "is to use Jews in connection with war work both in Nazi Germany and in Nazi Poland and Russia." Welles made this claim even though the State Department had received numerous reports of large-scale massacres by the Germans of Jews who could have been used for slave labor instead. Welles asked Wise to withhold public comment on the Riegner telegram until its veracity could be investigated. Wise complied. It was not until late November that Welles finally confirmed the accuracy of Riegner's report. At a November 24 press conference in Washington, Wise released the news. Simultaneously, Jewish leaders in London and Jerusalem unveiled new information from Europe describing how Jews in Poland and Russia were being "rounded up and taken away in sealed train cars" to "special camps at Treblinka, Belzec and Sobibor, in Southeastern Poland," where they are "mass-murdered." The reports also referred to "trainloads of adults and children taken to great crematoriums at Oswiecim, near Cracow." Oswiecim was the Polish name for Auschwitz.[287]

"Rescue Through Victory"

Acknowledging the horror was one thing; doing something about it was quite another. A delegation of Jewish leaders that met with President Roosevelt in early December found him unwilling to go beyond expressions of sympathy. After the meeting, Rabbi Wise told reporters the president was "profoundly shocked" by the Nazis' mass murder of European Jewry. According to Wise, Roosevelt said "the American people will hold the perpetrators of these crimes to strict accountability," and promised the Allies "are prepared to take every possible step" to "save those who may still be saved." In a note to presidential adviser David Niles the next day, Wise exulted: "We ought to distribute cards throughout the country bearing just four letters, TGFR (Thank God For Roosevelt), and as the Psalmist would have said, thank Him every day and every hour."[288]

But another member of the Jewish delegation, Adolph Held, of the Jewish Labor Committee, provided a rather different account to his colleagues. Held wrote that FDR joked around, made a few sympathetic remarks, and said he was "sure" the German people would rise up to "protest against the atrocities, against the whole Hitler system." After giving the Jewish leaders "a minute or two" to make suggestions, "the President then plunged into a discussion of other matters." Of the 29 minutes the delegation spent with Roosevelt, "he addressed the delegation for 23 minutes." As soon as FDR finished speaking, he "pushed some secret button, and his adjutant appeared in the room" to usher the Jewish leaders out. Held made no reference to any promise by Roosevelt to take "steps" to save the Jews, contrary to Wise's claim.[289]

Other accounts of meetings with Roosevelt on refugee matters during the 1940s indicate that this air of detachment was the rule rather than the exception. In October 1940, James McDonald, chairman of the President's Advisory Committee on Political Refugees, together with several colleagues met with FDR to plead for more visas. Henry M. Hart Jr., assistant to the Solicitor General, who was present, later recalled how "a very cordial Roosevelt spun a succession of stories. Whenever McDonald tried to confront the President with the refugee issue, Roosevelt would be reminded of something else and another anecdote would result. This entertainment continued until the half hour was up and [presidential aide Edwin] 'Pa' Watson came in to mention that the next appointment was due. Then followed a few rushed minutes of trying to present the problem before the group left."[290]

Nahum Goldmann, cochairman of the World Jewish Congress and Washington, D.C. representative of the Jewish Agency, gave a similar account when he briefed David Ben-Gurion and other Agency leaders in Jerusalem in 1944. Reporting on American Jewry's relationship with the president, Goldmann expressed frustration that "It takes six months just to get an appointment with the president. He spends the first ten minutes telling you anecdotes, and then he expects you to entertain him with anecdotes, and all that leaves is ten minutes to discuss serious issues. It is impossible to have serious political impact under these conditions."[291]

In the days following Rabbi Wise's announcement confirming the mass murder, the British government came under strong pressure from Jewish leaders and members of Parliament over its cautious response to the killings. To deflect the criticism, the British proposed to the Roosevelt administration that the Allies issue an official statement of condemnation. The first draft prepared by the British referred to "reports from Europe which leave no room for doubt" that systematic annihilation was underway. The State Department objected to that phrase on the grounds that—as one U.S. official complained—it could "expose [the Allies] to increased pressure from all sides to do something more specific in order to aid these people." The final statement, released on December 17, omitted the phrase "which leave no room for doubt."[292] It also contained no reference to taking any steps to rescue Jews. As one senior State Department official noted to his colleagues during the discussion over the wording, "The plight of the unhappy peoples of Europe, including the Jews, can be alleviated only by winning the war." This sentiment reflected the Roosevelt policy that would come to be known as "rescue through victory." The final proclamation strongly condemned the Nazis' "bestial policy of cold-blooded extermination" and warned that the perpetrators would face postwar punishment, but went no further. It was signed by the United States, Great Britain, the Soviet Union, and the governments-in-exile of eight German-occupied countries. Pope Pius XII declined to sign because, as the papal secretary explained, the Vatican preferred to condemn war crimes in general rather than single out any particular atrocities.[293]

Shattering the Silence

A Gallup poll in early 1943 asked the American public: "It is said that two million Jews have been killed in Europe since the war began. Do you think this is true or just a rumor?" Although just weeks earlier, the Allied leadership publicly confirmed that two million Jews had been systematically slaughtered, the poll found only 47% of Americans believed it was true, while 29% dismissed it as a rumor, and 24% had no opinion. A major part of the reason for the public's skepticism was the failure of the American news media to provide sustained, detailed, or prominent coverage of the Nazi genocide. Many newspapers relegated articles about the mass killings to their back pages. The most influential daily, the *New York Times*, published nearly 1,200 articles about the Holocaust between 1939 and 1945, but only 26 of them made page one, and in only six of those articles were Jews identified on the front page as the main victims of the killings. Some newspaper editors regarded the suffering of the Jews as incidental when compared to the travails of the world war. Other editors, remembering atrocity stories from World War I that turned out to be fabricated, were skeptical about the latest reports. Even when editors took the information about the mass murders seriously, news about the war effort naturally had priority. In the case of the *New York Times*, its publisher, Arthur Hays Sulzberger, was an assimilated Jew who instructed the staff to downplay news about Jews lest the newspaper be accused of pro-Jewish bias.[294]

In early 1943, a small Jewish activist group enlisted stars of Broadway and Hollywood to shatter the wall of silence surrounding the Holocaust. The group was spearheaded by Hillel Kook, a follower of Jabotinsky and comrade of Eliahu Ben-Horin in the Irgun Zvai Leumi's effort to smuggle Jewish refugees from Europe to Palestine. In the summer of 1940, Kook, then 27, came to the United States, initially to assist in Jabotinsky's campaign for the creation of a Jewish army to fight alongside the Allies against the Nazis. A nephew of Abraham Isaac Kook, the Chief Rabbi of Mandatory Palestine, Kook used the name "Peter Bergson" to shield his famous family from unwanted attention. When news of the mass murder was confirmed in the autumn of 1942, Bergson and his cohorts threw themselves into the struggle for the rescue of Europe's Jews. With a tiny office in midtown Manhattan and a skeleton secretarial staff, the Bergson Group teamed up with screenwriter Ben Hecht (famous for such Hollywood blockbusters as *Gone with the Wind* and *Scarface*) to create a theatrical production about the plight of Europe's Jews. They called it *We Will Never Die*, an allusion to a biblical verse about the eternity of the Jewish people. Hecht recruited stage and screen legends Edward G. Robinson, Paul Muni, Sylvia Sidney, and Stella Adler to star in the pageant. Moss Hart volunteered to direct, Billy Rose agreed to produce it, and world renowned composer Kurt Weill created an original score. The involvement of this all-star creative team ensured the production would be a sensation.

Promotional material for *We Will Never Die* featured an impressive Sponsoring Committee whose members included members of Congress from both parties, military and diplomatic officials, and the only living former president, Herbert Hoover. The ability of the Bergson Group to secure the endorsement of such individuals of prominence would prove to be one of its greatest strengths in the rescue campaign of 1943. So long as President Roosevelt believed the plight of Europe's Jews was of concern to Jews only, he was unlikely to feel under pressure to act, since Jewish support for his re-election was presumed to be a virtual certainty. "The problem is that when politicians have Jews in their pockets, they leave them there," the journalist Sidney Zion once quipped.[295]

To convince FDR to take rescue action, it was first necessary to demonstrate that a significant number of leading Americans, beyond the Jewish community, cared about the issue. Although new to the United States and not thoroughly familiar with American political culture, Bergson and his colleagues, grasped this basic fact about political strategy more quickly than some seasoned veterans of the major Jewish organizations. Building a bipartisan coalition for rescue became a top priority for the Bergson Group. Hence the fact that their list of sponsors for *We Will Never Die* featured a conservative Republican ex-president, Herbert Hoover, alongside such Roosevelt stalwarts as Bureau of the Budget director Harold D. Smith and

Peter Bergson (Hillel Kook)

War Production Board chairman Donald M. Nelson, constituted a significant political statement and a major step in the process of creating that vital coalition.

Allied leaders looked askance at *We Will Never Die*. The White House declined Billy Rose's request that it send a message to be read aloud at the premiere. The administration feared the publicity surrounding the show would increase pressure to admit Jewish refugees to the United States. The British ambassador in Washington, for his part, wrote to Foreign Minister Anthony Eden that the pageant was "by implication anti-British" because its appeal to the Allies to find havens for Jewish refugees could include letting them enter Palestine. London, in deference to Arab opposition, refused to open Palestine's doors.[296]

Most mainstream Jewish leaders were unhappy about the Bergsonites. Some feared the Bergson group's vocal activism would usurp their own role in the Jewish community. Others worried that dramatic public activities such as Hecht's pageant might provoke antisemitism. Some would not work with Bergson because their particular factions in the Zionist movement regarded him as their political rival since had been associated with Jabotinsky. In an attempt to secure co-sponsors for the pageant, Hecht convened a meeting of several dozen representatives of Jewish organizations, but none could be persuaded to cooperate.

Despite the naysayers, *We Will Never Die* succeeded beyond its creators' expectations. It played to audiences of more than 40,000 in two shows at Madison Square Garden on March 9, 1943, the second added at the last moment for the sake of the large crowd of would-be attendees who were unable to gain admittance to the first. In the months to follow, it was staged in Philadelphia, Boston, Chicago, the Hollywood Bowl in Los Angeles, and Washington D.C. The audience at the latter performance included First Lady Eleanor Roosevelt, six Supreme Court justices, numerous members of the international diplomatic corps, and an estimated 300 members of Congress. In addition to the more than 100,000 people who viewed the shows, the performances received substantial news media coverage. Mrs. Roosevelt was so moved that she devoted part of her next syndicated column to the pageant. For millions of American newspaper readers, the news about *We Will Never Die* was the first time they heard about the Nazi mass murders.

Militant Zionists on Capitol Hill

Ever since the British liberated Palestine from the Turks in 1918, Zionist leaders had focused their hopes, and their political strategy, on London. But the onset of

World War II convinced Revisionist Zionist leader Zev Jabotinsky that England's need for U.S. assistance would give Washington important leverage in determining the future of Palestine. In the spring of 1940, Jabotinsky headed for the United States, together with a number of his closest deputies. Some of them would later establish the Bergson Group. Others, including Eliahu Ben-Horin of *Parita* fame, became senior figures in the U.S. wing of the Revisionists, known as the New Zionist Organization of America (NZOA). Benzion Netanyahu, later the father of Israel's prime minister, worked with the Bergson faction for a time, then became executive director of the NZOA. An early Revisionist innovation was to develop relationships with key Republicans on Capitol Hill. This represented a departure from the usual approach of mainstream Jewish leaders such as Rabbi Wise, most of whom strongly supported President Roosevelt and for the most part refrained from building relationships with GOP members of Congress both out of ideological disdain and fear of appearing disloyal to the president.

In May 1940, the Revisionists sent Benjamin Akzin, a political scientist and legal scholar (and future president of Haifa University), to Capitol Hill to promote Jabotinsky's idea of establishing a Jewish army to fight alongside the Allies. Isolationist Democrats such as Sen. Burton Wheeler of Montana and conservative Republicans such as Sen. Henry Cabot Lodge of Massachusetts, each for his own reasons, responded sympathetically. Wheeler, Akzin found, had not been approached by the major Jewish organizations and as a result, the entire subject of Zionism was "terra incognita" for him. Akzin's angle was blunt: " I set him thinking that if he doesn't want [European Jews coming] here, he must find for us a State somewhere. It may work, after a few more talks. But, *entre nous*, he most definitely doesn't want us here." Sen. Gerald Nye (D-North Dakota), a hardline isolationist and nativist, agreed to author an article for a Revisionist magazine. Akzin even tried to secure an appointment with Martha Taft, wife of the Republican senator from Ohio, since she had, in Akzin's estimation, a 10% chance of becoming the First Lady.[297]

The Revisionists did not have sufficient resources to continue Akzin's work in Washington beyond that spring, but two years later, Benzion Netanyahu began traveling regularly to Washington to pick up where Akzin left off. He found close allies in prominent Republicans such as Senator William Langer, who agreed to serve as a keynote speaker at an NZOA rally in New York City, and to deliver a pro-Zionist speech in the Senate, ghostwritten by Akzin. Another was Connecticut congresswoman Clare Boothe Luce, wife of *Time* magazine's publisher, who signed on to a full-page Revisionist ad in the *New York Times* calling for rescue and Jewish

Benzion Netanyahu, in 1940

statehood. The NZOA also sent Ben-Horin to meet with Hoover and 1936 GOP presidential nominee Alf Landon and acquaint them with Revisionist concerns. These early contacts with two pillars of the Republican Party would later play a significant role in the evolving relationship between the GOP and American Jewry.[298]

When British Prime Minister Winston Churchill visited the United States in the spring of 1943, the NZOA placed a full-page ad in the *Times* headlined, "Mr. Churchill, Drop the Mandate!" It argued that since the British had failed to fulfill the Balfour Declaration's promise to facilitate creation of a Jewish national home, they should surrender their mandate over Palestine. Most mainstream Jewish leaders believed that despite setbacks such as the White Paper, England could be relied upon to eventually fulfill its promises regarding Palestine. Hence they were outraged by the NZOA's unorthodox position. Rabbi Wise told colleagues that the "hideous" advertisement had "deeply shocked" President Roosevelt and Secretary Hull, and "sticks in their craws." FDR told Samuel Rosenman, his closest Jewish adviser, that he and Churchill were "incensed" by the ad. The president instructed Rosenman to speak with Zionist leaders to see if they could prevent further such outbursts. Rosenman suggested to Wise that he arrange a meeting with the militants; Wise, appalled at the idea of treating the upstarts as equals, rejected the proposal.[299]

Bermuda: Rescue or Mockery?

Meanwhile, the rescue issue was at last long last gaining international attention. In the spring of 1943, a rising tide of calls in the British parliament, media, and churches for Allied assistance to Jewish refugees prodded the British Foreign Office and the State Department to discuss holding an Anglo-American conference on the refugee problem. The island of Bermuda was chosen as the locale. World Jewish Congress cochair Nahum Goldmann was correct when he surmised that the remote setting was selected precisely so that "it will take place practically in secret, without pressure of public opinion," far from the prying eyes of protesters and the news media. Like the abysmal Evian conference five years earlier, Bermuda was born of the Allies' desire to exhibit ostensible concern about the refugees without taking concrete steps to alleviate the Jews' plight. The Roosevelt administration rejected a request by the Joint Emergency Committee for European Jewish Affairs, a coalition of Jewish groups, to send a delegation to the conference. The JEC then presented Undersecretary Welles with a list of proposals for rescue action, but the proposals were ignored.[300]

The Bermuda conference opened on April 19, 1943. The American delegates' terms of reference guaranteed that no meaningful result would emerge from Bermuda. There was to be no special emphasis on the plight of the Jews, nor any policies adopted that would benefit Jews in particular. The U.S. would not agree to the use of any trans-Atlantic ships to transport refugees, not even troop supply ships that were returning from Europe empty. There would be no increase in the number of refugees admitted to the United States. The British delegates, for their part, refused to even discuss Palestine as a possible refuge, because of what Nahum Goldmann called "[their] policy, both foolish and immoral, of appeasing Arab Nazis." The British also shut down the idea of negotiating with the Nazis for the release of Jews, on the grounds that "many of the potential refugees"—"'potential corpses' would be a more appropriate term," a Bergson Group official later commented—"are empty mouths for which Hitler has no use." Their release "would be relieving Hitler of an obligation to take care of these useless people." Both sides also rejected the idea of food shipments to starving Jews as a violation of the Allied blockade of Axis Europe, even though they had previously made an exception for German-occupied Greece. All of these limitations left the delegates at Bermuda spending a large amount of time on very small-scale steps, principally the evacuation of 5,000 Jewish refugees from Spain to the Libyan region of Cyrenaica. Having achieved next to nothing, the two governments kept the proceedings of the conference secret, which only generated further suspicion. If anyone in the Jewish community still clung to the hope that Bermuda represented any change in Allied policy, they only needed to hear the message that Assistant Secretary of State Adolph Berle sent to a Jewish rally in Boston two days after Bermuda's conclusion: "Nothing can be done to save these helpless unfortunates" except to win the war.[301]

From the perspective of the Jewish community and others sympathetic to the refugees, Bermuda revealed before the public, for the first time, the Allies' deliberate failure to undertake rescue initiatives. Until Bermuda, American Jews could cling to the assumption that behind the scenes, the administration was aiding refugees to the extent that could be reasonably expected in wartime conditions. But by convening the Bermuda conference, the United States and Great Britain were, in effect, acknowledging that something more could be done. Certainly if the best minds of these two superpowers came together for the express purpose of determining the ways and means of rescue, then at least some ways and means would be found. Washington and London had inadvertently raised expectations even as they were hoping to bury the rescue issue, and now that they had failed to even minimally meet those expectations, there would be a response from the disappointed constituencies and their sympathizers, including Hoover. That response would have far-reaching consequences.

The failure of the Bermuda conference provoked the first serious public criticism of the administration's refugee policy. Congressman Samuel Dickstein (D-NY), chairman of the House Immigration Committee, declared: "Not even the pessimists among us expected such sterility." Rep. Emanuel Celler (D-NY) accused the delegates in Bermuda of engaging in "more diplomatic tight-rope walking," at a time when "thousands of Jews are being killed daily." Celler pointedly characterized Bermuda as "a bloomin' fiasco"—a slap at another Jewish Congressman, Sol Bloom (D-NY), who supported the State Department and served on the U.S. delegation to Bermuda.

Some mainstream Jewish leaders for the first time began to criticize the administration's refugee policy. Dr. Israel Goldstein of the Synagogue Council of America blasted the conference as "not only a failure, but a mockery," and bluntly added that "the victims are not being rescued because the democracies do not want them, and the job of the Bermuda conference apparently was not to rescue victims of Nazi terror but to rescue our State Department and the British Foreign Office from possible embarrassment." The Labor Zionist magazine *Jewish Frontier* charged that the delegates to Bermuda had acted "in the spirit of undertakers." Even Rabbi Stephen Wise characterized the Bermuda parley as "a woeful failure," although he held back from blaming the Roosevelt administration. The Joint Emergency Committee for European Jewish Affairs was slow to react to Bermuda—it took more than a month to compose its official response—but when it finally did, the JEC went further than any of its member-organizations had previously gone in challenging U.S. policy. Directly confronting the administration's "rescue through victory" philosophy, the JEC asserted: "To relegate the rescue of the Jews of Europe, the only people marked for total extermination, to the day of victory is...virtually to doom them to the fate which Hitler has marked out for them."[302]

The response that generated perhaps the most attention was a large advertisement placed by the Bergson Group in the *New York Times* on May 4. It was headlined "To 5,000,000 Jews in the Nazi Death-Trap, Bermuda was a Cruel Mockery." Coming just three days after the conference ended, the ad helped set the tone for other responses. "I think the most effective technique of all the methods we used was the ads," Rep. Will Rogers, Jr., a leading figure in the Bergson Group, later recalled. "They were hard-hitting and...they carried tremendous impact...I can remember when they appeared in the paper, even around the halls of Congress, there was conversation...I would go down to the floor of Congress and they would be talking about it. 'Look at this.' Or, 'Isn't this outrageous?' Or 'Shouldn't something be done?' Very effective. Very effective."[303]

It was an unorthodox tactic for that time. In the 1940s, mainstream Jewish organizations seldom used the medium of newspaper advertisements to advance their causes, mainly out of concern that aggressive showcasing of Jewish concerns could trigger an antisemitic backlash. The core leaders of the Bergson Group, by contrast, were foreigners who did not share the established Jewish leadership's worries about the status of Jews in American society. They placed more than 200 ads in newspapers around the country between 1942 and 1945, often featuring provocative headlines such as "How Well Are You Sleeping? Is There Something You Could Have Done to Save Millions of Innocent People—Men, Women, and Children—from Torture and Death?" and "Time Races Death: What Are We Waiting For?"

What made the Bermuda ad, and many of the other ads, especially effective was their inclusion of the names of VIP endorsers. A reader of the *New York Times*—whether a White House official or a straphanger in a Brooklyn subway—saw that the challenge to Bermuda was coming not only from Jewish activists but also prominent lawmakers and other public figures, including, once again, former president Hoover. As the rescue campaign rolled on, the quantity and breadth of VIP support rapidly expanded to include well known authors, actors, musicians, and artists.[304]

Some observers were startled by the political range of the Bergson Group's supporters. A columnist for the leftwing political journal *New Leader* wrote that he "nearly fell through the floor" when he "took a gander" at a list of its backers. "Nestling cheek by jowl on one piece of paper," he marveled, were "Congressman John Domengeaux, bitter Southern reactionary" and "Erwin Piscator, left-wing producer." There was "Lowell Thomas, Big Business propagandist" and "Mary Van Kleeck, leading Communist Party fellow traveller," among other odd political bedfellows. The British ambassador in Washington likewise noted with dismay "the large collection of eminent Americans whom it has managed to persuade to sign its proclamations." This "impressive list" of "misguided humanitarians of every stripe and colour" included not only "Congressmen, bishops [and] generals," but even "serving officials" of the U.S. government. The embassy even at one point appealed—unsuccessfully—to Undersecretary Welles to prohibit American government employees from signing the ads. The British were not the only ones paying attention to the ads. On one occasion in 1943, First Lady Eleanor Roosevelt told Bergson that FDR had complained that one of the ads was "hitting below the belt." Bergson replied that he was "very happy to hear that he is reading it and that it affects him."[305]

Recognizing the Emergency

The Bermuda conference represented the very embodiment of the "rescue through victory" approach. To counter it, the Bergsonites decided to hold a conference of their own. Their Emergency Conference to Save the Jewish People of Europe would serve as a kind of anti-Bermuda, something that would demonstrate the feasibility of rescue. Once again, Hoover was in the thick of it.

In late May, an internal Bergson Group committee began meeting to plan the nuts and bolts of the event. Among the chief items on the agenda was the preparation of a list of desired VIP speakers. Twenty-two names were chosen. Hoover's name topped the list.[306] Although there had been some previous contact between the Bergsonites and Hoover, resulting in the former president's name appearing on *We Will Never Die* publicity material and the Bermuda "Cruel Mockery" advertisement, this new initiative would go much further by inviting Hoover to be one of the keynote speakers at the conference. Despite his stature as a former president—and as the only living ex-president—Hoover was seldom invited to address gatherings of the mainstream Jewish organizations.

This was the result of the deep attachment that prominent Jewish leaders such as Rabbi Wise felt to President Roosevelt, the New Deal, and the Democratic Party. Wise sometimes privately referred to FDR as "the All Highest," "the Great Man," or other terms of reverence. "I still repeat the new American Hosanna, 'Thank God for Franklin D. Roosevelt'," Wise declared after reading the president's Rosh Hashana greeting to American Jewry in 1938. (Ironically, it was precisely those boilerplate holiday messages that symbolized the Jewish leadership's inability to secure meaningful policy changes from the president, in the view of Rabbi Dr. Abba Hillel Silver, who later sought to challenge Wise's leadership position. "We've had enough Rosh Hashana greetings from the president of the United States," Silver declared at a Zionist conference in early 1941. "We'd like to see some action on the matters which mean the most to us.")[307]

"The problem with you people," Sen. Arthur Vandenberg, Republican of Michigan, once told a group of Jewish leaders, "is that every time the Great White Father [FDR] waves his hand you jump right through the hoop." Wise and other Jewish leaders regarded Hoover, and the Republicans in general, as the antithesis of everything in which they believed. Roosevelt's Republican opponents were not merely individuals with whom one disagreed, but represented, as Wise put it, everything that was "inimical to the highest interests of democratic life." These Jewish leaders vehemently opposed Republican positions on domestic issues; vividly remembered the prewar isolationism that many Republicans embraced; and, in general, tended to identify Republicans as part of the blue-blood, Protestant, well-to-do social class with which they had little in common. Ironically, on a personal level, Franklin Roosevelt fit that cultural stereotype as much as Herbert Hoover, but the Democrats as a party were closely identified with labor unions, the concerns of the working class, and the interests of religious and ethnic minorities in a way that profoundly separated them from the Republicans in most Jewish eyes. Hence for many Jewish leaders, building a friendly relationship with Hoover was virtually unthinkable.[308]

Although the Jewish leaders' attitude may have been appreciated by the Democrats as an impressive display of ideological loyalty, as political strategy it could be a handicap by diminishing the Jewish community's leverage in its dealings with the White House. FDR and his advisers had little reason to believe there existed any credible threat of losing Jewish votes over his refugee policy. By closing the door to the Republicans, Jewish leaders limited their own political options. In effect, even if the president's policies disappointed them, they had nowhere else to go. So long as the president perceived that the Jews had no alternative, he felt little pressure to address their concerns with anything more than an occasional rhetorical gesture.

Bergson and his colleagues, by contrast, were not hampered by such political constraints. Unlike the established Jewish leaders, they were not American citizens nor did they envision a future for themselves in the United States. They were either residents of Palestine who intended to return there, or Europeans who intended to go to Palestine. Their future lay in the Jewish state they were laboring to bring into existence. They were not caught up in America's internal political or cultural debates. They harbored no instinctive reluctance to deal with any particular segment of American society. They adhered to a narrow agenda of Jewish and Zionist concerns, and felt no predilections about cooperating with those with whom they disagreed on other issues.

Moreover, the Bergson activists did not operate within the confines of the Jewish community. They did not even regard themselves as a Jewish organization. Instead, they consciously sought to craft a broad coalition of Americans of all political, religious, and ethnic hues. Of the twenty-two names on their wish list of speakers for the planned Emergency Conference, nineteen were non-Jews. Hoover was followed on the list by Max Lerner, the liberal academic and columnist for the leftwing daily newspaper *PM*. The third name was another Republican, 1940 presidential nominee Wendell Willkie. First Lady Eleanor Roosevelt was on the list, as was Supreme Court Justice Harlan Stone, a strong supporter of the New Deal; but so was Republican congresswoman Clare Boothe Luce.[309]

The Bergson Group's Jewish rivals observed the conference preparations with dismay. An aide to Rabbi Wise who saw the list of potential speakers reported that it was "a formidable list of names, including Hoover and Willkie...and if only half of them attend the Conference, its public effect will be devastating." The Joint's Joseph Hyman acknowledged to a Quaker refugee relief activist that the speakers at the Bergson conference would "include such imposing names as that of Herbert Hoover." Nonetheless, Hyman insisted, the absence of any established Jewish leaders made the event "not acceptable." When Rabbi Wise learned that the presiding Episcopal bishop, Henry St. George Tucker, had agreed to speak at the gathering, he tried to persuade the clergyman to withdraw. Tucker would not budge. Wise did, however, help convince Undersecretary of State Welles that the Bergsonites should be boycotted. On June 23, Welles urged U.S. ambassador Myron Taylor to stay away from the gathering on the grounds that "such leaders as

Rabbi Wise, who was with me this morning, are strongly opposed to the holding of this conference [and] have done everything they could to prevent it..."[310]

Bergson himself met with Hoover in June 1943, in the former president's suite at the Waldorf Astoria. Hoover's initial response to Bergson's invitation to speak at the conference was "yes, he would like to help, but that before he did he would like to check with the State Department because he would not take any stand on international issues without checking with the people there." Bergson knew the State Department would object:

> Being young and naive, and very intense on the subject, I came back at him, arguing that it was a question of the greatest emergency, that every day cost thousands of lives. I told him that only the other day, I read in the paper that he had disagreed with the State Department [on some matter]. "Let me assume," I said, "that the State Department tells you that the Jews can be killed and that you should do nothing about it. Why should you not take a stand against them?" "Let me think a little," he replied, in the same minute telling me that he would appear [at the Emergency Conference]. "You are right, young man," he said. "You are right. You convinced me."[311]

Hoover agreed to serve as honorary chairman of the Emergency Conference and to address the event via live radio hook-up from California.[312]

In the weeks to follow, a bipartisan array of VIPs joined Hoover on the list of honorary co-chairs of the Emergency Conference: Roosevelt's own secretary of the interior, Harold Ickes, as well as Republican National Committee chairman Harrison Spangler; influential newspaper editor William Allen White, a supporter of the New Deal, as well as newspaper magnate William Randolph Hearst, one of FDR's most vigorous Republican opponents; three U.S. Senators—all Democrats, itself an implicit shot across the administration's bow; labor leaders William Green of the AFL and Philip Murray of the CIO; civil liberties lawyer Arthur Garfield Hays (known for his role in the Scopes Trial as well as the trials of Sacco and Vanzetti and the Scottsboro Boys); and Bishop Tucker.

A separate list of more than 300 Conference Sponsors likewise featured an impressive range of Americans from disparate walks of life, including four U.S. Senators and twenty-seven members of the House of Representatives; university presidents and faculty; newspaper publishers; artists, musicians, and authors;

prominent Christian clergy, including the bishops of Kentucky, Iowa, New Jersey, and Los Angeles; prominent African-Americans such as poet Langston Hughes, author Zora Neale Hurston, and Bishop Edward Thomas Demby; and several Jewish figures of note who were not previously known as Bergson Group supporters, among them prominent Cleveland rabbi Armond Cohen and Mrs. Alice Brandeis, widow of the supreme court justice.

The advance publicity materials made clear that the Emergency Conference was intended as a challenge to the administration. The assembly "will attempt to do what no group of governmental or private experts has thus far attempted: [prepare] a comprehensive program for the salvation of European Jewry," an early press release announced. That declaration included a statement by Bergson Group chairman Senator Edwin Johnson (D-Colorado) pointedly taking aim at the rescue-through-victory philosophy: "Unless we take immediate and vigorous action...the invading armies of the United Nations [as the Allies were known] will find in Europe not a continent but a cemetery." In a similar spirit, a statement by five senators endorsing the conference, released by the Bergson Group shortly before the gathering, warned: "If we wait until the war is won [to help the Jews], there may be only corpses left to enjoy the fruits of victory." The first lines of *PM*'s coverage of the conference's opening day could not have been more explicit: "An emergency conference called to do what the Bermuda conference failed to do—provide a definite plan of rescue for the 4,000,000 Jews left in Europe—is underway..."[313]

On the sweltering morning of July 21, 1943, Dr. Maurice William, a Bergson supporter and refugee relief activist, rapped his gavel on the podium at Manhattan's Hotel Commodore, calling to order the more than 1,500 delegates on hand to participate in the Emergency Conference. William began by reading aloud sympathetic messages from First Leady Eleanor Roosevelt, Treasury Secretary Henry Morgenthau, Jr., Wendell Willkie, New York Governor Herbert Lehman, and Palestine Chief Rabbi Yitzhak Herzog. Congressman Will Rogers, Jr. followed with a pull-no-punches opening address in which he blasted the "incompetence, laxity, cruelty and deliberate self-indulgence in the diplomatic policy of the United Nations—and we might as well put the blame where it belongs, on England and the United States." Rogers said it was time to "take the Jewish problem out of the dossiers of the diplomats and place it in the heart of humanity." Those were strong words for a Democrat and staunch New Dealer to utter about an incumbent president from his own party.[314]

Each day's proceedings consisted of a series of panel discussions, some of them featuring addresses by prominent speakers. The discussions focused on practical ways to interrupt the mass murder process or facilitate escape. The panel on international relations, chaired by Max Lerner, urged the Allies to negotiate with Axis satellite regimes for the release of their Jews, and to provide financial aid to countries that temporarily sheltered escapees. The panel on military affairs, with retired Rear Admiral Yates Stirling, Jr. presiding, proposed Allied reprisal strikes to "intimidate" the Germans and their satellites "into discontinuance of their program of annihilation of the Jewish people."[315]

Members of the Relief and Transportation panel heard Louis D. Caplane of the *Norwegian Journal of Commerce and Shipping* explain that sufficient shipping was available in the Mediterranean to move tens of thousands of Jews from the Balkans to Palestine. Another speaker at that session, Perrin Galpin of the Food for Small Democracies movement, urged the Allies to ship food to starving Jews in Europe just as they had done for the populace of German-occupied Greece.[316]

The panel on public opinion, co-chaired by Herbert Moore of Trans Radio News and exiled Italian radio broadcaster Lisa Sergio, proposed to organize a committee of writers and publicists to "humanize" the plight of European Jewry for the American news media and public. The panel on religious affairs, addressed by Bishop Tucker and chaired by Virginia bishop James Cannon, called on America's churches to mobilize in support of the campaign "to bring the Jews out of their present Egypt of suffering into some Canaan of safety."[317]

The issue of immigration to the United States was discussed in earnest at the conference. Refugee advocates and members of Congress with a particular interest in immigration knew that the Hoover administration's edict screening out immigrants who were "likely to become a public charge" had been superseded in practice by the Roosevelt administration's policy of reducing immigration to far below the legal limits. Assistant Secretary of State Breckinridge Long described this approach as "postponing and postponing and postponing" issuing visas. An additional regulation imposed by the State Department in 1941 barred admission to anyone who had "close relatives" in Axis territory, on the theory that the Gestapo might blackmail them into becoming Nazi spies by threatening their kin. No instances of such blackmail were ever uncovered, but in the meantime the "close relatives" edict made it even harder for Jews to escape Hitler Europe. During the year before the conference (1942), the German-Austrian quota had been only about 18% filled; the Polish quota was 14% filled; and the French quota was 35%

filled. Altogether, between 1933 and 1945, a total of about 190,000 quota places from Germany and Axis countries would be left unused. On the third day of the Emergency Conference, Rep. Samuel Dickstein, a speaker on the panel on international relations, proposed combining all unused immigration quota slots from the previous five years into a single "refugee quota" to aid Jews escaping from Hitler. The delegates warmly applauded the Dickstein plan, but like so many refugee relief proposals that briefly surfaced on Capitol Hill in those years, it was strongly opposed by the administration and could not gain traction in Congress.

Bergson saved Hoover for the final, climactic evening of the conference, expecting that session would both attract the most substantial news media attention and help shape the public conversation about rescue that he hoped would follow the conference. Just prior to Hoover's remarks, conference chair Maurice William read aloud messages from President Roosevelt and Secretary of State Hull that were arguably at odds with the spirit of the conference. FDR informed the delegates that his administration had already undertaken "repeated endeavors to save those who could be saved." Hull, for his part, insisted "the final defeat of Hitler and the rooting out of the Nazi system is the only complete answer" to the plight of European Jewry. Hull claimed the Allies, at Bermuda, had already determined "those measures which have been found to be practicable under war conditions..."[318]

The juxtaposition of the messages from Roosevelt and Hull with Hoover's remarks highlighted the contrast between Roosevelt's approach and Hoover's. In every major respect, the former president threw his weight behind the rescue campaign and challenged the administration's refugee policy. The plight of the Jews was not merely a Jewish concern, Hoover emphasized, but "a great human problem that ranks with the other human problems" and that every person had an obligation to address. Moreover, consideration of the problem could not be postponed until after the war: it required immediate attention by the Allies, "as part of the war," through "systematic temporary measures."[319]

One step Hoover urged was negotiations, via "European neutrals," for the release of Jews from Axis countries. The Bergson Group, as well as mainstream Jewish organizations, had repeatedly urged such an approach, but the Roosevelt administration had consistently rejected it. Hoover also called for food shipments to starving Jews, a proposal the Allies had spurned on the grounds that the Germans might confiscate the goods, but which the Allies had permitted for the Greeks. Hoover, hearkening back to his vast experience providing food to starving Europeans in World War I, declared: "Does not this experience [in Greece] warrant its extension to other occupied countries? It would save the lives of thousands of Jews."

Hoover also called on the Allied leadership to organize havens around the world to which Jewish refugees could flee:

> The time has arrived when we should demand that a real solution be found and, further, that the United Nations undertake to finance and manage a real solution as part of the war.
>
> There are groups of Jews who have escaped into the neutral countries of Europe. They and any other refugees from the persecution of fascism should be assured of support by the United Nations. This step should go further. Definite refugee stations should be arranged in these neutral countries for those who may escape.

In this context, Hoover reiterated his earlier suggestion that the Central African uplands could serve as a site for Jewish resettlement. The concept of such temporary havens was critical to the Bergsonites' approach to rescue. They recognized that a major obstacle to rescue action was the Allies' fear that they would be forced to admit, as immigrants, the Jews whom they saved. Redefining havens as a strictly temporary measure could open up vast territories for refuge without having to determine, in advance, the refugees' long term status. Jews could be admitted on this basis to areas whose governments had previously objected, including the United States, Palestine, and Allied-control areas in North Africa. (Many American and British officials opposed bringing Jewish refugees to North Africa because of local Arab opposition.)

The most important demand of the Emergency Conference was its call for the creation of a new U.S. government agency "specifically charged with the task of saving the Jewish people of Europe." The Bergson Group had become convinced that so long as refugee policy was in the hands of the State Department, there was little chance any meaningful rescue steps would ever be taken. Deeply entrenched anti-immigration sentiment, and even antisemitism, throughout the State Department would inevitably serve as an effective counterweight to refugee advocates' pleas to the White House. The only way to break the logjam was to establish a government agency whose specific task was to save Jews. In order to advance that demand in the political arena, the conference concluded by transforming itself into the Emergency Committee to Save the Jewish People of Europe and launching an all-out publicity and pressure campaign for a new agency.

"How can the West rescue the Jews of Europe?" *New York Post* columnist Samuel Grafton asked in his commentary on the Emergency Conference. "The answer to that is that the West cannot do it at all, unless it starts to do it." He explained:

> It must make at least a beginning of setting up one man, or one agency, in one room, as an office in charge of rescuing the Jews. The situation is not that the West has failed in this task. The West hasn't even assigned the task.[320]

The Battle for Rescue Moves to Capitol Hill

There was not much political advantage, in the summer of 1943, for Hoover or other Republicans to champion the cause of U.S. action to rescue Jews from Hitler. Hoover himself, then 69, no longer harbored hopes of running for president again, and in any event it was too early on the political calendar for party activists or potential candidates to be seriously planning for the 1944 campaign. Moreover, any notion of the GOP seeking Jewish votes was at that point highly dubious, since there had been no serious signs of a rupture between American Jewish voters and the Roosevelt administration that the GOP might conceivably exploit. Jewish leaders' criticism of Allied refugee policy in the aftermath of the Bermuda conference represented only the first small murmurs of disappointment in a long-venerated president.

But in August, there were more, and louder, murmurs. Two separate presidential envoys to the Middle East, Lt. Col. Harold Hoskins and Brig. Gen. Patrick Hurley, had recently warned Roosevelt that the Bergson Group's Jewish army campaign, coupled with growing Jewish demands to open Palestine to refugees, could provoke Arab violence against Allied forces in the region. On the basis of that perceived threat, the State Department and British Foreign Office drafted an Anglo-American decree to ban all public discussion of Palestine for the remainder of the war. FDR approved the proposal, but before it was finalized, word began to leak out. Rabbi Wise, already convinced that "there is a cabal in the State Department" working against Zionism, hurried to the White House on July 23, only to find that Roosevelt "seemed completely in the dark with respect to such a statement [regarding Palestine]." Wise may not have been entirely taken in by FDR's act because, reflecting several months later on the plans for "that wretched statement," he confided to a friend that Roosevelt "seems to me to be completely and hopelessly under the domination of the English Foreign Office [and] the Colonial Office."

Alerted by Republican congressman Hugh Scott, Bergson's Emergency Committee lobbyists headed for Capitol Hill on their first mission, mobilizing members of Congress to oppose the Palestine statement. By the second week of August, the controversy had erupted into full public view. A syndicated column by top Washington investigative reporter Drew Pearson and a blistering denunciation by Congressman Emanuel Celler thrust the planned anti-Zionist decree into the national limelight.[321]

The escalating scandal created something of a political problem for Rabbi Wise and other Jewish supporters of FDR: the news that such a decree was afoot could sully the president's name in the Jewish community, and the actual adoption of the new Palestine policy would be catastrophic for Roosevelt's relationship with American Jewry. FDR "has come to have a very, very special place in the heart of Jews," Wise wrote to White House adviser Samuel Rosenman in late August. "They rightly look up to him, revere him, and love him...No one would more deeply sorrow than I, unless it be you, if this feeling of Jewish homage...should be changed. The issuance of that statement might change it." Moreover, Wise warned, the American Jewish Conference, a national gathering of Jewish organizations, was just days away; the assembly would be "thrown into a nasty uproar" and "regrettably unwise things may be said [about Roosevelt] in the course of the Conference" unless the decree were aborted. Indeed, Wise and his colleagues had organized the event precisely in order to secure a community-wide consensus in favor of opening Palestine's gates and creating a Jewish state. The proposed statement threatened to turn the conference into a flashpoint of resentment against the president. A flurry of behind-the-scenes lobbying by Wise, Roosevelt's Jewish advisers, and members of Congress, combined with the negative media coverage, succeeded in scuttling the plan.[322]

Ironically, the American Jewish Conference inadvertently generated a good deal of unflattering p.r. regarding the administration's refugee policy. The organizers' intention was to focus on Palestine, and the conference would be widely remembered in the years to follow as marking the rise to Zionist leadership of the activist faction led by Rabbi Dr. Abba Hillel Silver. But some news coverage of the conference focused more on the participants' expressions of disappointment over

Allied policy toward European Jewry. Stories in *PM*, for example, featured headlines such as "Conference Hears Allies Accused of Stalling on Jews" and "United Nations Delay On Aid Upsets Jews." The *New York Times*, which seldom put news of European Jewry's plight on its front page, did so on the second day of the conference, under the heading "Rescue at Once of Europe's Jews Demanded at Conference Here." Another day's coverage was headlined "Immediate Rescue of Jews is Urged, Conference Asks That as Many as Possible Be Assisted From Nazi Territory." Such articles not only reported the Jewish dissatisfaction over the abandonment of the Jews but probably helped accelerate it as well, by making it part of the public conversation, exactly at the time the administration was trying to downplay the issue so as to reduce public pressure for U.S. intervention.[323]

A series of pro-rescue initiatives in the early autumn kept the issue on the front burner. In September, at the instigation of Republican former congressman William S. Bennet, a prominent Bergson supporter, the National Republican Club and the National Democratic Club (the national networks of grassroots party activists) each adopted a resolution urging Congress to grant temporary admission to victims of religious discrimination. Although the proposal gained no traction on Capitol Hill, it was significant as a gesture of bipartisan sympathy for the plight of the Jews. In early October, the Bergson Group organized a march by four hundred rabbis to the White House. Arriving three days before Yom Kippur, the marchers were greeted on the steps of the Capitol by congressional leaders and Vice President Henry Wallace. But when they arrived at the White House, bearing a petition urging creation of a rescue agency, President Roosevelt refused to meet them. The snub backfired by triggering substantial news media coverage of the protest. Eight days later, Senator Warren Barbour, Republican of New Jersey, one of those who had greeted the marchers at the Capitol, introduced legislation to admit 100,000 Jewish refugees outside the quota system. Later that month, the Bergsonites staged a rally at Carnegie Hall to salute the people of Sweden and Denmark for rescuing some 7,000 Danish Jews from the Nazis. The standing room-only crowd heard a dramatic recounting of the rescue mission by Hollywood celebrities Orson Welles and Ralph Bellamy, as well as remarks by members of Congress and diplomats hailing the actions of the Swedes and Danes as evidence of the feasibility of rescue. A full page newspaper ad by the Bergson Group about the rescue operation was headlined "It Can Be Done!"[324]

The rallies, newspaper ads, and other protests made a strong impression on members of Congress, generating sympathetic discussion of the rescue agency proposal in Washington circles and on Capitol Hill. The Bergson Group's lobbyists, working both sides of the aisle, found support for their cause in both parties. In November, Rep. Rogers, a liberal Democrat, joined hands with Republican congressman Joseph Baldwin of New York to introduce a resolution, authored by the Bergsonites, urging the president to create a rescue agency. An identical version was introduced in the Senate by Sen. Guy Gillette of Iowa and eleven cosponsors, nine Democrats and two Republicans, Homer Ferguson of Michigan and presumed presidential contender Robert Taft of Ohio, neither of whom had previously exhibited any particular interest in Jewish affairs. Taft, in fact, had opposed the 1939 Wagner-Rogers bill to admit German Jewish refugee children. Rep. Sol Bloom, chairman of the House Committee on Foreign Affairs, tried to stall the Gillette-Rogers resolution by insisting that it be the subject of hearings. Hearings normally were reserved for legislation, not resolutions, since a resolution was only a recommendation rather than a law. Bloom, a staunch supporter of FDR's refugee policy, viewed the resolution as a "direct personal criticism of him and what he did as the American delegate to the Bermuda Conference," Oscar Cox of the Lend-Lease Administration explained to Secretary Morgenthau.[325]

The Gillette-Rogers resolution attracted bipartisan support. Prominent Democrats and New Dealers such as 1928 presidential candidate Al Smith and American Labor Party leader Dean Alfange endorsed the measure. So did three of the most prominent Republicans in the nation: Wendell Willkie, New York City mayor Fiorello La Guardia, and newspaper publisher William Randolph Hearst. La Guardia, in fact, came to Washington to testify in support of the resolution, and Hearst repeatedly published sympathetic editorials and news articles in his chain of thirty newspapers nationwide.

Rep. Bloom countered by bringing in Rabbi Stephen Wise, who asserted in his testimony that the resolution was "inadequate" because it made no reference to settling refugees in Palestine. Bergson and Rogers had deliberately omitted Palestine from the text because some members of Congress would not support a resolution challenging British policy in Palestine. "I understand that there are differences of opinion in Jewish circles," a frustrated Rogers wrote to Wise and other Jewish leaders afterwards. "But sincerely, gentlemen, those differences should be forgotten when a case of rescue is concerned."[326]

In the end, a blunder by Rep. Bloom and Assistant Secretary of State Breckinridge Long spoiled the administration's strategy for blocking the resolution. On November 26, testifying before the Foreign Affairs committee as to why a separate rescue agency was unnecessary, Long declared: "[W]e have taken into this country since the beginning of the Hitler regime and the persecution of the Jews, until today, approximately 580,000 refugees." Long's testimony was given behind closed doors, but wavering congressmen subsequently asked him to release it publicly, because they believed it would justify their decision to shelve the rescue resolution. Long, with Bloom's support, agreed to do so. Long's statistics made the front page of the *New York Times* and seemed to sway key members of Congress—until, a few days later, his figures were exposed as false. The actual number of refugees admitted was not more than 250,000, and many of them were not Jews. Long's errors set off a firestorm of criticism from the media, mainstream Jewish organizations, and members of Congress. The controversy deeply embarrassed the administration and provided additional momentum to the campaign for U.S. rescue action.[327]

Breckinridge Long

While the battle over rescue was raging in the halls of Congress, another struggle was underway behind the scenes, at the Treasury and State departments. Aides to Treasury Secretary Morgenthau discovered that senior State Department officials had been deliberately obstructing opportunities to rescue Jewish refugees, blocking the transmission of Holocaust-related information from Europe to the United States, and trying to cover up evidence of their actions. State Department officials took these steps because they feared the rescue of large numbers of Jews would put pressure on the United States to open its doors to them. As one official privately explained: "There was always the danger that the German government might agree to turn over to the United States and to Great Britain a large number of Jewish refugees. In the event of our admission of inability to take care of these people, the onus for their continued persecution would have been largely transferred from the German government to the Allied nations."[328]

On Christmas Day, 1943, Morgenthau aide Josiah E. DuBois, Jr. composed an 18-page report which he titled "Report to the Secretary on the Acquiescence of This Government in the Murder of the Jews." In careful, detailed, lawyerly language, DuBois exposed the State Department's record of obstruction. The report's searing conclusion: State Department officials "have been guilty not only

Henry Morgenthau, Jr., right, with President Roosevelt

of gross procrastination and willful failure to act, but even of willful attempts to prevent action from being taken to rescue Jews from Hitler...Unless remedial steps of a drastic nature are taken, and taken immediately...to prevent the complete extermination of the Jews [in Hitler Europe], this Government will have to share for all time responsibility for this extermination." DuBois pressed Morgenthau to bring the matter directly to the president, and warned the Treasury Secretary that if he did not act, DuBois would resign in protest and publicly expose the scandal.[329]

All this took place at the same time the controversy over Breckinridge Long's testimony was exploding on Capitol Hill and the rescue resolution was advancing in the Senate. The chairman of the Senate Foreign Relations Committee, Tom Connally of Texas, an administration loyalist, initially prevented the resolution from coming up for a vote, but just before Christmas, Connally took ill and his replacement, Senator Elbert Thomas of Utah—a staunch Bergson supporter—immediately placed the resolution before the committee. It passed unanimously. "It is not a Jewish problem alone," the Senators wrote in the preamble to the resolution. "It is a Christian problem and a problem for enlightened civilization. We have talked; we have sympathized; we have expressed our horror; the time to act is long past due."[330] It was precisely this concept—that everyone, not just Jews, should be concerned about the mass murder—that had guided the Bergson Group in its campaign for rescue and which Hoover had articulated in his address to the July 1943 Emergency Conference.

Surveying the political landscape, in those final days of 1943 and the beginning of 1944, Morgenthau could see trouble looming for the president. The Bergson Group's newspaper ads and rabbinical march, the swift criticism by mainstream Jewish groups of Long's testimony, and the groundswell of support among members of Congress for rescue action stung, and were likely to get worse. But had the public mood shifted sufficiently for Roosevelt to recognize the political problem he faced?

Chapter 6

Hoover and the Origins of the "Jewish Vote"

"There is no Jewish vote," Rabbi Stephen Wise wrote on the eve of the 1932 presidential election. "In the United States, there can never be a Jewish vote," Rabbi Isaac Landman told the 1933 convention of the Central Conference of American Rabbis. "The so-called Jewish vote is a myth," Rabbi Abraham Feinberg of Manhattan declared in a sermon quoted in the *New York Times* in 1937. Such statements were expressions of hope more than carefully reasoned assessments of American Jewish political behavior. Many Jewish leaders feared that the perceived existence of a "Jewish vote" would provoke antisemitic accusations that Jews were insular, selfish, or more loyal to a Jewish agenda than to broader American interests. Yet no matter how often some Jewish spokesmen denied its existence, many politicians, and many American Jews, continued to believe that issues of particular Jewish concern do sometimes motivate large numbers of American Jews to vote for, or against, a particular candidate for office.[331]

The fate of two World War I-era Jewish socialist candidates for office in New York City illustrates some early trends in American Jewish voting behavior. Between 1891 and 1914, an estimated 1.3-million Russian Jews, fleeing Czarist persecution, immigrated to the United States, most of them to New York City. A large portion lived in Manhattan's Lower East Side and worked in the garment industry and similar blue-collar trades. Naturally they were especially concerned with issues that directly affected them and their families, such as labor rights, and sometimes this translated into Jewish voters supporting socialist candidates at a rate much higher than the general voting populace. But Jewish support for socialist candidates was highly selective. Consider the case of Morris Hillquit, the Socialist Party's candidate for congress from the Lower East Side in 1908 and for mayor of New York City in 1917. Hillquit was Jewish but toed his party's line in favor of immigration restriction and rejected all vestiges of Jewish tradition, even to the point of having participated in "Yom Kippur Balls" at which young Jewish radicals demonstrated their antipathy for Judaism. Hillquit lost both in 1908 and 1917 by overwhelming margins. By contrast, attorney Meyer London, the Socialist Party's candidate for congress from the same Lower East Side district in 1914, was a Yiddish-speaking immigrant rights activist who often defended predominantly-Jewish labor unions free of charge. He won the 1914 race, and was reelected twice. For many New York Jewish voters, evidence of concern for particular Jewish interests trumped doctrinaire socialism.

On the national level, Jewish voters demonstrated no clear attachment to either party prior to 1928. In 1920, Republican Warren Harding won a plurality of the Jewish vote, an estimated 43%. In 1924, however, Democrat John W. Davis captured 51% of Jewish votes. In both contests, third party candidates ran relatively well among Jewish voters. In 1920, Eugene Debs, a Socialist, apparently won about twice as many Jewish votes as the Democratic nominee, James Cox; in 1924, Robert La Follette, candidate of the Progressive Party, likewise did well in many heavily-Jewish voting districts. In the 1928 race, with no third party in the mix, Democrat Al Smith won about 67% of the Jewish vote, to an estimated 33% for Hoover. For the reasons discussed in Chapter 3, Hoover made no real effort to attract Jewish voters in 1928 and only a last-minute attempt four years later.

In the 1932 race between Roosevelt and Hoover, American Jewish voters both rejected the Republicans and embraced the Democrats. On the one hand, they joined most other Americans in faulting what they saw as President Hoover's inadequate response to the onset of the Great Depression. At the same time, the Democratic Party was positioning itself as the champion of labor rights, which was still an important consideration for Jewish voters. Equally significant was the fact the Democrats were increasingly seen as the party that cared about religious and ethnic minorities; the fact that they were the only party to have ever nominated a presidential candidate from a minority faith certainly reinforced this perception. By taking sympathetic positions on issues of ethnic concern, placing ethnic candidates on local party tickets, and doling out patronage jobs accordingly, the Democrats consciously presented themselves as the party of inclusion.

A Jewish immigrant voter who personally experienced the terror of never knowing when Cossacks might burn down his house or maul his loved ones, naturally favored the party that seemed most likely to foster a tolerant and welcoming society. Although anti-Jewish violence on the scale of Czarist Russia was of course never duplicated in the United States, Jewish immigrants were reminded of the threat by the fact that dozens of antisemitic groups were active nationwide in the 1930s, the antisemitic demagogue Father Charles Coughlin reached huge radio audiences, polls showed many Americans harboring anti-Jewish prejudice, and there were periodic outbursts of antisemitic hooliganism, often perpetrated by Irish-American street gangs in New York City and Boston. Hence the Jewish relationship with the Democrats was anchored in a bedrock of hope that they would make America safe for the Jews. An estimated 85% of Jewish voters backed Franklin Roosevelt in 1932 and 1936, rising to 90% in 1940. These figures demonstrated consistent enthusiasm for Roosevelt among Jews and made the relationship between American Jewry and the Democrats seem unshakable.

Could 1944 be Different?

In view of these historical trends, was it conceivable that any significant number of Jewish voters might defect to the Republican candidate in the 1944 presidential election? Did the occasional expressions of Jewish disappointment over Roosevelt's response to the Holocaust in late 1943 represent anything more than the anguished cries of a small minority in the community? More to the point, given the high level of Jewish support for FDR in previous elections, was there any serious possibility of persuading Roosevelt that his failure to aid the refugees would cause him political harm? Was rescue indeed becoming, as White House aide Oscar Cox told Morgenthau in December 1943, "a domestic political problem" for the administration?[332]

Despite contemporary popular assumptions that overwhelming Jewish electoral support for the president in 1944 was a foregone conclusion, some observers at the time thought otherwise.

Internal Bergson Group memoranda from late 1943, for example, indicate that the Bergsonites were convinced the administration's stance on rescue, especially during the debate over the Gillette-Rogers resolution, could cost it Jewish votes. Although the Bergson activists were obviously an interested party, it seems clear that as a general rule, they had their fingers on the pulse of the Jewish grassroots to a greater extent than many of the established leaders. The Bergsonites often had a better sense of the sentiment on the 'Jewish street' because they tended to live in working-class neighborhoods and fraternize with the immigrant generation. It is noteworthy that the Bergson activists' remarks about the erosion of Jewish support for Roosevelt were not intended for publication but were made strictly behind the scenes in internal discussions; one may conclude that those remarks reflected their genuine sentiment rather than public posturing.

Eri Jabotinsky, for example, reported to his Bergson Group colleagues in October 1943 that there was evidence of an "anti-Democratic swing in New York City," which "is partly to be attributed to a growing opposition to the Roosevelt Administration among the masses of the Jewish population. According to a very serious census, undertaken by us (mostly through congregations) this swing is gaining momentum." Unless there was "a change of governmental policy" on rescue and Palestine, there would be substantial Jewish defections to the Republicans in forthcoming elections, he predicted.[333]

In December 1943, at the peak of the battle over the congressional rescue resolution, Jabotinsky again saw significant political implications:

> The Republicans are watching this fight very attentively. Mr. Willkie sent a statement which was read by a Republican Congressman at one of the first hearings, and in that statement Willkie expressed his unequivocal support of the Resolution. Furthermore, it is felt in Democratic as well as in Republican circles that the issue involved, if not handled carefully, may lose for the Administration a good million of Jewish votes, especially in New York City…The debate around the Resolution has certainly succeeded in awakening widespread Jewish interest, and the failure of this Resolution to be adopted by Congress would certainly create a deep rift between the Jews on the one side and the State Department, even the President, on the other side. It is typical today to hear public orators at Jewish public gatherings saying that Jesus was not the Messiah nor apparently is Mr. Roosevelt."[334]

Part of the reason the Bergsonites perceived a shift in Jewish attitudes toward Roosevelt is that they were devout readers of the Yiddish-language press. In late 1943, criticism of FDR's positions on European Jewry and Palestine appeared in some Yiddish dailies to an extent that challenges contemporary perceptions of unanimous adoration of Roosevelt among American Jews. "Lately there has been a tendency in certain circles of our overheated nationalists to talk much evil about Roosevelt," a columnist for the Yiddish-language *Forverts* complained in October. "In open comment it is voiced that Roosevelt has betrayed the Jews."[335] An article by columnist B.Z. Goldberg in *Der Tog* in December was bluntly titled "Does the

Roosevelt Administration Have the Jews in Its Vest-Pocket?," a question that would have been almost inconceivable only a few months earlier. He wrote:

> [T]he leaders of the Roosevelt administration [have] the impression that they can be sure of the Jews, that they have the Jewish vote in their vest-pocket, that they can be taken for granted and left out of mind. Someone should make it plain to official Washington that it is wrong to take the Jews for granted...[T]he Jews are beginning to take an account of what they have received from the [supposedly] philo-Jewish Roosevelt administration and the entire Jewish coterie—what did they get in practical terms?...[T]he greatest debit of the Roosevelt administration is its State Department...[T]ens and tens of thousands of Jews could have saved themselves from Germany and Austria [in the 1930s] according to the regulations of the land (quota), [but] the State Department, on its own authority, prevented the entry...Someone should remind the administration that it should not overlook the reckoning with the Jews—least of all in 1944."[336]

Within some mainstream Jewish leadership circles, too, there was talk of Jewish voters turning against FDR. At an August 10 meeting of the Joint Emergency Committee, one of Rabbi Wise's top aides, Lillie Shultz of the American Jewish Congress, asserted that the Jewish leadership had erred in its decision to "put all our eggs in one basket," that is, "the assumption that there is a friendly administration in Washington." As a result, "our proposals [to the administration] for action were couched in terms of appeal;" now a different political strategy was needed—

> The time has come, she said, to be critical of [the U.S. government's] lack of action and in view of the fact that this is the eve of a presidential election year, ways can be found to indicate to the administration, and possibly through the political parties, that the large and influential Jewish communities will find a way of registering at the polls [their] dissatisfaction over the failure of the administration to take any effective steps to save the Jews of Europe.

Shultz was not alone. The next speaker at that meeting, veteran American Zionist leader Morris Rothenberg, "expressed agreement with the point of view of Miss Shultz," according to the minutes. Evidently both Shultz and Rothenberg perceived a sufficient level of unhappiness over FDR in the Jewish community to presume that a threatened withdrawal of Jewish support would be taken seriously.[337]

Rabbi Wise and his colleagues in the Jewish leadership still strongly supported Roosevelt and eagerly looked forward to his re-election in 1944, but it is not entirely clear how confident they were, in the autumn of 1943, that most American Jews still felt as strongly as they did. Some of their private statements to senior Roosevelt advisers at the time indicated doubts regarding the firmness of Jewish electoral support for FDR. Nahum Goldmann, cochairman with Rabbi Wise of the World Jewish Congress, spoke to presidential aide Samuel Rosenman, in October 1943, about what he called "the developing resentment among the Jews of America to the negative attitude of our Government, the silence of the State Department on the White Paper, and in general, the 'changed' attitude which we have sensed within the past year, a resentment which is bound to make itself felt during the coming year."[338]

That same month, Congressman Celler raised the issue even more explicitly in a meeting with Secretary Hull and a lengthy memo to presidential secretary Marvin McIntyre concerning New York Governor Thomas Dewey, a likely candidate for the Republican presidential nomination in 1944: "The Jews in New York and other areas like Philadelphia, Chicago, Boston, Sanfrancisco [sic], Cleveland are greatly exercised over the failure of our Administration to condemn the MacDonald White Paper," he warned.

> Particularly I have in mind that we are naturally concerned with the New York local situation. Some of Governor Dewey's advisors in New York are eminent Jews. His closest advisor and original sponsor is a Jew. They, undoubtedly, are giving thought to the subject of Palestine and the advisability of prevailing upon the British Foreign Office to keep open the gates to that haven. It would not surprise me in the least to have Governor Dewey make a pronouncement in the not too distant future to the effect that Palestine cannot be liquidated as a homeland for the Jews and that the MacDonald White Paper must be abrogated since it is violative of the treaty and declaration of our Congress.

"[A]s far as the race of Abraham, Isaac and Jacob is concerned," Celler concluded, Dewey "would steal the show right from under our noses. He has lots of political canniness...I cannot too strongly emphasize the political echoes of such a pronouncement whether by the President or Dewey.[339]

The issue of Jewish votes in 1944 also figured into Secretary Morgenthau's calculations as he discussed with his aides whether to speak to the president about the Gillette-Rogers rescue resolution. At a January 15, 1944 meeting between Morgenthau, his senior staff, presidential adviser Ben Cohen, and Oscar Cox, Cohen had this to say about the idea of presenting the DuBois "Acquiescence of This Government" memorandum to the president:

> [T]here is also a factor which you don't want to put in the memorandum which will influence the President and will influence [Secretary of State] Hull. We all know that during this political year minorities are being exploited. It is not that the minorities are trying to exploit politics. There may be some of that, but all the politicians are trying to exploit the value of minority groups, and the situation has gotten to the point where something has to be done.[340]

Morgenthau did not respond specifically to Cohen's point, but there can be little doubt that the politically astute Treasury Secretary appreciated the possible electoral implications of the rescue controversy. Morgenthau understood this was the moment to push forward. The pressure in Congress and the shift in public opinion in favor of rescue, he said at the meeting, gave him the leverage he needed to convince the president that "you have either got to move very fast, or the Congress of the United States will do it for you."

No transcript exists of Morgenthau's January 16, 1944 meeting with FDR. In later writings and interviews, Morgenthau never indicated whether he specifically raised the question of how Jews might vote in November. But these four facts are clear:

First, as noted above, the president's top Jewish adviser, Samuel Rosenman, had in recent months been warned by Jewish leaders, on more than one occasion, about Jewish voters possibly turning against FDR, and both Secretary Hull and presidential secretary McIntyre received a similar warning from Congressman Celler.

Second, Roosevelt himself had conversed with Winston Churchill about the Jewish vote during Churchill's visit to the United States the previous May. When FDR spoke of the need to maintain good relations with Arab countries, Churchill replied that "there were more Jewish than Arab votes in the Anglo-Saxon countries and we could not afford to ignore such practical considerations."³⁴¹

Third, Roosevelt was likely aware of the budding relationship between some American Jews and Republican leaders. Hoover's address to the Bergson Group's Emergency Conference less than six months earlier had been amply covered in the *New York Times* and other major newspapers that the White House monitored. In addition, the leading presumed contenders for the Republican nomination, Wendell Willkie and Governor Dewey, spoke at Zionist rallies in the autumn of 1943. Vice President Henry Wallace noted in his diary on November 2 "how vigorously Willkie is going to town for Palestine." Willkie's message to that particular rally was striking. He called the failure to permit the rise of a Jewish state "a shameful blot on the conscience of mankind" and criticized the Allies for taking "no effective measures" to rescue Europe's Jews. No comparably aggressive pitch for Jewish votes had ever been made previously by a candidate for the Republican presidential nomination.³⁴²

Fourth, as a seasoned politician and himself a former governor of New York, FDR undoubtedly appreciated the size of the state's Jewish voting bloc (about 14%) and the significant role of New York, the state with the largest number of electoral votes (47), in determining the outcome of a presidential election. Except in 1876, no candidate had ever been elected president without carrying New York. The fact that Dewey was the popular governor of New York could have added to the president's sense that a major clash with the American Jewish community might cost him that crucial state.

With election day just ten months away, the last thing the president needed was a public scandal over the refugee issue. Morgenthau was, in effect, offering him a way out. The Treasury Secretary handed Roosevelt a condensed version of the DuBois "Acquiescence" report and urged him to unilaterally create a rescue agency in order to pre-empt the embarrassment of congressional action. FDR quickly assented. Within days of his meeting with Morgenthau, Roosevelt issued an executive order creating the War Refugee Board. Its mission: to undertake "effective measures for the rescue, transportation, maintenance and relief of the victims of enemy oppression." Even Breckinridge Long, arch-opponent of rescue action, thought the creation of the board was "a good idea—for local political reasons" —as he wrote in his diary— "for there are 4 million Jews in New York and its environs who feel themselves related to the refugees and because of the persecutions of the Jews, and who have been demanding special attention and treatment. This will encourage them to think the persecuted may be saved and possibly satisfy them—politically..."343

The Rescuers

Who would run the new agency? Morgenthau and his aides believed the War Refugee Board should be headed by an individual of international stature, someone whose prominence would both lend prestige to the Board and facilitate dealings with government officials. The ideal candidate also would be a take-charge type capable of effectively managing a government agency. They needed "a young Herbert Hoover," Secretary of War Henry Stimson suggested, a remark Morgenthau passed along to Roosevelt. The president "thought that was very funny," the Treasury Secretary later reported to his staff. Mentioning Hoover to Roosevelt probably was a mistake. FDR knew all too well how the fame Hoover gained from his food relief efforts during and after World War I paved his road to the White House. Reminding the president of the political implications of the War Refugee Board appointment would not help win FDR's support for the man Morgenthau and his aides wanted: Wendell Willkie. The 1940 Republican presidential nominee, like young Hoover, was a business executive who had never held elected office before rising to national prominence. Although soundly defeated by Roosevelt four years earlier, he was one of the leading candidates for the Republican nomination in 1944. Morgenthau and his aides believed Willkie would likely accept an offer to chair the new Board precisely because of what Treasury staff member Ansel Luxford called the "terrific political potentialities" of the position. Luxford predicted the person taking the job could turn out to be "another Herbert Hoover," that is, leading a humanitarian mission abroad would serve as a political springboard for him at home. "[W]hat Wendell Willkie needs now is a springboard to talk from," Morgenthau agreed. "Where can he speak today?...[But as chair of the War Refugee Board] he would come down and have a press conference every day." Roosevelt evidently shared that perception—and reached a conclusion the opposite of Morgenthau's. The White House quickly shot down Willkie's candidacy because, as presidential secretary Grace Tully put it, Willkie "has had all the build-up he has coming to him on that [recent global] trip."344

In the end, 29 year-old Treasury staffer John Pehle was chosen as executive director. Josiah DuBois was named general counsel. The Board received little government funding, and lacked the clout that a big-name leader would have brought to the enterprise. Nonetheless Pehle, DuBois, and their small but dedicated staff advanced the cause of rescue with determination and creativity. They energetically employed unorthodox means of rescue in Europe, including bribery of border officials and the production of forged identification papers and other documents to protect refugees from the Nazis. The WRB's agents saved the lives of 48,000 Jews by arranging for them to be moved from Transnistria, where they would have been in the path of the retreating German army, to safer areas in Romania. A year earlier, Samuel Grafton of the *New York Post* had asked rhetorically, "What could a special [rescue] agency do? After all, how many Jews can we get out of Rumania, and where we can send them? The spirit that begins by asking such questions will not rescue anybody, even itself. We take as many out of the Balkans as we can." The WRB answered Grafton's question.[345]

About 15,000 Jewish refugees, and about 20,000 non-Jewish refugees, were evacuated from Axis-occupied territory, and at least 10,000 more were protected through various WRB-sponsored activities. The Board orchestrated a series of condemnations and threats from the U.S., the Vatican, and other world leaders against the Hungarian government to bring an end to the deportation of Hungarian Jews to Auschwitz in July 1944, after 440,000 had been deported from around the country but before the approximately 100,000 Jews in Budapest had been taken. Emissaries of the Board persuaded Swedish businessman Raoul Wallenberg to go to Budapest where, with funds and other assistance from the WRB, he sheltered thousands of Jews. The Board also persuaded Roosevelt to admit one token group of 982 refugees outside the quota system—"a bargain-counter flourish in humanitarianism," the journalist I. F. Stone called it. Historians estimate that the War Refugee Board's efforts played a major role in saving about 200,000 Jews and 20,000 non-Jews. The Board's work demolished the Roosevelt administration's long-standing claim that there was no way to rescue Jews except by winning the war.[346]

Could the Republicans Woo the Jews?

The American Jewish Congress hailed the creation of the War Refugee Board as "a healing balm applied to the wound which has long tormented American Jewry." The American Jewish Conference proclaimed, "The action taken by our President promises life to people who were otherwise doomed to destruction..." Moreover, the establishment of the WRB halted the acrimonious congressional and public debate over rescue and put a stop to the escalating negative press coverage of the administration's refugee policy. Hence the creation of the Board should have put an end to any Republican hopes of attracting Jewish voters in the 1944 presidential election. Yet exactly the opposite happened: as the year 1944 unfolded, Jewish ties with the GOP deepened and the Republicans' perception that they could win substantial Jewish electoral support intensified.[347]

The evolution of the Jewish relationship with the Republican Party in 1944 was all the more remarkable in view of the obstacles the relationship needed to overcome. Until Pearl Harbor, most Republicans staunchly opposed going to war against Hitler. Fringe elements on the political right even flirted with antisemitism. A culture gap between white collar Republican WASPs and the blue collar Jewish working class made the GOP seem alien to Jews. Moreover, many American Jews still regarded Hoover's response to the Great Depression as coldhearted, in contrast with FDR's interventionist programs and social welfare initiatives.

Yet it was also possible to see those as yesterday's issues. Isolationism was now irrelevant; fighting Hitler was a consensus issue. Antisemites on the far right, such as Charles Lindbergh, were no longer a political force, and in any event, antisemitism in the political arena often emanated from southern Democrats such as Rep. John Rankin or Sen. Theodore Bilbo rather than anyone connected to the Republicans. As for the Depression, that was largely just a bad memory; those years were over, and Hoover's response fifteen years earlier was not an active concern among Jewish or other voters. And the sense that the GOP was inhospitable to Jews and Jewish concerns, and that FDR was the one who cared about the Jews, arguably had been undermined by the events of the previous year.

Throughout the year following the Allies' December 1942 declaration on the Nazi mass murders, virtually every public action taken by the Roosevelt administration in response to the Holocaust or related issues disappointed the Jewish community. In most cases, these were not matters in which grassroots Jews needed to read between the lines of a hard-to-find news brief to figure out what was happening; rather, these were high-profile controversies in which respected mainstream Jewish leaders or outspoken Jewish congressmen publicly bemoaned the administration's failures. The volume and frequency of these verbal blasts against the administration inevitably contributed to a perception among many Jews that Roosevelt's refugee policy was far from adequate. Certainly not every Jewish voter paid attention to every such pronouncement by Jewish communal spokesmen.

Still, the accumulation of such presidential disappointments and antagonistic Jewish pronouncements was bound to have some impact.

For example, after liberating North Africa in late 1942, the administration chose to leave old anti-Jewish laws in place so as not to anger local Arabs. This policy generated a spate of angry protests by Jewish leaders and months of articles in the New York daily *PM* and Jewish newspapers with headlines such as "Why State Dept. Holds Up Repeal of Nuremberg Laws." Similarly, the refusal of the Roosevelt administration to permit Jewish organizations to attend the Bermuda refugee conference in April 1943 sparked press reports about how Jewish groups were being "locked out" of the gathering. Bermuda was a significant magnet for unfriendly press coverage: "Jews Disappointed In Refugee Parley" was the headline of a *PM* report three days before the conference even opened, and Jewish newspapers reported the prescient hope of Hadassah's president that Bermuda "will not turn out to be a mockery." Two weeks later, "mockery" was indeed one of the most frequently-quoted adjectives in the public responses of Jewish leaders and Bergson rescue activists alike. Some normally staid Jewish newspapers could not help but resort to sarcasm: "Bermuda Conferees Agree to Another Conference," the *Baltimore Jewish Times* informed its readers. In the summer of 1943, a behind-the-scenes struggle between the Roosevelt administration and Jewish leaders, over plans for a U.S. declaration banning public discussion of Palestine for the duration of the war, burst into public view, thanks to Congressman Celler and Washington investigative journalist Drew Pearson. The administration backed down, but only after suffering yet another public relations black eye. In the autumn of that year came the denouement of the year-long deterioration of the administration's image in the eyes of the Jewish community: the 400 rabbis snubbed by the president, the administration's effort to block the rescue resolution, and the front-page scandal over Breckinridge Long's false testimony about the admission of refugees.[348]

Jewish criticism of the Roosevelt administration's refugee policy in 1943-1944 was often remarkably specific and focused, indicating that the holes in many of the administration's claims were becoming well known in the Jewish community, thus intensifying resentment over U.S. policy. No ships available to transport refugees? A *Baltimore Jewish Times* editorial pointed out that empty troop-supply ships were "frequently going out of their way to find ballast" to weigh them down on their return trips, and that the Allies had managed to find ships to bring tens of thousands of Polish refugees to Iran, Uganda, and Mexico—"the very ships [that] all the apologists for failure to aid the Jewish refugees denied were available." Refugees would take jobs away from Americans? Congressman Samuel

Dickstein revealed in a radio address that the Department of Agriculture was spending $30-million "to import into this country Mexican and other residents of this hemisphere to help to relieve our labor shortage." The immigration quota system was to blame? Immigration "has for years been held far below the legal quotas" by the Roosevelt administration as a matter of policy, the World Jewish Congress charged. "[T]he admission of immigrants has been obstructed by the piling up of formalities, questionnaires [and] inquiries...The whole thing could be summarily dropped, fully or in part, by a simple order of the chief executive." No room for large numbers of refugees, even on a temporary basis? Yet hundreds of thousands of Axis P.O.W.s, "the creatures that have been hurling babies into the gutters in the forced ghettos of Europe," were given "food, clothing, and medical attention at the expense of American citizens," a *Jewish Forum* editorial argued. "Why does [President Roosevelt] not accord Jews at least equal treatment with enemy aliens...?" Conditions in the war zone made it impossible to aid the Jews? "Allied bombings of the death camps and the roads leading to them" could interrupt the murder process, the U.S. Labor Zionist journal *Jewish Frontier* insisted; the *National Jewish Ledger* even more specifically urged the Allies to "order the bombing of gas execution chambers at Oswiechim [*sic*] and Birkenau..." That so much detail was known about the fate of the Jews and possible avenues for aiding them could only make the administration's seeming indifference all the more troubling to American Jews.[349]

Would the creation of the War Refugee Board suffice to overcome Jewish voters' sense of disappointment? Would its establishment restore Roosevelt's name to its previous untarnished status in the Jewish community? The Republicans had some reason to think not. First, there was no way for Jewish voters to know whether the Board would be granted meaningful powers, or would turn out to be more a gesture than genuine progress in addressing the problem, such as the disappointing President's Advisory Committee on Political Refugees that FDR created in 1938, or the toothless Intergovernmental Conference on Refugees, which grew out of the Evian conference. In fact, as it turned out, most of the WRB's successes were of necessity kept confidential until after the war, and thus had no impact on Jewish attitudes toward Roosevelt in 1944.

Second, throughout 1943, as the administration's statements and actions regarding European Jewry repeatedly stoked concerns in the Jewish community, prominent Republicans were assuming a leading role in support of rescue and Jewish statehood. For the first time since Hitler's rise to power more than a decade earlier, the GOP was presenting the Jewish community with a seemingly credible alternative to FDR on these issues. Hoover's high-profile involvement with the Bergson Group, the pro-Zionist statements made by Willkie and Dewey, and the participation of the Republican National Committee's chairman and prominent GOP members of Congress in Bergsonite and Revisionist activities, began to erode old assumptions in the Jewish community about Republican indifference toward Jewish concerns.

Third, even if Jewish concerns about rescue were at least briefly assuaged in January 1944 by the establishment of the War Refugee Board, an emotional and headline-grabbing fight between American Jewry and the Roosevelt administration over Palestine was just getting underway in early 1944. And that was where the Republicans would make their decisive move to seek the Jewish vote.

Palestine, the Jews, and the GOP

In an attempt to inject fresh energy into the lethargic American Zionist movement, Rabbi Dr. Abba Hillel Silver, a dynamic activist and fiery orator from Cleveland, was in September 1943 elevated to co-chairmanship, alongside Rabbi Wise, of the American Zionist Emergency Council (AZEC), the umbrella for the major U.S. Zionist groups. (The Bergson Group and the Revisionists were not part of the council.) Silver crafted a political strategy targeting the British closure of Palestine. England's White Paper of 1939, limiting Jewish immigration to 15,000 annually, was due to expire on March 31, 1944, at which time, according to previous British promises to the Arabs, all Jewish immigration would end. In a concerted attempt to open Palestine to Jews fleeing Hitler and pave the way for creation of a Jewish state, Silver sought to mobilize sufficient public and congressional support for Zionism to bring about U.S. pressure on Britain to change its policies.

Although not formally a Republican, Silver enjoyed a close relationship with Senator Robert Taft, a fellow-Ohioan. In January 1944, at Silver's behest, Taft introduced a resolution calling for free Jewish immigration to Palestine and establishment of a Jewish state. Silver's expanded staff of activists at AZEC headquarters in New York City mobilized Zionists around the country to flood Washington with mail supporting the resolution, while Silver's newly-hired lobbyists on Capitol Hill solicited congressional backers. The Roosevelt administration, claiming the resolution would provoke "enraged Arabs" to attack Allied troops in the Mideast, sent General George C. Marshall, the Army chief of staff, to testify against it at hearings of the Senate Foreign Relations Committee in late February and early March. Benzion Netanyahu's Revisionists responded with a double-page spread advertisement in *The New Republic* and elsewhere, accusing the administration of "bartering Jewish blood for Arab oil."[350]

Wise and Silver, apparently unaware of FDR's role in orchestrating the opposition to the Taft resolution, met with the president on March 9 in the hope of securing a public endorsement of Zionist goals. They emerged from the White House meeting to tell reporters they were authorized to say the president assured them "the American Government has never given its approval to the White Paper of 1939." They continued:

> The President is happy that the doors of Palestine are today open to Jewish refugees. When future decisions are reached full justice will be done to those who seek a Jewish National Home for which our Government and the American people have always had the deepest sympathy and today more than ever in view of the tragic plight of hundreds of thousands of homeless Jewish refugees.

Actually, the doors of Palestine were not exactly "open" to refugees; the Zionist leaders were putting the best face on a bad situation. They were alluding to the fact that, because of England's efforts to discourage Jewish immigration, there were still 30,000 immigration slots left unused from the maximum 75,000 (15,000 per year for five years) that had been authorized for the years 1939-1945. Hence until those 30,000 were used, the doors were technically "open," but not very wide and not for very long.

Rabbi Silver, who saw vice president Henry Wallace later that day, told him he was "very much pleased" with the meeting with Roosevelt. That evening, Wise proudly read the aforementioned statement aloud at a Zionist dinner in Washington. But at a cabinet session the next day, FDR related a very different version. "I told Silver where to get off," the president reported to his cabinet. "I said to Silver...If you people continue pushing this recommendation on the Hill, you are going to be responsible for the killing of a hundred thousand people." Vice President Wallace, in his diary, expressed bewilderment at the president's behavior. "I knew [from Silver] that the bulk of the President's conversation had undoubtedly been to cause Wise and Silver to believe that he was in complete accord with them and the only question was timing," Wallace wrote. "The President certainly is a waterman. He looks in one direction and rows the other with the utmost skill."[351]

FDR also led Silver and Wise to believe he would be willing to issue a pro-Zionist statement based on their conversation. Four days after their meeting, on March 13, the Zionist leaders sent the president a draft of the proposed statement. In the meantime, however, FDR hurried to assure Arab leaders he did not really mean what Wise and Silver were claiming he meant. On March 15, Secretary Hull sent a telegram—the draft of which had the words "Approved by the President" noted in the margin—to American ambassadors in the Arab world, instructing them to inform Arab leaders that FDR had spoken to Silver and Wise only of a "national home" rather than a state; that the U.S. "has never taken a position in regard to the White Paper;" and that nothing would be done regarding Palestine "without full consultation with both Arabs and Jews." Meanwhile, back on Capitol Hill, the administration's continuing pressure on congressional leaders succeeded in persuading both houses to bury Taft's Palestine resolution.[352]

President Roosevelt meeting with Ibn Saud, king of Saudi Arabia.

While all this maneuvering was underway, events on the ground in Europe took a dramatic turn for the worse. On March 19, the Germans occupied Hungary. The last major Jewish community in Europe that had been untouched by the Holocaust, 800,000 in number, was now within Hitler's grasp. The War Refugee Board staff immediately asked FDR to issue a statement warning Hungarians to refrain from assisting any Nazi persecution of Hungarian Jewry. Secretary of State Hull took advantage of the Board's request to get Roosevelt off the hook with regard to the proposed Wise-Silver statement. FDR agreed to issue the warning to Hungary, although only after the word "Jews" was removed from the first four paragraphs and downplayed elsewhere in the text. The warning was published on March 24, and even though it did not mention Palestine, Hull persuaded Roosevelt that the Zionist leaders' request "is really fully answered in the Statement of March 24, 1944," so there was no need to act on it.

The occupation of Hungary, and Roosevelt's response to it, triggered one of the most remarkable critiques of FDR's refugee policy during the entire Holocaust period—remarkable both for its content and for the fact that it appeared as an editorial in *Congress Weekly*, the official journal of Rabbi Wise's American Jewish

Congress. While Wise himself did not personally author the editorials, it is implausible, given his close supervision over everything in the organization, that it could have appeared without his knowledge and tacit approval. Twice the length of a typical *Congress Weekly* editorial, "Where Rescue is Yet Possible" began by praising the president's March 24 warning, then reminding readers "how little willingness and initiative to save the victims of these massacres was displayed until recently by those who had the power to save at least part of them." Addressing the Allied leaders directly, the editorial declared: "You cannot recompense a people for its millions left to be butchered by the enemy through your indifference to their fate and the red tape of bureaucratic approach to the matter of their rescue." The editorial pointed out that the American and British representatives who met in Bermuda "to evolve means for their rescue evolved nothing." Jewish refugees who had escaped to Hungary from elsewhere in Europe "escape[d] also from the indifference of the democratic nations, from the inhumanity of certain of their policies, from their strict adherence to rigid immigration regulations..." Yes, the War Refugee Board was eventually established—but only after "endless months of pleading and appealing." Now another one million Jews (the editorial's estimate of the Hungarian Jewish population) are "doomed to extermination" unless the Allies do something "more tangible...than a mere warning to the murderers." The Allies "have it in their power to translate the words of abhorrence of the crimes and sympathy for the victims into action of concrete meaning to the victims," beginning with immediate abrogation of the White Paper. Otherwise, the *Congress Weekly* editorial concluded, the warnings by President Roosevelt and other Allied leaders "will only be a means of easing their own conscience with respect to those who could have been saved but were not." That such bitter criticism of the president appeared in the journal of the organization headed by President Roosevelt's most loyal Jewish supporter was testimony to the depth of resentment in the Jewish community toward the administration's policies in the spring of 1944.[353]

The conflict between American Jews and the Roosevelt administration over Palestine continued to escalate in the weeks to follow, giving the Republicans reason to believe they might yet make inroads in the Jewish community. Twenty thousand protesters jammed Madison Square Garden for a March 21 rally for Palestine immigration. Senator Taft was one of the keynote speakers. This appears to have been the first time he was invited to address a Jewish gathering; his relationship with Silver and sponsorship of the Palestine resolution had opened an important new door. On April 7, two more large protests were held—a conference of Hungarian-Americans organized by the Bergson Group to focus on the threat to Hungarian Jewry, and an anti-White Paper rally attended by 1500 in Manhattan. Rallies held on April 19 to mark the anniversary of the Warsaw Ghetto revolt, including a march by 15,000 to New York City Hall, a mass meeting at Carnegie Hall, and a prayer service by "more than 5,000 weeping Jews" at the 'little Warsaw' synagogue on the Lower East Side, focused additional attention on Palestine and rescue—and, at least by implication, the dearth of U.S. action. Rabbi Silver, too, ratcheted up his public criticism of the administration. At a United Jewish Appeal meeting in June, Silver bluntly criticized the Allies' response to the Holocaust. "Governments, friendly governments, beguiled and misled us with vague promises and ineffectual rescue agencies and conferences," he declared. "Our own country failed to use even its unfilled immigration quotas to shelter our refugees...[S]o many perished who might have been saved."[354]

In addition to Taft, numerous prominent Republicans leaped into the fray. On the floor of the House, Ranulf Compton, Connecticut Republican and lead House sponsor of Taft's resolution, accused President Roosevelt of "appeasement of the Arabs." Pennsylvania governor Edward Martin and a number of Republican congressmen signed full-page Bergson newspaper ads blasting the Allies' Palestine policy. Wendell Willkie was reported (erroneously, as it turned out) to be preparing to represent the Bergson Group at forthcoming congressional hearings on Palestine. Connecticut GOP congresswoman Clare Boothe Luce was especially vociferous. Together with Republican senator Styles Bridges of New Hampshire and Hoover's close associate Hugh Gibson, Mrs. Luce headlined a Revisionist rally in New York City in April. There Luce charged that the British policy of choking off Palestine-bound Jewish immigration transports from Europe was to blame for the fact that "Jewish blood stains the blue Mediterranean red." Netanyahu reprinted excerpts from their speeches in large ads in the *New York Times* and *New York Post*. The following month, Luce introduced a congressional resolution calling for creation of temporary havens in the U.S. for refugees. "For 11 years now Americans have been deploring" the persecution of the Jews, but "while we deplored and lamented, millions of refugees were savagely murdered," she said. "Others escaped death only to wander as refugees across the face of a world which was sympathetic but coldly inhospitable. They have life but no place to live."[355]

Republican strategists might well have noticed that even some liberals who were usually supportive of the president were speaking out, too. "[I]t is easy to indulge in the luxury of blaming [the British for the Palestine shutdown] when our own American policy is also at fault," the editors of the leftwing New York City daily *PM* asserted, pointing to FDR's opposition to the Taft resolution. The president's March 24 statement asked Balkan countries to shelter Jews, but he had no "moral right" to do so when America was shutting its own doors, the editorial charged. Democratic congressman and former four-term mayor of Boston James Curley declared on the floor of the House that the Roosevelt administration had failed to fulfill "the promise of relief which it has held out" to the Jews. (April 26) James G. McDonald, chairman of Roosevelt's own President's Advisory Committee on Political Refugees, accused the Allies of "paying only lip service" to Hitler's Jewish victims and "acting as if refugee problems were relatively minor matters." (May 21) Edgar Ansel Mowrer of the *New York Post* charged that Britain's harsh closure of Palestine "is, of course, supported by President Roosevelt." (May 21) I.F. Stone, in *The Nation,* blamed Britain and the U.S. for the failure of a plan to rescue 20,000 Jewish children and contended that the temporary shelters proposal was a test "of Mr. Roosevelt's courage and good faith" as well as his willingness "to face a few sneering editorials" from far-right newspapers. (June 9)[356]

Even FDR's announcement of plans to admit some refugees became an occasion for criticism. In the spring of 1944, the War Refugee Board, the Bergson Group, and other refugee advocates pressed the administration to create what they called "free ports" for Jews fleeing Hitler—temporary havens in the United States where refugees could stay until the end of the war, just as certain goods were permitted to stay temporarily in U.S. harbors without paying taxes. Roosevelt eventually agreed to grant temporary shelter to a single group of 982 Jewish refugees. In addition to the expected expressions of gratitude from the Jewish community, Roosevelt's gesture was derided by I.F. Stone, in *The Nation*, as "a bargain-counter flourish in humanitarianism." Congressman Samuel Dickstein, chair of the House Immigration Committee, said "the President's project did not go far enough." Marie Syrkin, in *Jewish Frontier,* contended that it was "impressive neither as a practical measure of alleviation nor even as a gesture." *Morgen Zhurnal* columnist Jacob Gladstone characterized it as "no more than a token, a symbolic gesture, a Christian Science rescue, and the conscience of the world may continue to doze..." An editorial in the *National Jewish Ledger* called the admission of such a small number "an insult and an affront to a greatly afflicted and martyred people." The *Ledger* took particular aim at the president's failure to speak out on the need for the British to open Palestine, asserting: "[H]is silence is sad, tragic, and bitterly disappointing." This sort of criticism, which was unheard of in the Jewish community just months earlier, became more acceptable as the grim news from Hungary began to reach the United States. Newspaper headlines in May such as "Jews in Hungary Fear Annihilation" and "Savage Blows Hit Jews in Hungary," gave way by June to "Hungary Plans Jewish Extermination," "Six Trains Carry Deported Jews from Hungary to Extermination Camp in Poland," and "100,000 Hungarian Jews Have Been Executed in Polish Death Camp, Underground Reports." Such news reinforced the sense among many American Jews that their brethren in Europe had been abandoned.[357]

These domestic and international developments in the spring of 1944 combined to rejuvenate the long-dormant relationship between the Republican Party and American Jewry. The tragedy of Hungarian Jewry was unfolding before the eyes of the world; it was too early to tell if the War Refugee Board would be empowered to save them, or would prove to be another meaningless gesture; President Roosevelt was in effect siding with the British and the Arabs on Palestine, while Republicans were emerging as the Jews' allies; and prominent Jews and others were openly criticizing the administration on rescue and Palestine. This was exactly the moment when the Palestine issue might well prove to be a "vote catcher," as British officials called it.

That characterization was not inaccurate, although it may have been something of an oversimplification. In addition to the hope of attracting Jewish votes for their party's candidates, Hoover, Taft, and the other Republicans who proved receptive to Zionist appeals appear to have genuinely believed in the merits of the cause. Some of the Republicans who embraced Zionism were inclined to do so because of their Christian religious beliefs; some were more interested in the possibility that a Jewish state would serve as a pro-American bulwark against Soviet penetration of the Middle East; others were simply moved by pity for Hitler's victims or a feeling of guilt over the Free World's abandonment of European Jewry. Undoubtedly there were some cynics in the Republican Party who jumped on the Jewish vote bandwagon for less admirable reasons, such as a desire to have the Jewish refugees go to Palestine so they would not come to the United States. Moreover, the fact that a primary target of Jewish protests was Great Britain, a country that many American conservatives had long regarded with suspicion, made it a little easier for Palestine to become part of the GOP's list of concerns. On the other hand, the fact that many of these Republicans advocated opening America's doors wider to Jews fleeing Hitler, a position that traditionally was unpopular among most of the GOP's constituents, indicates that their sympathy for the Jews was motivated by more than political self-interest.[358]

During the weeks preceding the Republican National Convention, scheduled to take place in Chicago at the end of June, Netanyahu and his colleagues undertook what they called "a systematic campaign of enlightenment" among the

Alf Landon, right, with Herbert Hoover in 1943.

Republican leadership. They spoke repeatedly with Hoover, Landon, Luce, Senators Taft, Bridges, and Albert Hawkes (of New Jersey), and GOP insiders such as Hugh Gibson and George Sokolsky, explaining the Zionist case and urging inclusion of a pro-Zionist plank in the party platform. Such a plank would be a first for either party. Taft chaired the convention's resolutions committee, and Hawkes and Luce were members of it as well. Luce and Sokolsky were among those who had a hand in drafting the plank on Palestine.[359]

The Maverick from Connecticut

Mrs. Luce is an intriguing figure, both because her role in facilitating the Republican embrace of Zionism is generally unknown, and because she defied many of her era's stereotypes about women, Republicans, and Christian supporters of Zionism. Talented and ambitious, Clare was a child actress, then a suffragist, before shifting to journalism in the early 1930s. She went from editorial assistant at *Vogue* to managing editor of *Vanity Fair* in just three years, then left the magazine and carved out a successful career as a playwright, a profession relatively few women had penetrated. In the meantime, she married the immensely wealthy

Clare Boothe Luce, after winning re-election to Congress in 1944.

and influential publisher of *Time*, *Life*, and *Fortune*, Harry Luce. Clare visited the front lines of war-torn Europe and Asia in 1940-41 as a correspondent for *Life*. She was a Republican, but unlike the isolationists who dominated the party prior to World War II, she criticized FDR for failing to build up the U.S. armed forces sufficiently in the 1930s to deter Nazi aggression.[360]

Mrs. Luce's foreign policy knowledge and experiences abroad helped her win a congressional seat in Connecticut in 1942, one of just eight women to serve in the U.S. House of Representatives that term. Her election was another important step forward in bringing women into American political life, although—perhaps not surprising given the temper of the times—even some of Luce's supporters often remarked on her looks and charm rather than her skills or character. "She is representing our Fourth District down there and giving the boys something to ogle to boot," a friendly Connecticut newspaper columnist offered. Her opponents could be cruder. President Roosevelt himself was not above half-jokingly referring to her as "that loose woman."[361]

Luce seems to have had little or no knowledge of, or interest in, Jewish affairs or Palestine until she went to Washington. She later attributed the kindling of her concern about the Jews to Pierre van Paassen's 1943 book *The Forgotten Ally*, a copy of which was given to her by a Jewish friend. An acclaimed journalist and fervent Christian Zionist, van Paassen, a Dutch expatriate, was involved with both the Bergson Group and the Revisionist Zionists. His book recounted the mistreatment of Europe's Jews, made the case for the Jewish right to Palestine, and argued that a Jewish Palestine could play a crucial role in the Allies' war effort. Luce said it was this "remarkable" volume that awakened in her "a lively interest" in "the great injustice that has been done and is being done" to the Jews. That, she recalled, is what "caused me to take up the case of the Jew in Palestine" and "the intolerable condition in which the Jews in Europe finds himself today" and led her to "resolve to do what I can to right that wrong."[362]

Although she did not explicitly link them, it could be that Luce's views on discrimination against women and African-Americans, and her sense of solidarity among mistreated minorities, also influenced her view of the Jews. "The position of the Negro in American society is the great test of democracy itself," she maintained. Luce blasted "Southern-reactionary Democrats" as "the greatest factor in the retarding of Negro advancement by this Congress." She viewed the struggle for black rights and women's rights through the same prism, explaining (in 1944):

> Although it is a very, very different thing, I am a woman in politics and, in some measure, although not nearly so tragic a measure, discrimination against women in politics exists just as it does against Negroes. There are 130 million Americans, 70 million of whom in this country are women. Nevertheless, there are only seven women in the House. There is no woman today in the Cabinet or any high position

of authority in the Government. There is no woman Senator....[I]t will be fifty years at least before a woman could be Vice President, no less President. Women are also segregated and discriminated against and treated as something other than "man." Any woman in public life knows, although as I say not with the same keen sense of tragedy, what it is like to be of a different race. "Jim Crowism" is practiced daily in political life—on women.[363]

In the months after she read van Paassen's book, Luce began taking part in protests over the plight of the Jews. She provided a long quote that was included in a Revisionist ad in the *New York Times* urging rescue and Jewish statehood; served as a co-sponsor of the Bergson Group's Emergency Conference to Save the Jewish People of Europe; published a strongly pro-Zionist statement in the Revisionist journal *Zionews*; delivered the aforementioned critique of the British at the Revisionist dinner in New York City; and introduced a congressional resolution urging temporary haven for Jewish refugees in the United States.[364]

It was not, however, Luce's budding interest in Jewish affairs that brought her to the attention of the national Republican leadership. It was her charismatic personality, impressive record of accomplishment in multiple fields, and graceful manner that made her an almost irresistible candidate for the 'new face' of the GOP. Luce's communication skills, especially her knack for turning a clever political phrase—her description of postwar liberal visions of a universal world order as "globaloney" instantly became part of the political lexicon—made her the party's choice for keynote speaker at the June 1944 Republican convention. She was the first woman to be given that honor by either party. Her remarks would immediately precede those of the only living ex-president. Hoover had long been fond of Luce; after she won re-election, he sent her a note that read, "That was a grand victory; I wish we had more men like you." He reviewed her convention address in advance and found it "beautiful and powerfully affecting." Hoover hailed her as "the Symbol of the New Generation."[365]

Netanyahu developed a close relationship with Luce, especially in the aftermath of her 1944 address to the Revisionist dinner, which he predicted would "go down in history as one of the great expressions of the American conscience." The Revisionists distributed tape recordings of her speech to radio stations around the country, and printed the text in a booklet that was sent to several thousand newspaper editors, Jewish community leaders, and other interested parties. Luce was so proud of the address that she had her office print up its own edition of the booklet for distribution to her constituents. On the eve of her departure for the GOP assembly in Chicago, in June 1944, Luce told Netanyahu, only half-joking, "I'm going now, to do your work at the convention."[366]

A Tale of Two Conventions

GOP activist George Sokolsky, too, had a hand in drafting the Palestine plank of the Republican platform, although he was not formally a member of the Resolutions Committee as was Luce. The son of Russian Jewish immigrants, Sokolsky graduated from the Columbia School of Journalism and traveled to Russia in 1917 to cover the political upheaval there. As a critic of the Communists, he ended up having to flee to China, where he carved out a career for himself as a correspondent for American and British newspapers and assistant editor of the English-language *North China Star*. Returning to the United States in 1931, the energetic and enterprising Sokolsky used his lively *New York Sun* column and considerable social networking skills to establish himself as a lecturer, author, and all-around self-made expert on international affairs. At the same time, his sharp criticism of the Roosevelt administration on a variety of issues brought him into senior circles of Republican Party activists. Sokolsky was also drawn to the Revisionist Zionist cause, and played an important role in introducing Netanyahu and his colleagues to leading Republicans with whom he was on a first name basis, including Hoover. At the 1944 Republican convention, Sokolsky wore both hats.[367]

Rabbi Abba Hillel Silver delivering the invocation at the 1944 Republican Convention.

Another important source of pressure with regard to the Palestine plank was Rabbi Silver. He understood how a Republican endorsement of Zionism might influence the Roosevelt administration's policies. "[O]ur good friends here [in Washington], upon whom we have been relying so much [i.e. the Roosevelt administration and the Democratic Party], will not move on their own accord, inspired by the moral righteousness of our cause," Silver reported to World Zionist Organization president Chaim Weizmann in March. "Our friends might be inspired to move and take some definite action as a result of the pressure of five million Jews in a critical election year."³⁶⁸

Thanks to his relationship with Sen. Taft, Silver was invited to deliver the invocation at the Republican convention. He arrived in Chicago a week earlier, together with several aides, and vigorously lobbied Taft, expected nominee Governor Dewey, and members of the resolutions committee regarding the Palestine plank. The combined power of the relationships that the Revisionists had established with Hoover, Landon, Sen. Owen Brewster of Maine, and others; the involvement of Luce and Sokolsky; and the lobbying by Silver and his team, produced significant results. The final text of the plank actually went further in some respects than the various Zionist factions had requested:

> In order to give refuge to millions of distressed Jewish men, women and children driven from their homes by tyranny, we call for the opening of Palestine for their unrestricted immigration and land ownership so that in accordance with the full intent and purpose of the Balfour Declaration and the resolution of Congress in 1922, Palestine may be reconstituted as a free and democratic Commonwealth. We condemn the failure of the President to insist that the Palestine Mandatory carry out the provisions of the Balfour Declaration and the Mandate while he pretends to support them.

"I hope you are satisfied with the Republican plank on Palestine," Sokolsky cabled Netanyahu. "It was an amazing job that we got through." Netanyahu was more than satisified. Although he had not specifically sought to have criticism of the president included in the text, he was pleased that the drafters did so. Rabbi Silver, fearing the anti-Roosevelt statement went too far, tried but failed to have that sentence deleted from the plank. Rabbi Wise, on the other hand, dashed off a letter to the president in which he declared he was "deeply ashamed" of the "utterly unjust" wording of the Republican plank. "[Y]ou may be sure," he wrote, "that American Jews will come to understand how unjust it is." Wise also publicly condemned the Republican plank as an "unjust aspersion" upon Roosevelt. Netanyahu, in his journal *Zionews*, responded: "It seems that to Dr. Wise and his friends, partisan politics are more important than truth and the interests of their people and their country."³⁶⁹

Of greater political consequence was the response of the Jewish press. In an age when newspapers were the primary medium through which the Jewish community learned of political developments, it was significant that New York City's Yiddish-language dailies, from the politically conservative *Morgen Zhurnal* to the socialist *Forverts*, gave the Republican plank front-page coverage. The two major English-language Jewish news services further reinforced the impression that the Republicans were going out on a limb for the Jewish people. The Jewish Telegraphic Agency's report on the adoption of the plank quoted only Silver, not Wise. A follow-up story two weeks later reported that the American Zionist Emergency Council had praised the GOP's plank. (The council's statement had actually said, in deliberately guarded language, that it was praising only "the section" in the plank concerning Palestine—meaning not the reference to FDR—but that nuance appears to have been lost in the story.) The Independent Jewish Press Service (IJPS), for its part, quoted both Silver and Wise, but gave Silver about twice as much space as his rival. Several days later, it ran follow-up reports about how the State Department and the Arab world were upset at the Republicans, developments which could only make Jewish voters look even more favorably on the GOP. The IJPS also published an article about how Congressman Emanuel Celler was pressing the Democrats to match the GOP plank. In addition, the press service ran a political gossip column reporting that "opposition to a [pro-Zionist] plank [at the Democratic convention] has been whittled down as a result of the Republicans' action"—a further indication to Jewish voters of another possible benefit from the Republicans' action. All in all, it was probably the best coverage the Republican Party had received in the Jewish news media in more than a decade. For Republican election strategists angling for the Jewish vote, it was a significant achievement.[370]

The Republican move put strong pressure on the Democrats, for the first time, to compete for Jewish sympathies and treat the Jewish vote as if it were up for grabs. Rabbi Wise traveled to Chicago in July to press delegates at the Democratic convention to adopt a Palestine plank similar to that of the Republicans. At first things did not go well. Wise's pre-conference request for a meeting with FDR to secure his "personal and administration support of [the] Zionist program" and affirmation of his desire to bring about "maximum rescue [of] Jewish civilians" fell on deaf ears at the White House. On the second day of the convention, an agitated Wise buttonholed assistant attorney general Norman Littell to report that members of the platform committee were resisting his pleas for a pro-Zionist plank. "It will hurt the president," Wise warned him. "It will lose the President 400,000 or 500,000 votes." Wise emphasized that the GOP had adopted "a satisfactory plank" on Palestine. Rep. Celler, who was a member of the Resolutions

Committee, likewise warned the Democratic party leadership that they could lose Jewish votes in the November presidential election if they failed to match the Republicans' stance on Palestine. A large Revisionist advertisement in the *Chicago Daily News* reminded the delegates of the GOP plank and pressed them to support "immediate and effective action on behalf of a Jewish Palestine."

Synagogue Council of America president Israel Goldstein, who accompanied Wise at the convention, later recalled how they positioned themselves near a revolving door directly downstairs from the room where the platform was being discussed, "so that every politician that came in would be bound to bump into Wise."

> [H]e knew most of them by their first names...And he collared every one of these politicians and I was standing there at his side as a kind of junior assistant and the two of us together would indoctrinate that person in the two or three minutes that were available, and that person was on his way to the meeting of the Platform Committee which was upstairs. So by the time he got to his meeting, he had already had some indoctrination at the hands of Wise plus Goldstein—mostly Wise.

Wise may have felt a need to protect the president from Jewish defections, but for Goldstein, securing a pro-Zionist plank from the Democrats was simply canny politics: "[Silver] was playing off the two parties against one another. It was a fine strategy and it worked, because the result was that we got very good planks in both party platforms." The Democrats agreed to endorse "unrestricted Jewish immigration and colonization" of Palestine and the establishment of "a free and democratic Jewish commonwealth." Now both parties stood unequivocally in support of rescue and statehood.[371]

By the early fall, however, Wise was worried that without a pro-Zionist declaration by Roosevelt personally, the platform plank might not impress Jewish voters. "There are things afoot which I do not like, designed to hurt you," he wrote to the president in September 1944. "Nearly everything can be done to avert them if [Rabbi Silver and I] can talk to you and have from you a word which shall be your personal affirmation of the Palestine plank in the Chicago platform of the Party." Ten days later, having received no response from the president, Wise wrote to Rosenman:

> I may say to you in confidence that it would be definitely helpful to THE cause if we could see the Chief with the least possible delay, and

get from him a statement that would be little more than one of assent to the plank in the Democratic platform, together with some word that would indicate that either in this or his next term of office he will do what he can to translate that platform declaration into action together with the British Government.

Believe me, dear Judge, that I would not press this as I do if I did not have reason to fear that fullest advantage might be taken of the Chief's failure to speak on this at an early date. It would be a mistake to let that word come just before the election; the sooner the better, as you well understand.

It took the White House three more weeks, but finally, knowing that Governor Dewey was going to send a pro-Zionist message to a national Zionist convention in Atlantic City on October 15, President Roosevelt did, too. In a message that was read to the delegates by Senator Robert Wagner, FDR referred sympathetically to the goal of "establishment of Palestine as a free and democratic Jewish commonwealth," and pledged to "help to bring about its realization." The Zionist delegates, who reportedly wept "tears of joy" upon hearing the president's statement, did not know that FDR watered down Wagner's original draft. He had removed "undivided" from before "Palestine," and changed "do all in my power" to "help."[372]

On election day, more than 90% of American Jews cast their ballots for President Roosevelt. This overwhelming Jewish electoral support for FDR, despite the rumblings of discontent heard in late 1943 and much of 1944, was facilitated by several factors. One was a nervous minority group's understandable human longing for reassurance. Most American Jews revered Roosevelt and naturally wanted to believe the feeling was mutual. It was inconceivable that the man renowned as a humanitarian could be indifferent to the plight of their massacred coreligionists; indeed, that was one of the reasons most Jews had been so slow to criticize the Roosevelt administration's refugee policies in earlier years. It was far more comforting to believe that the failure to rescue was the fault of wily State Department bureaucrats operating without the president's knowledge. Roosevelt's establishment of the War Refugee Board fit neatly into this narrative and was seen as proof of the president's concern for the plight of the Jews, even if the Board's actual record was not a matter of a public knowledge.

Thomas E. Dewey, left, with Wendell Willkie

An incident during the 1944 campaign involving the Republican vice presidential candidate, Ohio Governor John W. Bricker, probably contributed further to the avalanche of Jewish backing for Roosevelt's re-election. Two weeks before election day, Bricker, who had previously endorsed the "free ports" proposal, suddenly declared that bringing the 982 refugees to the United States outside the immigration laws was unconstitutional. He also accused FDR of misleading Congress into thinking that most of those admitted would be "palefaced women and frail children"; in fact, according to Bricker, the majority were men—"and not laboring men either, but writers, lawyers, artists and intellectuals generally." Bricker's outburst confirmed for some Jews that, as one Jewish periodical put it, "certain sections of the Republican Party" still subscribed to "anti-foreignism (read anti-Semitism)." That made it even easier for Jewish voters to continue regarding the Democratic Party as Jewry's natural home.[373]

Narrowly interpreted, the election results might be seen as confirmation that nothing had changed in the relationship between American Jewry and the major political parties. In fact, however, the events of the summer of 1944 fundamentally altered the dynamics of American Jewry's role in presidential politics as well as the relationship between the United States and the Jewish state-to-be. In 1944, for the first time in history, the Republicans and Democrats adopted planks pledging support for Jewish statehood and actively competed for Jewish electoral support on that basis. Support for Jewish statehood was elevated to a status above partisanship. There would be no turning back. Every four years since then, both parties have reaffirmed that position. Thanks to the events of 1944, competition for the "Jewish vote" emerged as a factor in presidential politics, and bipartisan support for the Jewish state would become an integral part of American political culture.[374]

Zionism's Bipartisan Roots

The parties' embrace of Jewish statehood in 1944 was anchored in a widespread sympathy for Zionism among grassroots American Christians that dated back to the previous century. The Blackstone Memorial of March 1891, a petition urging President Benjamin Harrison to help facilitate creation of a Jewish state, attracted the signatures of more than 400 prominent Americans, most of them Christians, including the speaker of the House of Representatives, the chairman of the House Foreign Relations Committee, and the chief justice of the Supreme Court. Christian Americans were taking an increasing interest in the Holy Land, thanks to reports brought back by the large number of archaeologists, bible scholars, missionaries, and tourists—including former President Ulysses Grant—who visited Palestine in the mid and late 1800s. These visits coincided with the spread, in the United States, of a strand of Protestant thought known as dispensationalism, according to which the return of the Jews to the Holy Land and reestablishment of their state is a necessary stage in the imminent Second Coming process. That belief remains a significant part of American Protestantism to this day.

Even for the many Christians who did not embrace dispensationalism, religious sentiments often underlay their sympathy for Jewish national aspirations. Whether it was Woodrow Wilson, the deeply religious son of a Presbyterian minister, endorsing the Balfour Declaration, or Herbert Hoover, the devout Quaker raised on Bible stories, embracing the Zionist cause, the romantic ideal of the Holy Land reborn proved irresistible to American Christians of various denominations. A well-known photograph of notable participants in the founding conference of the American Palestine Committee, a Christian Zionist group established in 1932, illustrates the diversity of mainstream Protestants who were enamored of the Palestine cause: Vice President Charles Curtis, a Methodist, is pictured alongside, among others, Supreme Court Justice Harlan F. Stone, an Episcopalian; Illinois Congressman Henry T. Rainey, a Presbyterian; and Utah Senator William H. King, a Mormon.[375]

King and fellow-Utah Senator Elbert Thomas, both former missionaries and arguably the two most prominent Mormons in America during the 1930s-1940s, stood out as ardent champions of rescuing Jews from Hitler and establishing a Jewish state. Both were motivated by their faith in Mormon prophecies about the return of the Jews from exile. King was one of the few members of Congress to urge severance of diplomatic relations with Germany in response to Kristallnacht; supported the 1939 Wagner-Rogers bill to admit 20,000 refugee children; and in 1940 sponsored legislation to open Alaska to Jewish refugee immigration. Thomas, for his part, delivered numerous speeches calling for rescue, co-chaired the Bergson Group's Emergency Conference to Save the Jewish People of Europe, and played a key role in advancing the Gillette-Rogers rescue resolution in the Senate.[376]

King and Thomas were Democrats with no political incentive to stand up for the Jews. They represented a state with a miniscule number of Jewish voters. Supporting refugee immigration, U.S. rescue action, or pressure on the British over Palestine meant going directly against the wishes of the Roosevelt administration. Their religious convictions trumped ordinary political considerations. Other dissident Democrats who defied the administration by promoting rescue and statehood were inspired by somewhat more secular considerations: admiration for the efforts of the Zionist pioneers and, especially, sympathy for Hitler's victims. A relatively small number of politicians, from both parties, may have been motivated to support Zionism out of hope for Jewish electoral support, but more often that was not the case. Senator Gillette, for example, represented Iowa, which had few Jewish residents, while Congressman Rogers went to Washington intending to serve only one term. Likewise on the Republican side, the most vocal pro-Jewish voices in the Senate typically belonged to the likes of Owen Brewster of Maine and Charles Tobey of New Hampshire, who had no electoral incentive to take an interest in Jewish issues. There were many similar examples on both sides of the aisle.

In adopting party planks endorsing Jewish statehood, the national leaders of the Republican and Democratic parties were embracing and elevating an issue that, on its merits, was already close to the hearts of many of their congressmembers and had already been a bipartisan issue for many years. Now, for the first time, it was becoming an electoral issue as well.

Chapter 7

Republicans, Democrats, and the Birth of Israel

At the 1944 Democratic convention, President Roosevelt replaced Vice President Henry Wallace with Missouri Senator Harry S. Truman. How America's Palestine policy would have evolved in a Roosevelt-Truman administration is a matter of conjecture, although it did not augur well that Roosevelt, in remarks to Congress on March 1, 1945, said of his recent meeting with Saudi Arabia's king that "I learned more about the whole problem, the Moslem problem, the Jewish problem, by talking with Ibn Sa'ud for five minutes than I could have learned in an exchange of two or three dozen letters." But six weeks later, FDR died suddenly and Truman became the 33rd president of the United States. Now the vexing Palestine dilemma fell into Truman's lap—and the new competition from the Republicans for the Jewish vote, inaugurated by the 1944 GOP platform, would play a major role in determining Truman's Palestine policy. Truman himself had been involved in drafting the Democrats' 1944 Palestine plank—a transparent appeal to Jewish voters—so there can be little doubt that he understood, clearly and early on, the role domestic politics played in addressing this thorny issue.[377]

In the aftermath of the Allied victory over Germany in May 1945, the new president was confronted by the problem of tens of thousands of Holocaust survivors languishing in the Displaced Persons camps that had been established by the American and British occupation forces. American Zionists, grief stricken at the revelations of the full extent of the Nazi genocide and furious at England's continuing White Paper policy, pressed the Truman administration to call for opening Palestine's doors to the DPs. This increasingly militant mood in the Jewish community was a boon for Rabbi Abba Hillel Silver, who had resigned from the American Zionist leadership after a clash with Rabbi Wise in December 1944 over the congressional resolution on Palestine; Silver had wanted to revive the resolution, while Wise deferred to the Roosevelt administration's desire to bury it.

Now, as rank-and-file Zionists "boiled with indignation" (as Pierre van Paassen put it) over the plight of the DPs and British policy in Palestine, Silver was swept back to the helm of the American Zionist movement. This set the stage for intensified confrontation between American Jewry and the Democratic administration. Silver launched a series of nationwide publicity efforts and lobbying campaigns to secure U.S. support for Jewish statehood, including establishing more than 400 local Zionist emergency councils and sponsoring a pro-Zionist broadcast on over 200 radio stations each week. Although these protests never explicitly encouraged Jewish voters to turn Republican, the political implications of this escalating controversy were obvious to the White House.[378]

President Truman wavered on Palestine, caught between his British ally and the Jewish community whose votes the Democrats needed. Adding to the pressure on the president was the fact that Palestine itself was in flames. Previously rivalrous Jewish underground militias in 1945 formed a United Hebrew Resistance to wage guerrilla warfare against the British ruling forces. Jewish attacks, British retaliation, and calls from Democratic and Republican members of Congress alike for U.S. intervention pushed the controversy to the forefront of Truman's concerns.

With the number of DPs swelling daily as refugees from elsewhere in Europe streamed to the relative safety of the Allied camps, and with winter not far off, the Truman administration dispatched University of Pennsylvania Law School dean Earl G. Harrison to Europe and Palestine to survey the situation. Harrison's report to the president, delivered in September 1945, found the DPs suffered from inadequate medical care, shelter, food, and clothing. Some had nothing to wear but German SS uniforms. Conditions were so poor, Harrison wrote, that "we appear to be treating the Jews as the Nazis treated them except that we do not exterminate them." He recommended permitting 100,000 DPs to immigrate to Palestine. The British resisted this demand for fear of angering the Arab world. For Truman, Harrison's proposal represented an opportunity to support a humanitarian gesture without having to take a stand on Palestine's political status; he endorsed the 100,000 call. American public opinion, shocked by newsreel footage of the liberated death camps and sympathetic to the suffering of the survivors, strongly supported opening Palestine's doors. Rabbi Silver's publicity campaigns, supplemented by rallies and newspaper ads from the Bergson Group and Netanyahu's Revisionists, further solidified U.S. public support for the Zionist cause.

The Republican platform of 1944 cast a long shadow over the administration's Middle East policy considerations in 1945. The GOP had put the Democrats on notice that as far as it was concerned, the Jewish vote was up for grabs. Now, as Truman and his political advisers nervously eyed the upcoming, hotly-contested New York City mayoral race, they had to consider the likelihood that Jewish voters might see the election as an opportunity to cast protest votes against the Democrats over Palestine and the DPs. The fact that the Republican nominee, Judge Jonah Goldstein, was Jewish and that the Liberal Party was also endorsing Goldstein, only intensified the Democrats' worries. Harrison's recommendation offered the president a way to score political points and assume the mantle of humanitarianism without taking a definitive stand on the complicated question of Palestine's future. Truman thus endorsed the Harrison proposal, much to London's consternation. British foreign minister Ernest Bevin privately complained to his colleagues that the increasing influence of Jewish voters on the Truman administration was making it harder for England to decide long-term policy on Palestine.[379]

The British had hoped to keep the United States from playing any role in resolving the Palestine problem, but in view of what he called "the propaganda in New York," Bevin concluded there was no choice but to involve the Americans. The British proposed creation of an Anglo-American Committee of Inquiry on Palestine, with each government appointing six delegates. The Truman administration assented but, much to London's annoyance, Secretary of State James Byrnes insisted on postponing establishment of the committee for electoral reasons. Citing the "intense and growing agitation about the Palestine problem in the New York electoral campaign," Byrnes informed London that the announcement would have to wait until after the November 6 vote, lest it "inflame" New York's Jews against the Democratic candidate. Presidential adviser Samuel Rosenman wrote Truman: "Why in the world there has to be a statement on October 25th [as the British at one point proposed], ten days before the election in New York, I cannot possibly imagine." Apprehension over the Jewish vote, before a single ballot had been cast, was already influencing U.S. foreign policy. The election results seemed to confirm the wisdom of the administration's strategy: Goldstein was handily defeated by the incumbent Democratic mayor, William O'Dwyer.[380]

A second Palestine-related decision was also delayed until after the election. At Silver's request, Senators Taft and Wagner re-introduced their Palestine resolution in October 1945. Truman and Secretary Byrnes initially gave the sponsors the impression that the administration did not object to the resolution, but at the end of November—that is, after the New York City election—Secretary Byrnes informed the Senate Foreign Relations Committee that the president opposed Taft-Wagner. Democratic senators from states with large numbers of Jewish voters—California, New York, Pennsylvania, Illinois, and Connecticut—complained to Byrnes that their reelection in 1946 would be endangered by Truman's position. Worried about the political implications of Truman's Palestine policy, Robert Hannegan, chairman of the Democratic National Committee, forwarded to the president a letter he received from the mayor of Jersey City, NJ, warning that Jews in his state were "disgusted and resentful against President Truman and the State Department in their actions towards the Jews.[381]

A remark by Truman that same month at a meeting with American envoys to the Middle East, in Washington, D.C., indicates his sensitivity to the issue of Jewish votes. According to one participant in the meeting, when complaints were aired about the dangers of U.S. policy tilting in favor of the Zionists, Truman replied: "I'm sorry gentlemen, but I have to answer to hundreds of thousands who are anxious for the success of Zionism; I do not have hundreds of thousands of Arabs among my constituents."[382]

Peace Plans for Palestine

In the aftermath of World War II, a variety of peace plans for Palestine were put forth by interested parties. The mainstream Zionist movement contended that economic progress in Palestine, combined with unflinching Anglo-American insistence on the creation of a Jewish state, would convince the Arabs to make peace with the Jews. At the other end of the spectrum, a small group called *Ihud* (Unity), led by Hebrew University president Judah Magnes, promoted a plan for a binational Arab-Jewish Palestine with immigration limits that would prevent the Jews from becoming a majority. The leftwing Zionist group Hashomer Hatzair also proposed a binational Arab-Jewish state, but without immigration restrictions. The British government and the U.S. State Department backed the Morrison-Grady Plan, to give the Jews and Arabs autonomy under British rule (see below). The United Nations eventually stepped in with a plan of its own, to partition Palestine into Jewish and Arab states. Given the temper of the times, perhaps it is no surprise that Hoover, too, came up with a plan for Palestine. As a humanitarian relief activist, Hoover genuinely sympathized with the plight of the survivors of Nazism. As an engineer, he always looked for practical solutions to international conflicts, such as his proposal for a Jewish haven in Central Africa, as a temporary refuge for those fleeing from Hitler. Now, together with the erstwhile Eliahu Ben-Horin, Hoover formulated another plan for Palestine.

Ben-Horin, along with several other Revisionists, was hired by Abba Hillel Silver when Silver returned to the helm of the American Zionist movement in the summer of 1945. One of Ben-Horin's early assignments was to secure a public statement from Hoover endorsing Jewish statehood. Hoover surprised him by proposing to instead issue a statement calling for the resettlement of Palestinian Arabs in fertile but undeveloped parts of Iraq, in order to make room for a state with a Jewish majority in Palestine. A number of governments had in recent years sought to address ethnic conflicts through population transfers. The Norwegian diplomat Fridtjof Nansen was awarded the Nobel Peace Prize for bringing about the Greco-Turkish population exchange of 1923, which was imposed by the two regimes on largely unwilling communities. More recently, the U.S., Great Britain, and the Soviet Union had decided at the August 1945 Potsdam conference to transfer millions of ethnic Germans out of Poland, Hungary, and Czechoslovakia.

In November 1945, with Ben-Horin's assistance, Hoover released a 400-word news release outlining his "solution by engineering instead of by conflict" in Palestine. The proposal attracted minimal press coverage and was almost completely ignored in diplomatic and political circles at home and abroad except, not surprisingly, in Baghdad, where it was condemned as the devil's handiwork. The Hoover plan never had any serious chance of realization, since the Palestinian Arabs, having prospered from Jewish development of the country, were unlikely to voluntarily relocate; Iraq and other Arab regimes would not cooperate in any scheme beneficial to the Jews; and the superpowers would not take steps that would alienate the Arab world and endanger access to the region's oil.

Still, in the context of American Jewry's postwar shift away from the Truman administration and the Democratic Party, the proposal was not entirely without significance. Mainstream Zionist leaders had never advocated moving Arabs out of Palestine, and the American Zionist Emergency Council refrained from endorsing Hoover's plan, yet at the same time expressed appreciation for the former president's sympathy "at a time when Jewry seems to have been deserted by most of its friends." The Yiddish daily *Der Tog* published a sympathetic front-page news report about Hoover's proposal, while the editors of the rival *Morgen Zhurnal* hailed Hoover as "a humanitarian" who had suggested "a very practical solution" to the Palestine conflict "We should appreciate the friendship and encourage the plans of Herbert Hoover and other national and international personalities who are willing to help us," the *Morgen Zhurnal* asserted. If nothing else, these Jewish responses to the Hoover plan may have further enhanced the growing sense within the American Jewish community that the Republicans could be seen as genuine friends of the Jewish people and Zionism.[383]

Republicans for Palestine

As the conflict between England and world Jewry over Palestine continued to heat up in late 1945, Truman's senior advisers, and even the president himself, repeatedly cited the possibility of Jewish defections to the GOP as a major consideration in determining Palestine policy. There were, of course, important additional factors influencing Truman's thinking on Palestine. The danger of Soviet influence in the postwar Middle East worried the administration. Relations with the oil-rich Arab world could not be ignored. The large and rapidly-increasing number of Holocaust survivors in Allied DP camps was a source of constant pressure on the White House. The president's sometimes rocky relationship with the State Department officials to whom he derisively referred as "striped-pants boys" was also part of the mix. But in the end, a party preparing for midterm congressional elections, and a president thinking ahead to his own re-election campaign, had to take seriously the possibility that a significant number of their traditional Jewish constituents might switch sides.

Hoover himself was not a part of the escalating postwar political struggle over Palestine. From 1946 to 1947, he was preoccupied with his role as chairman of Truman's Famine Emergency Committee (which examined postwar food shortages in Europe and Asia), and from 1947 to 1949 he headed the president's Commission on the Organization of the Executive Branch. Numerous other Republicans, however, did assume public roles in support of the Zionist cause following the 1944 party plank endorsing Jewish statehood. Twelve senators signed a Revisionist-organized pro-Zionist statement on the eve of the United Nations founding conference in San Francisco in May 1945; the majority of them were Republicans. Of the eighty-one "Congressional Sponsors" listed on the letterhead of the American League for a Free Palestine, a Bergson committee that lobbied for Jewish statehood, 40% were Republicans. Five of the seven U.S. Senators on the "Congressional Advisory Board" of the Political Action Committee for Palestine, a Bergson offshoot, were Republicans. When Netanyahu mobilized 80 members of the House to sign a pro-Zionist letter to Truman in the summer of 1945, one-third were Republicans—a minority, to be sure, but a significant number for a party that until recently had been widely regarded as intrinsically cold to Jewish interests.

Republican ex-congressman William Bennet became vice-chair of Bergson's Emergency Committee to Save the Jewish People of Europe. Edward Martin, Republican governor of Pennsylvania and chairman of the influential National Governors Conference, signed more than a dozen different Bergson newspaper ads. When Abba Hillel Silver returned to the helm of the American Zionist Emergency Council in the summer of 1945, following a seventh-month absence because of his struggle with Rabbi Wise, the AZEC substantially expanded its Washington lobbying activities, including increased outreach to Republicans. Now, unlike when Wise was the movement's sole leader, leading Republicans routinely appeared at mainstream Zionist rallies, signed Palestine proclamations, delivered pro-Zionist speeches on Capitol Hill, and took part in a variety of other efforts that helped rouse American public support for Jewish statehood and increased pressure on the British and the Truman administration. This high profile Republican involvement with Zionism served as a constant reminder to Truman of the danger of the Democrats losing Jewish votes.

At the same time, prominent Jewish leaders and organizations became increasingly bold in their criticism of the Democratic administration. In his keynote address to the February 1946 national gathering of the American Jewish Conference—the coalition of most mainstream Jewish groups—Dr. Silver charged that while President Truman may have intended to be "helpful," in fact he had "unfortunately proved otherwise." After calling for admission of 100,000 refugees to Palestine, Truman had "weakened and acceded to the delaying device of [the Anglo-American] committee of inquiry." After indicating his support for the Taft-Wagner resolution, Truman "changed his mind and opposed Congressional action." American Jews sometimes had no choice but "to go counter to the wishes even of a President or of a State Department, and to challenge and oppose an administration which fails to fulfill its public pledges," Silver advised. He warned the conference delegates to "be on guard against accepting substitutes or appeasement gifts from the Administration," such as appointing a Jew "to this or that important post in government or mak[ing] inexpensive good-will gestures in our direction." The Palestine resolution adopted by the delegates did not mince words: "Our own administration has failed to advance the rightful aspirations of the Jewish people which were endorsed by every President of the United States since President Wilson and twice by the Congress of the United States." Netanyahu's Revisionists, in a series of newspaper ads in late 1945 and early 1946, likewise took direct aim at the the president and his administration, rather than just the British or the State Department. "President Truman Joins With Britain in Blocking Jewish Freedom," one was headlined. A second declared: "Our Government is Following Britain in the Betrayal of the Jews."[384]

Return of the Mufti

With emotions over Palestine and the DPs running at a fever pitch in the Jewish community, even something seemingly as unrelated to U.S. politics as the postwar status of the Grand Mufti of Jerusalem could have an impact on the mood of American Jewish voters. Despite his role in the 1929 pogroms in Palestine, the Mufti, Haj Amin el-Husseini, was not prosecuted by the British Mandate authorities, a decision that came back to haunt them when in 1936 he spearheaded a nationwide wave of Arab violence against Palestine's Jews and British forces. Fleeing the country ahead of a British arrest warrant in 1937, Husseini eventually made his way to Germany, where he spent the war years broadcasting pro-Nazi propaganda to the Arab world, recruiting Bosnians for an all-Muslim division of the SS, and organizing parachute-drops of Axis saboteurs into Palestine. During the war, American Jews were generally aware that the Mufti was in Berlin and aiding the Nazis, but a series of exposes in the *New York Post*, *PM*, and *The Nation* in early 1946 revealed his activities in much greater detail, including his intervention to stop a prisoner exchange with the Germans that would have saved the lives of 4,000 Jewish children.[385]

In May 1945, Bergson Group lobbyists at the founding conference of the United Nations, in San Francisco, persuaded Yugoslav delegates that their government should indict the Mufti for war crimes committed by members of his Bosnian "Handschar" unit of the SS. Belgrade announced the indictment in July. In the meantime, Husseini was arrested by the French and placed under house arrest in a villa near Paris. But as months passed with no sign that the French intended to prosecute or extradite the Mufti, American Jewish leaders grew alarmed at the prospect that a man who had devoted his life to waging war against Jews might escape justice and even return to lead the Palestinian Arab struggle against Jewish statehood. The American Zionist Emergency Council turned to the Truman administration, arguing in a 13-page memorandum to the State Department in September that there was sufficient evidence for the U.S. itself to indict the Mufti as a war criminal. When that appeal produced no results, the AZEC sponsored large advertisements in the *New York Times* and elsewhere which indirectly criticized the administration by charging that members of the Anglo-American Committee of Inquiry had suppressed pro-Nazi testimony given at one of its Jerusalem hearings by the Mufti's senior deputy.[386]

In late May 1946, Husseini departed the residence where he was supposedly under house arrest and boarded a plane to Cairo without interference. The French said they could not understand how he escaped; the British colonial authorities ruling Egypt made no effort to arrest him; and the Truman administration remained silent. The Mufti controversy added fuel to the fire of an AZEC rally at Madison Square Garden on June 13, which had originally been called as a protest against British policy. Now speakers dished out criticism of the Truman administration alongside their denunciations of the British. Even Rabbi Wise, normally the most reserved in his public remarks concerning the president, called on President Truman to "speak sharply and act decisively in relation to the [Palestine policy of] the British Government." A newspaper ad by the Revisionists directly accused the Truman administration of tolerating the Mufti's 'escape': "The American people have a right to know why their Government permits itself to be a party to this infamous conspiracy." It was not that the fate of the Mufti per se became a major issue among American Jews in 1945-1946. But it was yet another exasperating turn of events in an accumulation of developments that soured the mood in the Jewish community and could inflame Jewish voters against the president and his party.[387]

Truman and the Midterm Elections

The possibility of a Democratic setback in the upcoming midterm congressional elections weighed heavily on the White House in the summer of 1946. After President Truman declined to meet with a delegation of congressmen from New York, Rep. Emanuel Celler warned a senior Truman aide that the president's refusal "will give political ammunition to the upstate Republicans who wanted to attend [the meeting] and you remember New York faces a very crucial election... [I]t is bad politics for the President not to meet with them..." Truman reluctantly agreed to see them.[388]

Politics intruded again as the president considered a Palestine partition plan that grew out of the Anglo-American Committee of Inquiry. The proposal, known as the Morrison-Grady Plan after its respective British and American co-authors, recommended dividing the country into semiautonomous Jewish and Arab provinces under continued British rule. American Jewish leaders rejected the plan, while the British government and the State Department favored it. Truman personally considered Morrison-Grady "really fair," according to Henry Wallace—now serving as secretary of commerce—but there were other factors to consider: the chairman of the New York State Democratic Committee, Paul Fitzpatrick, told the president, "If this plan goes into effect it would be useless for the Democrats to nominate a state ticket this fall." Wallace warned the president on July 29 that Rabbi Silver had been "working with the Republicans" to whip up emotions on Palestine. And a July 30 letter from Ed Flynn, former chairman of the Democratic National Committee, current head of the Democratic Party in the Bronx, NY, and a frequent adviser to President Truman on election matters, cautioned that if the administration took an anti-Zionist line, "the effects will be severely felt in November."[389]

Wallace described in his diary how at the July 30 cabinet session, the president displayed "a sheaf of telegrams about four inches thick" that he had received from pro-Zionist protesters. "Jesus Christ couldn't please them when he was here on earth, so how could anyone expect that I would have any luck?," Truman complained. That the president of the United States would link the behavior of contemporary Jews to that of Jews from 2,000 years before, and that he would perpetuate timeworn prejudices about Jewish behavior toward Jesus and Jewish insatiability, may seem jarring to the modern ear. But in fact, Truman's near-legendary plain-spokenness always included a dose of antisemitism. In letters he wrote to his fiance during his army days, Truman referred to New York City as a "kike town," described his astute management of the army canteen's finances as his "Jewish ability," and called his canteen business partner Eddie Jacobson his "Jew clerk." In a 1935 letter, he referred to someone who "screamed like a Jewish merchant." A July 1947 Truman diary entry (discovered in 2003) included this passage: "The Jews have no sense of proportion nor do they have any judgement on world affairs...The Jews, I find are very, very selfish. They care not how many Estonians, Latvians, Finns, Poles, Yugoslavs or Greeks get murdered or mistreated as D[isplaced] P[ersons] as long as the Jews get special treatment. Yet when they have power, physical, financial or political neither Hitler nor Stalin has anything on them for cruelty or mistreatment to the under dog."[390]

None of these remarks were known to the Jewish public at the time; had they been, undoubtedly they would have generated a widespread and irreversible antipathy toward Truman among American Jews. The one allegation of an anti-Jewish remark by the president that was reported at the time came in a March 1948 column by renowned Washington investigative reporter Drew Pearson, who claimed Truman had, in a private conversation, "shout[ed] that New York Jews were disloyal to the country." The president responded, at a press conference, that Pearson was "a liar out of the whole cloth," although Pearson's claim seems less implausible in light of the other unkind remarks about Jews that Truman is now known to have made. In any event, despite his private negative feelings about Jews, in the end Truman made his decision on the Morrison-Grady proposal based on cold political calculations: that July 30, 1946 cabinet session concluded with the president opting to reject the plan, in deference to Vice President Wallace's warning that Morrison-Grady was "political dynamite." Wallace later noted in his diary: "I emphasized the political angle because that is the one angle of Palestine which has a really deep interest for Truman." The president later complained to Senator Elbert Thomas of Utah that "I thought we had the [Palestine] matter settled" via the Morrison-Grady plan, but "the New York Jews knocked that out..."[391]

Undersecretary of State Dean Acheson bluntly informed the new British ambassador in Washington, Lord Inverchapel, that the president could not support Morrison-Grady because "intense Jewish hostility" had turned the issue into a serious political problem for Truman. Secretary Brynes complained to Navy Secretary James Forrestal that White House aides had turned Truman against Morrison-Grady by emphasizing that "the [expected] Republican candidate [for president, Gov. Dewey] was about to come out with a statement in favor of Zionist claims on Palestine" and Democratic congressional candidates would lose in New York if Truman backed down on Palestine.[392]

Inverchapel reported back to Foreign Minister Bevin that Truman's rejection of Morrison-Grady was "solely attributable to reasons of domestic politics." He compared it to the administration's insistence on delaying the announcement of the Anglo-American Committee on Palestine until after the previous year's New York City mayoral election. Based on a briefing by State Department officials, Inverchapel concluded that since Rabbi Wise was a Democrat and Rabbi Silver was pro-Republican, "neither therefore could afford to compromise without the certainty that the other would at once derive political benefit from his decision." Thus, "with both leaders solidly opposed to [Morrison-Grady], the administration dared not take the risk of antagonising the powerful Zionist lobby in an election year."[393]

Concern about Jews turning Republican resonated even to the point of causing internal rifts within the British government. Lord Inverchapel became so worried about the fact that Zionists "are so strong in this country and exercise so great an influence on domestic politics" that he pressed London to make gestures to appease Jewish sentiment, such as inviting Jewish leaders to visit unauthorized immigrants to Palestine whom the British were holding in detention camps in Cyprus. London rejected the proposal.

By September, Truman was convinced that, as he wrote the First Lady, "the Jews and crackpots seem to be ready to go for Dewey." Rabbi Wise seemed to share that view. Still a force of some influence despite Silver's return to the Zionist helm, Wise complained to a colleague in October about "the creatures who dare to ask us to vote against every Administration candidate" because of Palestine. "Unless the Silvers...are stopped now," Wise worried, "we shall have a frank Jewish vote on all problems"—meaning that there would emerge a solid Jewish voting bloc that would publicly acknowledge its preference for candidates favorable to Jewish interests, a strategy Wise believed would cause antisemitism.[394]

Matters reached a critical point in early October (1946), when White House adviser David Niles informed the president that Dewey planned to deliver a strongly pro-Zionist speech to a United Palestine Appeal gathering on October 6. Niles urged Truman to act first, since "the Jewish vote in New York is going to be crucial." On October 4, the eve of Yom Kippur, barely a month before the 1946 midterm congressional elections, Truman issued a statement in which, for the first time, he expressed support for creation of a Jewish state, although its size and other details were left undefined.

"Domestic politics in general and the New York State campaign in particular," James Reston of the *New York Times* wrote on October 7, "are generally believed here to be the reason why Mr. Truman opposed [the Morrison-Grady plan] and why he insisted on putting out his Palestine statement" before Yom Kippur. Eliahu Epstein of the Jewish Agency's Washington office agreed that Truman's move was influenced by "the activity of the Republican candidates in the forthcoming elections, and especially in New York, who overtly showed their determination to make the Palestine issue one of the focal points of attack on Truman and the Democratic administration." Congressman Celler, for his part, was delighted by Truman's statement: "It should also have a very desirable political effect upon our chances in New York," he wrote the president. To Rabbi Silver, it was "a smart election move," although he was not convinced it represented a sincere change in U.S. policy. Secretary of State Acheson confided to Inverchapel that Truman decided to issue the statement to pre-empt Dewey. The Yom Kippur statement did not, however, produce the desired results. Dewey himself overwhelmingly defeated Democratic U.S. Senator James Mead in the New York gubernatorial race, and Republican senate nominee Irving Ives easily beat his Democratic opponent, Jewish ex-governor Herbert Lehman. Normally Democratic New York City went Republican for the first time in eighteen years. Overall, the Republicans gained 55 seats and took over control of the House of Representatives.[395]

Truman and the United Nations Partition Plan

Exhausted by Jewish guerrilla warfare in Palestine and the growing international pressure in support of Jewish statehood, the British announced in February 1947 that they intended to withdraw from Palestine and turn the problem over to the United Nations. A UN Special Committee on Palestine studied the issue that summer and recommended partitioning Palestine into separate Jewish and Arab states. The Zionist movement embraced the proposal, despite the miniscule size of the proposed Jewish state, because it offered national sovereignty at long last; Arab leaders rejected it because they opposed a Jewish state of any size.

The failure of the British to set a date for their pullout, their continued use of harsh measures to stamp out Jewish rebels in Palestine, and the ongoing closure of Palestine's gates to Jewish immigrants raised doubts among American Jews as to London's true intentions. The situation also stimulated Jewish criticism of the Truman administration for not adopting an explicitly pro-Zionist policy. An editorial in the *Boston Jewish Advocate* asserted that "If the United States says the word firmly enough, it can tell Mr. Bevin what to do, and he'll do it." Likewise, the *Kansas City Jewish Chronicle* charged that it was the silence of Truman administration officials that made it possible for England, "a once great country, now exhausted by war, to imitate Hitler in a policy of depravity that has no parallel in modern English history." Truman, in his memoirs, recalled that the White House was "subjected to a constant barrage" of pro-Zionist criticism during the period preceding the UN vote. "I do not think I ever had as much pressure and propaganda aimed at the White House as I had in this instance," he wrote.[396]

The political angle was very much on the president's mind. Truman complained to his aide David Niles on May 13 that he "could have settled this Palestine thing if U.S. politics had been kept out of it." In his memoirs, he recalled feeling "disturbed and annoyed" that "a few of the extreme Zionist leaders" were "engaging in political threats." Truman's advisers repeatedly reminded him in the summer and autumn of 1947 that there would be serious political consequences if Truman failed to back the UN partition plan. The outgoing chairman of the Democratic National Committee, postmaster general Robert Hannegan, and his successor, Senator J. Howard McGrath, told Truman on September 4 that if he failed to support the Zionist position, it would cost him two or three states in the 1948 election, resulting in his defeat. McGrath likewise told Defense Secretary James Forrestal that "there were two or three pivotal states which could not be carried [in 1948] without the support of people who were deeply interested in the Palestine question." Later that month, New York State Democratic leaders Fitzpatrick and Flynn met with party treasurer Karl Sherman and New York City Mayor William O'Dwyer to review the electoral damage Truman would suffer if he did not support Jewish statehood; Flynn then telephoned the president to directly reiterate their concerns.[397]

On October 11, the Truman administration announced it would support the UN partition plan. More than that, Truman and his aides intervened to secure the support of wavering countries for the General Assembly's November 29 vote on partition. Although the U.S. already supported partition, Clark Clifford in November again underlined the electoral issue in a memorandum to the president about the 1948 race: "The Jewish vote, insofar as it can be thought of as a bloc, is important only in New York. But, (except for Wilson in 1916) no candidate since 1876 has lost New York and won the Presidency, and its 47 votes are naturally the first prize in any election." After the partition plan was adopted by the General Assembly (by a vote of 33 to 13), Leo Sack, one of Dr. Silver's top lobbyists in Washington, told the AZEC leadership that the "great victory" was won "[not] because of the devotion of the American Government to our cause" but strictly because of "the sheer pressure of political logistics."[398]

"Statehood or Extermination"

In the aftermath of the UN vote, Arab violence against Jews in Palestine intensified. Faced with the prospect of U.S. forces being dragged into the conflict, Truman began to backtrack. The administration resisted calls to enforce partition, threatened to cancel the citizenship of any Americans who volunteered to fight for

Palestine Jewry's armed forces, and, less than a week after the UN vote, announced an embargo on arms to the Middle East. The embargo primarily affected the Jews, since the Arab states were receiving weapons from other countries. It was implemented so zealously that the U.S. rejected even a request for armored plates to shield Jewish civilian buses from Arab attackers. Dr. Silver warned that as a result of the embargo, "the situation in Palestine may become as bloody and disastrous as Spain [in the 1930s]." In a heartfelt appeal to Truman to drop the embargo, Chaim Weizmann wrote: "The choice of our people, Mr. President, is between Statehood and extermination." Truman's refusal to budge created yet another point of tension between American Jewry and the administration during the early months of 1948, further eroding the goodwill Truman had attained among Jewish voters when he supported the partition proposal.[399]

Jewish organizations and members of Congress vigorously protested the embargo. Jewish trade unionists brought the State Department an anti-embargo petition bearing 100,000 signatures. Republican senators Albert Hawkes, Arthur Vandenberg, and Raymond Baldwin were the featured speakers, alongside Tel Aviv mayor Israel Rokeach, at a Jewish War Veterans event focusing on the demand to lift the embargo. Republican Senator Owen Brewster bluntly called the administration's policies an attempt "to frustrate the United Nations decision to establish a Jewish state." Brewster and fellow-Republican senator Charles Tobey were among thirteen prominent Christians signing a full-page ad in the *New York Herald Tribune* that denounced the embargo and asked whether the Truman administration, after supporting the UN vote on statehood, intended "to leave the Jewish people there defenseless?" Many Democrats also spoke out strongly against the embargo, a fact which underlined the bipartisan nature of support for Jewish statehood. Former governor Herbert Lehman accused the Truman administration of "giving aid and comfort to the Arabs," while Democratic Senator James Murray of Montana accused the administration of "unbecoming timidity toward the Arabs and thinly-disguised disapproval towards the Jews." Murray and Rep. Emanuel Celler mobilized 41 members of Congress to sign a letter denouncing the embargo. New York Democratic Senator Robert Wagner and Liberal Party leader (and longtime Bergson Group activist) Dean Alfange co-founded a Committee to Arm

Left to right: Robert Taft, Wendell Willkie, Arthur Vandenberg

the Jewish State. These developments intensified the perception among some Jewish voters that the Truman administration favored the Arabs.[400]

A February 1948 election to fill a vacant congressional seat in a heavily-Jewish district of the Bronx provided an early test of the Jewish electorate's mood. Democratic nominee Karl Propper, fully backed by the local party machine (headed by the aforementioned Truman confidante Ed Flynn), was heavily favored to defeat political unknown Leo Isacson, nominee of the American Labor Party and supporter of Henry Wallace's splinter Progressive Party. Wallace repeatedly visited the district to campaign for Isacson, hammering away on the Palestine issue. Truman "talks Jewish but acts Arab," Wallace charged, urging Jewish voters to reject Propper as a way of sending the administration a message about its Palestine policy. They did. Isacson swamped Propper, 55% to 31%. Jewish voters had fired a loud warning shot at the administration. Would Pennsylvania be next? U.S. Senator Francis Myers of Pennsylvania warned Truman in early March that his Jewish constituents were furious about the administration's Palestine policy and that several local party leaders had recently resigned.[401]

A blunder by the president in March brought Jewish criticism of the administration to a fever pitch. Worried by growing signs that partition might not be enforceable, Truman evidently agreed (although he later denied it) to a State Department proposal to abandon partition in favor of imposing a temporary international trusteeship over Palestine. The U.S. ambassador at the United Nations, Warren Austin, announced the new policy on March 19, but apparently neglected to coordinate his timing with the White House. American Jews were furious at the change in policy, and the embarrassed president scrambled to persuade Jewish leaders that he was not to blame and that, in any event, it did not necessarily represent a shift in policy. Truman aide Eben Ayers worried that "the political effect" of Truman's stumble "may be terrificly [*sic*] bad," and he was right: the White House was flooded with thousands of angry letters and telegrams and the Jewish press was filled with sharp denunciations of the administration's about-face. New York Congressman Arthur Klein called it "the most terrible sell-out of the common people since Munich." Brooklyn Democratic Party activists threatened to lead a revolt against Truman at the 1948 Democratic convention. Moreover, in addition to the torrent of Jewish protests, Truman faced a barrage of criticism from editors, pundits, and political figures over the broader problem of the administration appearing to be confused and divided on a sensitive strategic issue. "We who thought the United States had been fumbling and bumbling along [regarding Palestine] were very much mistaken," an editorial in *PM* asserted. "Behind the mask of the bumbler was the face of the deceiver." Mutual Radio commentator Cecil Brown accused the White House of "gutless fear of Russia," while NBC's Clifton Utley predicted Truman's retreat from the partition plan would lead to a Soviet takeover of Italy. "Just as the Republicans were getting set to kill him off next November," House Ways and Means Committee chair Robert Doughty charged, "up comes Truman and commits suicide on them."[402]

Meanwhile, developments on the ground jacked up the pressure on Truman several more notches. The British set a date of May 15 for their withdrawal from Palestine, and momentum toward a Jewish declaration of statehood built up rapidly in the weeks to follow. Now Truman wrestled with the question of when, or whether, to recognize the new state that was likely to be proclaimed as soon as the British departed. Senior State Department officials, who strongly opposed Jewish statehood, worried—with justification—that Palestine was becoming "a football of domestic politics." A memo to the president in May from adviser Max Lowenthal warned that if a Jewish state were proclaimed without U.S. recognition, American Jews and prominent Republicans would lead a chorus of protests. For Truman to extend recognition only later, after the protests, would be widely regarded as little better than "climbing on the bandwagon." The result, Lowenthal predicted, would be that the administration would "pay a high political price [in Jewish votes] for it is especially important in a [presidential] election year..."[403]

A crucial meeting between Truman, senior White House aides, and top State Department officials was held on May 12. Secretary of State George Marshall made the case against U.S. recognition: a Jewish state would lead to war, the Arab world would be inflamed, and pressure would be put on the U.S. to intervene. In response, Clark Clifford, citing the upcoming presidential election, urged speedy American recognition as a way for Truman to win back skeptical Jewish voters. Undersecretary of State Robert Lovett countered that such a "transparent attempt to win the Jewish vote" would backfire by undermining the president's credibility.[404] At meeting's end, Truman appeared still to have not made up his mind. During the next twenty-four hours, phone calls to the president from Bronx Democratic leader Ed Flynn; former New York governor Herbert Lehman; and Jacob Arvey, an important Jewish supporter of Truman's and a political leader in Chicago, emphasized the acclaim the president would receive among American Jews if quick recognition were extended. John A. Kennedy, a friend of Truman's who met with the president at about this time, recalled asking Truman if he intended to recognize the Jewish state, to which the president responded, "Well, how many Arabs are there as registered voters in the United States?" He answered that question on May 15 by recognizing the State of Israel just minutes after its proclamation.[405]

Left to right: George C. Marshall, President Harry Truman, Dean Acheson

Truman's decision undoubtedly was the product of multiple factors. He himself cited the danger that the Soviets would gain influence with the new Jewish state if they were the first to recognize it. The path to recognition was certainly made smoother when Secretary Marshall, dejectedly acknowledging the inevitability of the Jewish state's creation, belatedly informed Truman he would remain neutral, rather than continuing to oppose recognition. Although difficult to quantify, there was also the personal factor, that is, the influence of Truman's closest Jewish friend, Kansas City businessman Eddie Jacobson. Truman's personal sympathy for the victims of the Holocaust, and some lingering religious sentiment about the restoration of the Jews to the Holy Land, probably also figured in the mix. But behind all these considerations lay the stark reality of a rapidly approaching presidential election in which the Jewish voters of New York, and perhaps several other states, could play a critical role. For four long years, beginning with the adoption of the 1944 Republican platform, senior GOP figures from Herbert Hoover on down had championed the Zionist cause and thereby transformed the Jewish vote into a real factor in American politics. Assistant Secretary of State Loy Henderson, who opposed recognition, later conceded that Truman might well have lost the 1948 election if he had done otherwise. "In so far as internal political considerations played a role, we should bear in mind that many of the leaders of the Republican Party, including Dewey...were almost constantly criticising Truman for failure to give full support to the Zionists," Henderson wrote. "If Truman had taken positions that would have resulted in a failure to establish the Jewish State, he would almost certainly have been defeated in the November [1948] elections..."[406]

Leon Feuer, the chief AZEC lobbyist in Washington during those tumultuous years, dismissed as "a legend" the notion that Eddie Jacobson's influence was what caused Truman to recognize Israel:

> Those kinds of political gestures simply do not take place. What occurred was more prosaic but far more in line with the political realities. Truman was a candidate for President. He knew that the election of 1948 would be, as it was, uncomfortably close. He suspected that the Jewish vote in the populous states would be crucial. He knew all about, and as a politician respected, even if he was often visibly annoyed by, the pressure of the tremendously effective and responsive nationwide organization which Silver had created. He had an opportunity, by recognizing Israel, to make a grab for those votes, State Department or not. He saw his main chance and he took it. It was as simple and natural as that.[407]

Even U.S. recognition of Israel might not have been enough to avert a major clash with Jewish voters over the embargo issue, if in the weeks preceding the election, American Jews believed Israel's existence was endangered by Truman's refusal to provide military assistance. In late May, former Secretary Harold Ickes charged that Truman's recognition would be exposed as nothing more than "a political move, with his eye on the coming November election," unless he lifted the embargo. "Nothing could be more inconsistent," Ickes wrote, than for the Truman administration to endorse Israel's existence and then leave the Jewish State defenseless in the face of threats to its existence. To the administration's chagrin, Congressman Emanuel Celler led a successful effort at the Democratic convention in July to include a plank calling for lifting the arms embargo. Events on the ground in the Middle East, however, were already making the embargo a non-issue. The same week as the convention, a series of Israeli military operations turned the tide in the War of Independence. Israeli forces secured the Jerusalem-Tel Aviv corridor, captured the cities of Ramle and Lod, repulsed a major Egyptian attack on Negba, conquered the lower Galilee, including Nazareth, and, for the first time, bombed Damascus. American Jews following the news of the first Arab-Israeli war could rest assured that Israel's existence had been secured, and that the continuing embargo no longer posed a serious threat.[408]

The final tally in 1948 shows Truman's margin of victory was so thin that a significant shift of Jewish votes to Dewey in three key states could have tipped the election to the Republican. Truman won Ohio, with 25 electoral votes, by just 7,107 votes; California, also with 25 electoral votes, by 17,865; and Illinois, with 28 electoral votes, by 33,612. If Dewey had won all three, he would have been elected president. Although a Jewish electoral shift of the magnitude necessary to affect the outcome in this way was unlikely, the fact that it was even within the realm of possibility dramatized a new political reality: in a close election, American Jews were already approaching the point of having sufficient numbers in certain states to play a decisive role.

Conclusion

Herbert Hoover never had more than a handful of Jewish associates, nor much more than a cursory familiarity with Judaism or Jewish affairs. Growing up in 19th century Iowa and Oregon, he may have never even met a Jew until he was an adult. Yet again and again throughout his public career, Hoover chanced to find himself in a position to have a significant influence on matters of Jewish concern.

Hoover's campaign to feed the destitute masses of wartorn Europe encompassed some of the continent's largest Jewish communities and saved many Jews from starvation. He also utilized his position to press Poland's leaders for action against local pogromists.

Over the years, Hoover gradually forged ties with a small but influential group of Jews, not for the sake of political or other gain, but because of their common humanitarian interests. These relationships helped ensure that Hoover would remain aware of Jewish issues and concerns throughout his career in public service.

As president, Hoover endorsed Zionism and never wavered from that stance, despite strong anti-Zionist (and sometimes antisemitic) pressure from his own State Department. Despite his role in the initial imposition of Depression-era restrictions on immigration, Hoover spoke out for the admission of German Jewish refugees to the United States before World War II. There is more than a touch of irony in the fact that Hoover lost the White House because he was widely perceived as insufficiently sensitive to the public's suffering, while Franklin Roosevelt enjoyed a reputation as a humanitarian and champion of 'the little guy.' Despite their respective public images, it was Hoover who instructed America's ambassador in Berlin to intervene on behalf of German Jews, and FDR who ordered the next ambassador to respond only in the most limited fashion. It was Hoover who urged opening America's doors to Jewish refugee children, and Roosevelt who kept those doors closed.

Similarly, during the years of the Nazi genocide, 1941-1945, Hoover repeatedly spoke out for the Jews, while Roosevelt repeatedly turned away. Hoover lent his name to the Bergson Group's efforts to publicize the plight of European Jewry, at a time when the Roosevelt administration was trying to keep the tragedy out of the news. Hoover signed newspaper advertisements urging rescue action, at a time when FDR claimed rescue was impossible. Hoover put forth plans for Jewish refugee resettlement, and for a Jewish Palestine, which testified to the depth of his concern for the Jewish people.

Despite Hoover's record on Jewish concerns, most mainstream Jewish leaders refrained from building ties to the former president or other prominent Republicans. As staunch supporters of President Roosevelt—whom Rabbi Stephen Wise called "the All Highest"—they would not be seen in the company of FDR's opponents. Jewish voters, too, felt they had little in common with a Republican Party that was a bastion of isolationism and WASP privilege.[409]

The Democrats, meanwhile, were increasingly perceived as the party of ethnic inclusion and labor rights. While President Roosevelt did precious little to aid Germany's Jews, by the late 1930s he was at least moving America to preparedness for conflict with Hitler. Thus in the 1930s and early 1940s, there was little chance of the GOP making inroads among Jewish voters. By late 1943, however, the Roosevelt administration was seen by many as indifferent to the Nazi genocide of European Jewry, while prominent Republicans were pushing for rescue. The president avoided an election-year scandal in 1944 over the abandonment of the Jews, and headed off the possibility of significant Jewish defections to the Republicans, by creating the rescue agency that Republicans and dissident Democrats in Congress were demanding.

With Jewish support for the president apparently softening, Benzion Netanyahu's Revisionists and Rabbi Abba Hillel Silver saw in the president's waffling on Palestine an opportunity to advance the Zionist agenda at the 1944 GOP convention. Hoover, Senator Taft, Congresswoman Luce, and the other Republicans involved in the Palestine plank discussions saw an opportunity to challenge FDR and siphon some Jewish votes from the Democrats.

Once support for a Jewish Palestine was enshrined in the Republican platform, the Democrats realized they needed to match it with a Zionist plank of their own. Thus what began as a brief coincidence of interests between the Republicans and Jewish activists ended up leaving a permanent imprint on American political culture. There would be no turning back from the pro-Zionist planks of 1944, because their removal would mean severely alienating a small but important segment of the electorate. Bipartisan support for Zionism —and, after 1948, for Israel—became a fixture of both platforms, and a staple of American politics, ever since.

This is not to suggest that support for Jewish statehood in 1944, and for Israel in subsequent years, was based on nothing more than jockeying for votes. Both parties' support for Zionism always reflected the genuine sympathy of their leaders and policymakers for a cause rooted in moral values that they shared. But there are many issues party officials might personally endorse that are not necessarily elevated to the status of planks in their party's platform. Zionism in America benefited from a fortunate combination of humanitarian appeal, shared core values, election-year political opportunity, and creative lobbying by its advocates.

Nonetheless, the Republican pitch for Jewish votes proved unsuccessful in 1944; Governor Dewey received only 10% of Jewish votes against FDR. Nor did Dewey fare any better four years later against Harry Truman. Without Israel or other major Jewish concerns as election issues, the Jewish vote for Republican presidential nominees continued to remain low in subsequent years, shifting only minimally according to the circumstances of a specific race. Dwight Eisenhower, with his image as a non-political war hero rather than a traditional Republican, won about 25% of Jewish votes in 1952 and 1956. The Republicans' share of the Jewish vote dropped to less than 20% when the GOP chose more conservative candidates in 1960 (Richard Nixon), 1964 (Barry Goldwater), and 1968 (Nixon again). In 1972, it rose to 35%, as some Jewish voters rejected the sharply leftwing positions of the Democratic nominee, George McGovern.[410]

The watershed year for the GOP and Jewish voters was 1980, not because so many Jews were enamored of Republican nominee Ronald Reagan, but because of deep dissatisfaction in the Jewish community over President Jimmy Carter's policies toward Israel. It was the only presidential election in American history when Israel was a major campaign issue, and the first time since 1920 that the Democratic nominee did not win a majority of Jewish votes. An estimated 40% of Jews backed Reagan; 40% supported Carter; and 20% voted for independent John Anderson. In subsequent elections, when Israel was not an issue of contention between the candidates, the level of Jewish support for the Democratic incumbent or nominee returned to its traditional level, between 70% and 80%.

The concentration of Jewish voters in certain key electoral states creates the possibility that, given the right combination of circumstances, they could have a decisive impact on the outcome of a future presidential election. Such a scenario would require, first of all, a close contest nationwide, in which the results could be determined by the outcome in one or two states with large Jewish populations and significant numbers of electoral votes. Pennsylvania, for example, with 20 electoral votes, has a Jewish populace of about 300,000, constituting approximately

4% of the state's voters in a presidential race. The Democratic candidate has won Pennsylvania in the last five presidential races, but in 2004, Democrat John Kerry beat George W. Bush by just 51-49% (about 145,000 votes). In Florida, which has 29 electoral votes, the last three presidential races have been close, especially George W. Bush's 537-vote margin of victory in 2000. Florida has about 640,000 Jewish residents, who make up 6% to 8% of those who cast ballots on election day. Ohio, which has 18 electoral votes, has a Jewish population of about 150,000, an estimated 2% to 3% of the voters. Since 1976, the Republicans have won Ohio five times, the Democrats four; some races have been extremely close, such as Jimmy Carter's margin of 11,000 over President Gerald Ford in 1976, and Bill Clinton's victory by 90,000 votes in 1992.

New York has by far the largest number of Jewish voters of any state, but a narrow race there is not as likely as elsewhere. New York has gone for the Democratic candidate in the last six presidential races, and seven out of the last nine. On the other hand, three of those contests were sufficiently close that a significant shift among Jewish voters would have tipped the state to the other candidate. In 1976, if New York City's 800,000 Jewish voters had gone 52-48 for Carter—they actually went 70-30—that would have been enough for President Ford to overcome Carter's New York State margin of 288,767 votes and win the state, and with it, the election. However, there was no Israel issue in the 1976 race (unlike Carter vs. Reagan in 1980); in fact, if anything, Ford was seen as being not especially sympathetic to Israel. Hence Jewish voters had little motivation to support the Republican incumbent. Reagan beat Carter in New York by just 166,459 votes in 1980, and Michael Dukakis topped George H.W. Bush in New York in 1988 by 266,011 votes. Theoretically, both margins were small enough to have been overcome by a large shift in Jewish votes, although in those two instances, the outcome in New York would not have changed the overall result of the national race.[411]

Political analysts took a particular interest in the September 2011 special election in New York City's heavily-Jewish 9th congressional district. The Obama administration's Israel policy was a major issue in the race, and large numbers of Jews voted Republican, resulting in a surprise victory for the underdog GOP candidate. The circumstances were somewhat similar to the 1948 special election in the Bronx, in which many Jewish voters deserted the Democrats over the Truman administration's Palestine policy (see Chapter 7).

Yet in the end, the Bronx result was not a harbinger of Jewish electoral trends in the 1948 presidential election. Jewish voters, including those in New York

State, overwhelmingly supported Truman. That was because of another important factor in the distribution of the Jewish vote: Democratic presidents facing possible Jewish defections invariably strive to repair their relationship with the Jewish community by making political gestures in the months preceding the election. In 1944, FDR established the War Refugee Board, admitted 982 Jewish refugees outside the quota laws, and publicly reaffirmed his support for Zionism. In 1948, President Truman promptly extended recognition to the new State of Israel, putting an end to the threat that the Bronx election seemed to pose. In 1980, President Carter promised, if re-elected, to refrain from pressuring Israel any further, but a majority of Jewish voters nonetheless deserted him. Whether Jewish voting patterns in 2012 will more closely resemble those of the 1940s, or 1980, remains to be seen.[412]

Bibliography

Allerfeldt, Kristofer. "Rejecting the United States of the World: The consequences of Woodrow Wilson's new diplomacy on the 1921 Immigration Act," *European Journal of American Culture* 26 (2007), 145-165.

Allswang, John M. *The Political Behavior of Chicago's Ethnic Groups, 1918-1932.* North Stratford, NH: Ayer Company, 1980.

American Relief Administration: Documents of the ARA European Operations, 1918-1919. Vol. XVIII Poland. Stanford, CA: Stanford University, 1932.

Baker, Mark. "Lewis Namier and the Problem of Eastern Galicia," *Journal of Ukrainian Studies* 23 (1998), 59-104.

Bauer, Yehuda. "When Did They Know?," *Midstream* 14 (April 1968), 51-58.

Bauer, Yehuda. *My Brother's Keeper: A History of the American Jewish Joint Distribution Committee, 1929–1939.* Philadelphia: Jewish Publication Society of America, 1974.

Bauer, Yehuda. *American Jewry and the Holocaust: The American Jewish Joint Distribution Committee, 1939–1945.* Detroit: Wayne State University Press, 1981.

Baumel, Judith Tydor. *Unfulfilled Promise: Rescue and Resettlement of Jewish Refugee Children in the United States, 1934–1945.* Juneau, AK: The Deli Press, 1990.

Baumel-Schwartz, Judith. *The "Bergson Boys" and the Origins of Zionist Militancy.* Syracuse: Syracuse University Press, 2005.

Becker, Hortense. "American Jewish Personalities: James Becker and East European Jewry after World War I," *American Jewish Archives* 47 (1994), 279-312.

Ben-Ami, Yitshaq. *Years of Wrath, Days of Glory: Memoirs from the Irgun*. New York: Shengold, 1983.

Ben-Horin, Eliahu. *The Middle East: Crossroads of History*. New York: W.W. Norton, 1943.

Berman, Aaron. *Nazism, the Jews, and American Zionism*. Detroit: Wayne State University Press, 1990.

Berman, Gerald S. "Reaction to the Resettlement of World War II Refugees in Alaska," *Jewish Social Studies* 44 (Summer-Fall 1982), 271-282.

Bickerton, Ian J. "President Truman's Recognition of Israel," *American Jewish Historical Quarterly* 58 (December 1968), 173-240.

Blum, John L. *The Price of Vision: The Diaries of Henry A. Wallace, 1942-1946*. Boston: Houghton Mifflin, 1973.

Bogen, Boris D. *Jewish Philanthropy: An Exposition of Principles and Methods of Jewish Social Service in the United States*. New York: MacMillan, 1917.

Bogen, Boris D. *Born a Jew*. New York: MacMillan, 1930.

Brandeis on Zionism: A Collection of Addresses and Statements by Louis D. Brandeis. Washington, D.C.: Zionist Organization of America, 1942.

Breitman, Richard and Kraut, Alan M. *American Refugee Policy and European Jewry, 1933–1945*. Bloomington and Indianapolis: Indiana University Press, 1987.

Breitman, Richard, Stewart, Barbara McDonald, and Hochberg, Severin, eds. *Advocate for the Doomed, Volume 1: The Diaries and Papers of James G. McDonald 1932-1935*. Bloomington and Indianapolis: Indiana University Press, 2007.

Breitman, Richard, Stewart, Barbara McDonald, and Hochberg, Severin, eds. *Refugees and Rescue, Volume 2: The Diaries and Papers of James G. McDonald 1935-1945*. Bloomington and Indianapolis: Indiana University Press, 2009.

Brinkmann, Tobias. "From Immigrants to Supranational Transmigrants and Refugees: Jewish Migrants in New York and Berlin before and after the Great War." *Comparative Studies of South Asia, Africa and the Middle East* 30 (2010), 47-57.

Brinner, William and Rischin, Moses, eds. *Like all the Nations? The Life and Legacy of Judah L. Magnes*. New York: State University of New York Press, 1987.

Carenen, Caitlin. "The American Christian Palestine Committee, the Holocaust, and Mainstream Protestant Zionism, 1938-1948." *Holocaust and Genocide Studies* 24 (Fall 2010), 273-296.

Carlton, David. *MacDonald versus Henderson: The Foreign Policy of the Second Labour Government*. London: Macmillan, 1970.

Castle, Alfred L. *Diplomatic Realism: William R. Castle, Jr., and American Foreign Policy, 1919-1953*. Honolulu: Samuel N. and Mary Castle Foundation, 1998.

Clements, Kendrick A. *The Life of Herbert Hoover: Imperfect Visionary, 1918-1928*. New York: Palgrave Macmillan, 2010.

Clubb, Jerome and Allen, Howard. "The Cities and the Election of 1928," *American Historical Review* 74 (1969) 1205-1220.

Coffman, Elesha. "The 'Religious Issue' in Presidential Politics," *American Catholic Studies* 119 (Winter 2008), 1-20.

Cohen, Naomi W. *Not Free to Desist: The American Jewish Committee, 1906-66*. Philadelphia: Jewish Publication Society, 1972.

Cohen, Naomi W. *The Year After the Riots: American Responses to the Palestine Crisis of 1929-1930*. Detroit: Wayne State University Press, 1988.

Craig, Lloyd. *Aggressive Introvert: A Study of Herbert Hoover and Public Relations Management, 1912-32*. Columbus: Ohio State University Press, 1972.

Crum, Bartley. *Behind the Silken Curtain: A Personal Account of Anglo-American Diplomacy in Palestine and the Middle East*. London: Victor Gollancz Ltd., 1947.

Dalin, David G. "Louis Marshall, the Jewish Vote, and the Republican Party," *Jewish Political Studies Review* 4 (Spring 1992), 55-84.

Dawes, Charles G. *Journal as Ambassador to Great Britain*. New York: Macmillan, 1939.

Dekel-Chen, Jonathan L. *Farming the Red Land: Jewish Agricultural Colonization and Local Soviet Power, 1924-1941*. New Haven: Yale University Press, 2005.

Dodd, Jr., William E. and Dodd, Martha eds. *Ambassador Dodd's Diary, 1933-1938*. New York: Harcourt Brace and Company, 1941.

Eddy, William A. *FDR Meets Ibn Saud*. New York: American Friends of the Middle East, 1954.

Efrati, Nathan. *American Jewry and the Yishuv, 1890-1918: The "Zionism" of Non-Zionist American Groups*. Jerusalem: American Jewish Archives, 1993.

Eldersveld, Samuel J. "The Influence of Metropolitan Party Pluralities in Presidential Elections since 1920: A Study of Twelve Key Cities," *American Political Science Review* 83 (December 1949), 1189-1206.

Esco Foundation for Palestine, Inc. *Palestine: A Study of Jewish, Arab, and British Policies*. New Haven: Yale University Press, 1947.

Evensen, Bruce J. Truman, *Palestine, and the Press: Shaping Conventional Wisdom at the Beginning of the Cold War*. New York: Greenwood Press, 1992.

Feingold, Henry L. *The Politics of Rescue: The Roosevelt Administration and the Holocaust, 1938–1945*. New Brunswick, NJ: Rutgers University Press, 1970.

Feingold, Henry L. "Roosevelt and the Resettlement Question," in Gutman, Yisrael and Zuroff, Efraim, eds. *Rescue Attempts During the Holocaust: Proceedings of the Second Yad Vashem International Historical Conference*. Jerusalem: Yad Vashem, 1977, 123-181.

Feingold, Henry L. *Bearing Witness: How America and Its Jews Responded to the Holocaust.* Syracuse, NY: Syracuse University Press, 1995.

Ferrell, Robert H., ed. *Dear Bess: The Letters from Harry to Bess Truman 1910-1959.* New York: W.W. Norton, 1983.

Fink, Carole. "Louis Marshall: An American Jewish Diplomat in Paris, 1919," *American Jewish History* 94 (March-June 2008), 21-40.

Fink, Carole. *Defending the Rights of Others: The Great Powers, the Jews, and International Minority Protection, 1878-1938.* Cambridge: Cambridge University Press, 2004.

Friedman, Saul S. *No Haven for the Oppressed: United States Policy toward Refugees, 1938–1945.* Detroit: Wayne State University Press, 1973.

Fuchs, Lawrence H. "American Jews and the Presidential Vote," *American Political Science Review* 49 (June 1955), 385-401.

Galpin, Perrin C., ed. *Hugh Gibson 1883-1954: Extracts from His Letters and Anecdotes from His Friends.* New York: Belgian American Educational Foundation, 1956.

Gamm, Gerald H. *The Making of New Deal Democrats: Voting Behavior and Realignment in Boston.* Chicago: University of Chicago Press, 1986.

Ganin, Zvi. "Activism versus Moderation: The Conflict between Abba Hillel Silver and Stephen Wise during the 1940s," *Studies in Zionism* 5 (Spring 1984), 71-95.

Garland, Libby. "Not-quite-closed Gates: Jewish Alien Smuggling in the Post Quota Years," *American Jewish History* 94 (September 2008), 197-224.

Gartner, Lloyd P. "The Two Continuities of Antisemitism in the United States," in Shmuel Almog, ed., *Antisemitism through the Ages* (New York: Oxford University Press, 1998),

Geismar, Maxwell, ed. *Unfinished Business: James N. Rosenberg Papers*. Mamaroneck, NY: Vincent Marasia Press, 1967.

Gelfand, Lawrence L., ed. *Herbert Hoover: The Great War and its Aftermath, 1914-23*. Iowa City: University of Iowa Press, 1979.

Genizi, Haim. "James G. McDonald: High Commissioner for Refugees, 1933-1935," *Wiener Library Bulletin* 30 (1977), New Series Nos. 43/44, 40-52.

Genizi, Haim. *American Apathy: The Plight of Christian Refugees from Nazism*. Ramat Gan, Israel: Bar-Ilan University Press, 1983.

Gilbert, Martin. *Auschwitz and the Allies*. New York: Holt Rinehart and Winston, 1981.

Gitleman, Zvi. ed. *The Quest for Utopia: Jewish Political Ideas and Institutions Through the Ages*. Armonk, NY: M. E. Sharpe, 1992.

Guysenir, Maurice G. "Jewish Vote in Chicago," *Jewish Social Studies* 20 (October 1958).

Handlin, Oscar. *A Continuing Task: The American Jewish Joint Distribution Committee, 1914-1964*. New York: Random House, 1964.

Halperin, Samuel. *The Political World of American Zionism*. Detroit: Wayne State University Press, 1961.

Hassett, William D. *Off the Record with F.D.R. 1942-1945*. New Brunswick, NJ: Rutgers University Press, 1958.

Hecht, Ben. *A Child of the Century*. New York: Scribner's, 1954.

Hostetler, Michael J. "Gov. Al Smith Confronts the Catholic Question: The Rhetorical Legacy of the 1928 Campaign," *Communication Quarterly* 46 (Winter 1998), 12-24.

Heinze, Andrew R. "Clare Boothe Luce and the Jews: A Chapter from the Catholic-Jewish Disputation of Postwar America," *American Jewish History* 88 (September 2000), 361-376.

Hershman, Ruth, ed., *The American Jewish Conference: Proceedings of the Third Session: February 17-19, 1946 - Cleveland, Ohio*. New York: American Jewish Conference, 1946.

Higham, John. *Strangers in the Land: Patterns of American Nativism 1860-1925*. New York, 1963.

Hirschmann, Ira A. *Life Line to a Promised Land*. New York: Vanguard Press, 1946.

Hoff-Wilson, Joan. *Herbert Hoover: Forgotten Progressive*. Boston: Little Brown & Company, 1975.

Hoover, Herbert C. *American Individualism*. New York: Doubleday, Page & Co., 1922.

Hoover, Herbert C. *The Challenge to Liberty*. New York: Charles Scribner and Sons, 1934.

Hoover, Herbert C. *Addresses Upon the American Road*. Stanford, CA: Stanford University Press, 1951.

Hoover, Herbert C. *The Memoirs of Herbert Hoover: Volume I - Years of Adventure, 1874-1920*. New York: Macmillan, 1952.

Hoover, Herbert C. *The Memoirs of Herbert Hoover - Volume II: The Cabinet and the Presidency, 1920-1933*. New York: Macmillan, 1952.

Hoover, Herbert C. *The Memoirs of Herbert Hoover - Volume III: The Great Depression, 1929-1941*. New York: Macmillan, 1952.

Hoover, Herbert C. *An American Epic: Famine in Forty-Five Nations - Volume II - The Battle on the Front Line, 1914-1923*. Chicago: Henry Regnery, 1961.

Hoover, Herbert C. and Gibson, Hugh. *The Problems of Lasting Peace* (Garden City, NY: Doubleday, 1943), 235-236.

Ickes, Harold L. *The Secret Diary of Harold L. Ickes, Volume 3: The Lowering Clouds 1939-1941*. New York: Simon and Schuster, 1954.

Israel, Fred L. ed. *The War Diary of Breckinridge Long*. Lincoln, NE: University of Nebraska Press, 1966.

Isaacs, Stephen D. *Jews and American Politics*. Garden City, NY: Doubleday, 1974.

Jacobs, Travis and Berle, Beatrice, eds. *Navigating the Rapids: The Diaries of Adolf Berle*. New York: Houghton Mifflin, 1973.

Kapiszewski, Andrzej. "Polish-Jewish Conflict in America during the Paris Peace Conference: Milwaukee as a Case Study," *Polish American Studies* 49 (1992), 5-18.

Kaufman, Menahem. *An Ambiguous Partnership: Non-Zionists and Zionists in America, 1939-48*. Detroit: Wayne State University Press, 1991.

Kaufman, Menahem *The Magnes-Philby Negotiations, 1929: The Historical Record*. Jerusalem: Magnes Press, 1998.

Key Jr., V. O. *Public Opinion and American Democracy*. New York: Alfred A. Knopf, 1961.

Kolinsky, Martin. *Law, Order and Riots in Mandatory Palestine, 1928-35*. New York: Palgrave Macmillan, 1993.

Kutnick, Jerome M. *Non-Zionist Leadership: Felix M. Warburg, 1929-37*. Ph.D. dissertation: Brandeis University, 1983.

Litt, Edgar. "Status, Ethnicity, and Patterns of Jewish Voting Behavior in Baltimore," *Jewish Social Studies* 22 (July 1960), 159-164.

Leff, Laurel. *Buried by* The Times: *The Holocaust and America's Most Important Newspaper*. New York: Cambridge University Press, 2005.

Lipstadt, Deborah E. *Beyond Belief: The American Press and the Coming of the Holocaust, 1933–1945*. New York: The New Press, 1986.

Littell, Norman M. *My Roosevelt Years*. Seattle and London: University of Washington Press, 1987.

Lookstein, Haskel. *Were We Our Brothers' Keepers? The Public Response of American Jews to the Holocaust, 1938–1944.* New York: Hartmore House, 1985.

Lowenstein, Sharon R. *Token Refuge: The Story of the Jewish Refugee Shelter in Oswego, 1944–1946.* Bloomington: Indiana University Press, 1986.

Lukacs, John. "Herbert Hoover Meets Adolf Hitler," *The American Scholar* 2 (Spring 1993), 235-238.

Macmillan, Margaret. *Paris 1919: Six Months that Changed the World.* New York: Random House, 2002.

Maisel, L. Sandy ed. *Jews in American Politics.* New York: Rowman & Littlefield, 2001.

McKercher, B. J. C. *Esme Howard: A Diplomatic Biography.* New York: Cambridge University Press, 1989.

Meacham, Jon. *Franklin and Winston: An Intimate Portrait of an Epic Friendship* (New York: Random House, 2003.

Medoff, Rafael. *The Deafening Silence: American Jewish Leaders and the Holocaust.* New York: Steimatzky-Shapolsky, 1987.

Medoff, Rafael. "Herbert Hoover's Plan for Palestine: A Forgotten Episode in U.S. Middle East Diplomacy," *American Jewish History* 79 (Summer 1990), 449-476.

Medoff, Rafael. *Militant Zionism in America: The Rise and Impact of the Jabotinsky Movement in the United States, 1926–1948.* Tuscaloosa, AL: University of Alabama Press, 2002.

Medoff, Rafael. *Blowing the Whistle on Genocide: Josiah E. DuBois, Jr. and the Struggle for a U.S. Response to the Holocaust.* West Lafayette, IN: Purdue University Press, 2009.

Miller, Orlando W. "Jewish Refugees for Alaska 1933-1945." *Western States Jewish History* 36 (Fall 2003), 43-64.

Miller, Orlando W. "Jewish Refugees for Alaska 1933-1945—Part II," *Western States Jewish History* 36 (Summer 2004), 338-352.

Millis, Walter, ed. *The Forrestal Diaries*. New York: Viking Press, 1951.

Morgenthau, Henry III. *Mostly Morgenthaus: A Family History*. New York: Ticknor & Fields, 1991.

Morse, Arthur D. *While Six Million Died: A Chronicle of American Apathy*. New York: Random House, 1967.

Nash, George H. *The Life of Herbert Hoover: The Engineer, 1874-1914*. New York: W.W. Norton, 1983.

Nash, George H. *The Life of Herbert Hoover: The Humanitarian, 1914-17*. New York: W.W. Norton, 1988.

Nash, George H. "Herbert Hoover: Humanitarian in Europe," *Iowa Heritage Illustrated* 84 (2003), 58-67.

Nash, George H. "Determined Humanitarians: Herbert and Lou Henry Hoover in Europe," in *Uncommon Americans: The Lives and Legacies of Herbert and Lou Henry Hoover*. New York: Praeger, 2003.

Nash, George H. "Herbert Hoover: Humanitarian in Europe," *Iowa Heritage Illustrated* 84, no. 2 (2003): 66.

Nash, Lee, ed. *Understanding Herbert Hoover: The Humanitarian, 1914-17*. New York: W.W. Norton, 1988.

Neumann, Emanuel. *In the Arena*. New York: The Herzl Press, 1976.

Neuringer, Sheldon Morris. "American Jewry and United States Immigration Policy, 1881–1953." Ph.D. dissertation, University of Wisconsin, 1969.

Neustadt-Noy, Isaac. "The Unending Task: Efforts to Unite American Jewry from the American Jewish Congress to the American Jewish Conference." Ph.D. dissertation, Brandeis University, 1976.

Norwood, Stephen H. *The Third Reich in the Ivory Tower: Complicity and Conflict on American Campuses.* New York: Cambridge University Press, 2009.

Nurenberger, M.J. *The Scared and the Doomed: The Jewish Establishment vs. the Six Million.* Ontario: Mosaic Press, 1985.

O'Connor, Raymond G. *Perilous Equilibrium: The United States and the London Naval Conference of 1930.* Lawrence, KS: University of Kansas Press, 1962.

Ogilvie, Sarah A. and Miller, Scott. *Refuge Denied: The St. Louis Passengers and the Holocaust.* Madison, WI: University of Wisconsin Press, 2006.

Oren, Michael B. *Power, Faith, and Fantasy: America in the Middle East, 1776 to the Present.* New York: W.W. Norton, 2007.

Paassen, Pierre van. *The Forgotten Ally.* New York: Dial Press, 1943.

Patenaude, Bertrande M. *The Big Show in Bololand: The American Relief Expedition to Soviet Russia in the Famine of 1921.* Stanford: Stanford University Press, 2002.

Penkower, Monty Noam. "Ben-Gurion, Silver, and the 1941 UPA National Conference for Palestine: A Turning Point in American Zionist History," *American Jewish History* 69 (September 1979), 66-78.

Penkower, Monty Noam. *The Jews Were Expendable: Free World Diplomacy and the Holocaust.* Urbana and Chicago: University of Illinois Press, 1983.

Penkower, Monty Noam. *The Holocaust and Israel Reborn: From Catastrophe to Sovereignty.* Urbana and Chicago: University of Illinois Press, 1994.

Penkower, Monty Noam. *Decision on Palestine Deferred: America, Britain and Wartime Diplomacy 1939-1945.* London: Frank Cass, 2002.

Perl, William R. *The Four-Front War: From the Holocaust to the Promised Land.* New York: Crown, 1978.

Pfau, Richard. *No Sacrifice Too Great: The Life of Lewis L. Strauss.* Charlottesville: University Press of Virginia, 1984.

Plesur, Milton. *Jewish Life in Twentieth-Century America: Challenge and Accommodation.* Chicago: Welson-Hall, 1982.

Problems of World War II and Its Aftermath - Part 2: The Palestine Question, Problems of Postwar Europe. Washington, D.C.: Government Printing Office, 1976.

Rafaeli, Alex. *Dream and Action: The Story of My Life.* Jerusalem: Achva, 1993.

Raider, Mark A., Sarna, Jonathan D., and Zweig, Ronald W. eds. *Abba Hillel Silver and American Zionism.* London: Frank Cass, 1997.

Raider, Mark A. "The Aristocrat and the Democrat: Louis Marshall, Stephen S. Wise, and the Challenge of American Jewish Leadership," *American Jewish History* 94 (March-June 2008), 91-113.

Raphael, Marc Lee. *Abba Hillel Silver: A Profile in American Judaism.* New York: Homes & Meier, 1989.

Rapoport, Louis. *Shake Heaven and Earth: Peter Bergson and the Struggle to Rescue the Jews of Europe.* Jerusalem: Gefen, 1999.

Reznikoff, Charles. *Louis Marshall, Champion of Liberty.* Philadelphia: Jewish Publication Society of America, 1957.

Rischin, Moses *"Our Own Kind": Voting by Race, Creed, or National Origin.* Santa Barbara, CA: Fund for the Republic, 1960.

Rosenstock, Morton. *Louis Marshall: Defender of Jewish Rights.* Detroit: Wayne State University Press, 1965.

Sarna, Jonathan D. *American Judaism: A History.* New Haven: Yale University Press, 2004.

Sarna, Jonathan D. "American Jewish Political Conservatism in Historical Perspective," *American Jewish History* 87 (June-September 1999), 113-122.

Sarna, Jonathan D. "Two Jewish Lawyers Named Louis," *American Jewish History* 94 (March-June 2008), 1-19.

Schlup, Leonard and Blochowiak, Mary Ann. *Henry C. Hansbrough: Political Maverick of the Northern Plains*. Akron, OH: Midwest Press, 2007.

Segev, Tom. *One Palestine, Complete: Jews and Arabs Under the British Mandate*. New York: Metropolitan, 2000.

Sharp, Alan. "Some Relevant Historians: The Political Intelligence Department of the Foreign Office, 1918-1920," *The Australian Journal of Politics and History* 34 (1988), 359-368.

Sheean, Vincent. *Personal History*. Garden City, New York: Country Life Press, 1935,

Shogan, Robert. *Prelude to Catastrophe: FDR's Jews and the Menace of Nazism*. Chicago: Ivan R. Dee, 2010.

Shover, John L. "The Emergence of a Two-Party System in Republican Philadelphia, 1924-1936," *Journal of American History* 60 (March 1974), 985-1002.

Silver, Matthew. "Louis Marshall and the Democratization of Jewish Identity," *American Jewish History* 94 (March-June 2008), 41-69.

Smith, Richard Norton. *An Uncommon Man: The Triumph of Herbert Hoover* .New York: Simon and Schuster, 1984.

Smith, Sharon Kay. "Elbert D. Thomas and America's Response to the Holocaust," Ph.D. dissertation, Brigham Young University, 1992.

Snetsinger, John H. *Truman, the Jewish Vote, and the Creation of Israel*. Stanford, CA: Hoover Institution Press, 1974.

Snyder, Timothy. *The Reconstruction of Nations: Poland, Ukraine, Lithuania, Belarus, 1569-1989*. New Haven: Yale University Press, 2003.

Stember, Charles H. et al, *Jews in the Mind of America*. New York: Basic Books, 1966.

Strum, Harvey. "Henry Stimson's Opposition to American Jews and Zionism," *Patterns of Prejudice* 18 (October 1984), 17-24.

Szajkowski, Zosa. "Private and Organized American Jewish Overseas Relief (1914-38)," *American Jewish Historical Quarterly* 57 (September 1967), 52-106.

Szajkowski, Zosa. "Private and Organized American Jewish Overseas Relief and Immigration (1914-38)," *American Jewish Historical Quarterly* 57 (December 1967), 191-253.

Szajkowski, Zosa. "Private American Jewish Overseas Relief (1919-1938): Problems and Attempted Solutions," *American Jewish Historical Quarterly* 57 (March 1968), 285-352.

Szajkowski, Zosa. "Disunity in the Distribution of American Jewish Overseas Relief 1919-1939," *American Jewish Historical Quarterly* 58 (March 1969), 376-407.

Szajkowski, Zosa. "Disunity in the Distribution of American Jewish Overseas Relief 1919-1939 (Conclusion)," *American Jewish Historical Quarterly* 58 (June 1969), 484-506.

Szajkowski, Zosa. " 'Reconstruction' vs. 'Palliative Relief' in American Jewish Overseas Work (1919-1939), *Jewish Social Studies* 32 (1970), 111-147.

Urofsky, Melvin I. "Stephen S. Wise in Historical Perspective," *The American Zionist* 44 (May 1974), 31-36.

Urofsky, Melvin I. *We Are One! American Jewry and Israel.* Garden City, NY: Doubleday, 1978.

Urofsky, Melvin I., ed., *Herzl Year Book - Volume 8: Essays in American Zionism.* New York: Herzl Press, 1978.

Urofsky, Melvin I. *A Voice That Spoke for Justice: The Life and Times of Stephen S. Wise.* Albany, NY: State University of New York Press, 1982.

Voss, Carl Hermann, ed. *Stephen S. Wise: Servant of the People: - Selected Letters.* Philadelphia: Jewish Publication Society of America, 1970.

Voss, Carl Hermann. "The American Christian Palestine Committee," in Melvin I. Urofsky, ed. *Herzl Year Book - Volume 8: Essays in American Zionism* (New York: Herzl Press, 1978), 242-262.

Waldman, Morris D. *Nor By Power*. New York: International Universities Press, 1953.

Weil, Martin. *A Pretty Good Club: The Founding Fathers of the U.S. Foreign Service.* New York: W.W. Norton, 1978.

Wentling, Sonja. "Prologue to Genocide or Epilogue to War? American Perspectives on the Jewish Question in Poland, 1919-21." *The Journal of the Historical Society* 8 (December 2008), 523-544.

Wentling, Sonja. "Hoover, Palestine, and American Jews." *American Jewish Archives* 53 (2001), 45-64.

Wentling, Sonja. "The Engineer and the *Shtadlanim*: Herbert Hoover and American Jewish non-Zionists, 1917-28," *American Jewish History* 88 (September 2000), 377-406.

Wise, Stephen S. *Challenging Years: The Autobiography of Stephen Wise*. New York: Putnam's Sons, 1949.

Wyman, David S. *Paper Walls: America and the Refugee Crisis, 1938–1941*. Amherst: University of Massachusetts Press, 1968.

Wyman, David S. *The Abandonment of the Jews: America and the Holocaust, 1941–1945.* New York: Pantheon, 1984.

Wyman, David S. *America and the Holocaust*. 13 vols. New York: Garland, 1993.

Wyman David S., ed. *The World Reacts to the Holocaust*. Baltimore: Johns Hopkins University Press, 1996.

Wyman, David S. and Medoff, Rafael. *A Race Against Death: Peter Bergson, America, and the Holocaust.* New York: The New Press, 2002.

Zucker, Bat-Ami. *In Search of Refuge: Jews and U.S. Consuls in Nazi Germany, 1933–1941.* London and Portland, ME: Vallentine Mitchell, 2001.

Zucker, Bat-Ami. *Cecilia Razovsky and the American-Jewish Women's Rescue Operations in the Second World War.* Portland and London: Vallentine Mitchell, 2008.

Zuroff, Efraim. *The Response of Orthodox Jewry in the United States to the Holocaust: The Activities of the Vaad-ha-Hatzala Rescue Committee, 1939–1945.* New York: Yeshiva University Press, 2000.

About the Authors

Dr. Sonja Schoepf Wentling is associate professor of history at Concordia College in Moorhead, Minnesota. A Herbert Hoover Presidential Fellow, Class of 1997-1998, she has written about U.S. foreign policy, Zionism, and East European Jewish history for numerous scholarly journals, including the *Journal of World History*, the *Journal of American Ethnic History*, *American Jewish History*, and *American Jewish Archives*.

Dr. Rafael Medoff is founding director of The David S. Wyman Institute for Holocaust Studies. A Herbert Hoover Presidential Fellow, Class of 1988-1989, he is author or editor of fourteen books on American Jewish history, Zionism, and the Holocaust, including *Jewish Americans and Political Participation*, which was named an "Outstanding Academic Title of 2003" by the American Library Association's *Choice Magazine*.

Notes

1. Richard Pfau, *No Sacrifice Too Great: The Life of Lewis L. Strauss* (Charlottesville: University Press of Virginia, 1984), 1-10.
2. Oral History Interview with Admiral Lewis L. Strauss by Raymond Henle, 13 February 1967, 9, Name and Subject File I, Lewis L. Strauss Papers [hereafter LLS], Herbert Hoover Presidential Library, West Branch, Iowa [hereafter HHPL].
3. Herbert Hoover, *The Memoirs of Herbert Hoover: Volume I - Years of Adventure, 1874-1920* (New York: The Macmillan Company, 1952), 225.
4. Ibid., 208.
5. Quoted in Nash, *The Life of Herbert Hoover: The Engineer, 1874-1914* (New York: W.W. Norton, 1983), 571.
6. George H. Nash, "Herbert Hoover: Humanitarian in Europe," *Iowa Heritage Illustrated* 84 (2003), 66.
7. Herbert Hoover, *The Challenge to Liberty* (New York: Charles Scribner and Sons, 1934), 5
8. Hoover, *Memoirs - Volume 1*, 8.
9. Joan Hoff-Wilson, *Herbert Hoover: Forgotten Progressive* (Boston: Little Brown & Company, 1975).
10. Stanford University was to Hoover the epitome of a western institution as opposed to an eastern institution. Hoover's educational philosophy just like his attitude toward life emphasized pragmatism rather than a classical education. See Hoff-Wilson; and Nash, *The Life of Herbert Hoover: The Humanitarian, 1914-17* (New York: W. W. Norton & Company, 1988), 3, 275.
11. George H. Nash, "The Social Philosophy of Herbert Hoover," in *Understanding Herbert Hoover: Ten Perspectives* (Stanford, CA: Hoover Institution Press, 1987), 28.
12. Hoover, *Memoirs - Volume I*, 138-39.
13. George H. Nash, "Herbert Hoover: Humanitarian in Europe," *Iowa Heritage Illustrated* 84 (2003), 58.
14. Hoover, *Memoirs - Volume I*, 144-148.
15. Hoover's speech, on 1 December 1914, is quoted in Nash, Lee, ed. *Understanding Herbert Hoover: The Humanitarian, 1914-17* (New York: W.W. Norton, 1988), 95; Hugh Gibson, *A Diplomatic Diary* (New York (Hodder and Stoughton, 1917), 232; Ben S. Allen, "Feeding Seven Million Belgians," *World's Work*, April 1915, copy in Reprint File, HHPL (cited in Nash, *The Humanitarian*, 94).
16. Hoover had grown increasingly annoyed with German tactics of obstruction. Delays in granting travel permits to CRB workers in Belgium for up to weeks at a time seriously endangered the CRB's very purpose of supervising the distribution of food and establishing that the Germans were not cheating. German submarine warfare put CRB ships in danger, again hampering relief efforts to the Belgian civilian population. In addition, the German army's intent to requisition food and harvest further complicated Hoover's humanitarian mission. See Nash, *The Humanitarian, 1914-17*, 95, 103-131.
17. Lloyd Craig, *Aggressive Introvert: A Study of Herbert Hoover and Public Relations Management, 1912-32* (Columbus: Ohio State University Press, 1972); Richard Norton Smith, *An Uncommon Man: The Triumph of Herbert Hoover* (New York: Simon and Schuster, 1984), 89-90.
18. Pfau, 19.
19. Hoover, *Memoirs - Volume I*, 428.
20. Ibid., 428-29.

21 Hoover, *Memoirs - Volume I,* 425; Herbert Hoover, *An American Epic: Famine in Forty-Five Nations - Volume II - The Battle on the Front Line, 1914-1923* (Chicago: Henry Regnery, 1961). Murray N. Rothbard takes a somewhat more cynical approach to Hoover's humanitarianism. He argues that Hoover's relief program was neither non-political nor purely humanitarian. According to Rothbard, Hoover effectively used food as a political and diplomatic weapon in the service of Wilsonian principles, that is, to oppose Bolshevism on the left and contain reaction on the right. See Murray N. Rothbard, "Hoover's 1919 Food Diplomacy in Retrospect," in *Herbert Hoover: The Great War and its Aftermath, 1914-23*, ed. Lawrence L. Gelfand (Iowa City: University of Iowa Press, 1979), 87-110; Nash, "Herbert Hoover, Humanitarian in Europe," 64; Timothy Walch, "Introduction," *Uncommon Americans: The Lives and Legacies of Herbert and Lou Henry Hoover*, 1; George H. Nash, "Determined Humanitarians: Herbert and Lou Henry Hoover in Europe," in *Uncommon Americans*, 55.

22 Rosenwald to Hoover, 16 February 1928, File: "Jewish Matters," Commerce Papers, HHPL.

23 Lewis Strauss, "Herbert C. Hoover and the Jews of Eastern Europe," *The American Hebrew* (23 April 23, 1920, in Name and Subject File I, LLS; Wise to Hoover, 2 October 1919, File: Correspondence--Wise, S., Post-Commerce Papers, HHPL.

24 Quoted in Nash, "Herbert Hoover: Humanitarian in Europe," 65.

25 Strauss, "Herbert C. Hoover and the Jews of Eastern Europe."

26 Hortense Becker, "American Jewish Personalities: James Becker and East European Jewry after World War I, " *American Jewish Archives* [hereafter AJA] 47 (1994), 287.

27 Cited in Pfau, 10.

28 Oral History Interview with Admiral Lewis Strauss by Raymond Henle, 13 February 1967, at Long Boat Key, Sarasota, Florida," Name and Subject File I,14-17, LLS.

29 Ibid. If we are to believe Lewis Strauss, this incident was the only one in his long acquaintance with Hoover that involved a discussion about Judaism or any differences in the two men's religious beliefs.

30 Hoover, *Memoirs - Volume I*, 280; Henle interview; Hoover to Strauss, 6 October 1962, Name and Subject File I, LLS.

31 Henle interview, 12-14.

32 Pfau, 26.

33 Ron Chernow, *The Warburgs: The Twentieth-Century Odyssey of a Remarkable Jewish Family* (New York: Vintage, 1994).

34 Warburg radio broadcast over station WJZ, 30 October 1928, File: "Campaign of 1928, Felix Warburg," LLS.

35 Jonathan L. Dekel-Chen, *Farming the Red Land: Jewish Agricultural Colonization and Local Soviet Power, 1924-1941* (New Haven: Yale University Press, 2005), 91-92.

36 James Becker diary entry, January 1919, cited in Becker, "American Jewish Personalities," 295-296; Becker to his parents, 18 April 1919, File: "Correspondence 1917-1919," Box 1, Folder 2, James H. Becker Papers [hereafter JHB], American Jewish Archives, Cincinnati.

37 Becker, 283-305.

38 According to Zosa Szajkowski, "with the creation of the Joint Distribution Committee, organized relief for Jews overseas became one of the most important aspects of communal Jewish life in the United States." As early as October 1914, Orthodox Jews had created the Central Relief Committee (CRC), while the American Jewish Committee in collaboration with the leaders of the Zionist Provisional Committee founded the American Jewish Relief Committee (AJRC). The two organizations joined forces in November 1914 as the Joint Distribution Committee of the American Funds for Jewish War Sufferers (JDC). In November 1915, they merged with the labor-organized People's Relief Committee (PRC). See Zosa Szajkowski, "Private and Organized American Jewish Overseas Relief (1914-38)," *American Jewish History Quarterly* [hereafter AJHQ] 57 (1967), 56.

39 Boris Bogen, *Born a Jew* (New York: MacMillan, 1930), 168-169; "Born a Jew" (undated draft), Folder 10, Box 7, Boris Bogen Papers [hereafter BBP], American Jewish Archives, Cincinnati.

40 Carole Fink, *Defending the Rights of Others: The Great Powers, the Jews, and International Minority Protection, 1878-1938* (Cambridge: Cambridge University Press, 2004), 101-130; Tobias Brinkmann, "From Immigrants to Supranational Transmigrants and Refugees: Jewish Migrants in New York and Berlin before and after the Great War," *Comparative Studies of South Asia, Africa and the Middle East* 30 (2010), 52; Bogen to Joint Distribution Committee, 23 January 1919, File: "Joint Distribution Committee," Box 183, Felix M. Warburg Papers [hereafter FMW], American Jewish Archives, Cincinnati.

41 Boris D. Bogen, *Jewish Philanthropy: An Exposition of Principles and Methods of Jewish Social Service in the United States* (New York: MacMillan, 1917), 251. Gilbert S. Rosenthal, "Tikkun ha-Olam: The Metamorphosis of a Concept," *Journal of Religion* 85 (April 2005), 240, sees a connection between 20th-century Jewish philanthropy and the ancient concept of "tikkun ha-olam," which he defines as "improving and bettering society through legislation, social action, and activism and highlighting the human component to achieve these goals, with a dash of eschatology thrown in."

42 The establishment of the Agricultural Experiment Center in Atlit in 1910 as an American corporation marked the beginning of a more active involvement of the non-Zionist German-Jewish elite in the Holy Land and laid the foundations for a relationship between American Jewish non-Zionists and Palestine. American Jewish leaders such as Jacob Schiff and Louis Marshall put aside their ideological differences with Zionism in order to address pressing Jewish needs. See Nathan Efrati, *American Jewry and the Yishuv, 1890-1918: The "Zionism" of Non-Zionist American Groups* (Annual Lecture at the American Jewish Archives, Jerusalem: 1993) and Menahem Kaufman, *An Ambiguous Partnership: Non-Zionists and Zionists in America, 1939-48* (Detroit: Wayne State University Press, 1991), 12-14. Their non-Zionism did entail a strong commitment to the *yishuv* in Palestine as a viable center of Jewish life, culture, and learning.

43 Jonathan D. Sarna, "Two Jewish Lawyers Named Louis," *American Jewish History* [hereafter AJH] 94 (March-June 2008), 1-13; Mark A. Raider, "The Aristocrat and the Democrat: Louis Marshall, Stephen S. Wise, and the Challenge of American Jewish Leadership," *AJH* 94 (March-June 2008), 92; Kaufman, *An Ambiguous Partnership*, 14-16; Charles Reznikoff, *Louis Marshall, Champion of Liberty* (Philadelphia: Jewish Publication Society of America, 1957), xvii; Sarna, "Two Jewish Lawyers Named Louis," 9-10. Matthew Silver holds a somewhat different view of Marshall's leadership style. He argues that "Marshall's legacy combines and anticipates liberal-activist and conservative poles of American Jewish politics that consolidated in the decades after his death." See Matthew Silver, "Louis Marshall and the Democratization of Jewish Identity," *AJH* 94 (March-June 2008), 41 and Naomi W. Cohen, *Not Free to Desist: The American Jewish Committee, 1906-66* (Philadelphia: Jewish Publication Society, 1972). Peter Y. Medding argues that traditional Jewish politics, the characteristic pattern of politics of the corporate Jewish communities in Europe from the medieval period until emancipation, never existed in the United States. Emancipation gave rise to modern Jewish politics, which involved the pursuit by Jews of the benefits of citizenship, liberty and equality as a matter of right. It also reflected the political mobilization of the Jewish masses, even though notables resorted to personal and non-public representation at times in order to address Jewish issues. See Peter Y. Medding, "The 'New Jewish Politics' in the United States; Historical Perspectives," in *The Quest for Utopia: Jewish Political Idea and Institutions through the Ages*, ed. Zvi Gitelman (New York: M. E. Sharpe, 1992), 119-53 and Jonathan Frankel, "Modern Jewish Politics: East and West, 1840-1939," in *The Quest for Utopia*, 83.

44 Marshall to Fink, 4 September 1919, File: "September 1919," Box 1589, Louis Marshall Papers [hereafter LMP], American Jewish Archives, Cincinnati.

45 Kristofer Allerfeldt, "Rejecting the United States of the World: The consequences of Woodrow Wilson's new diplomacy on the 1921 Immigration Act," *European Journal of American Culture* 26 (2007), 145-148. Allerfeldt argues that the bitter league fight and ultimate rejection of the treaty contributed to the creation of a more tribal society in America, which in turn facilitated the passage of more restrictive legislation toward immigrants of Eastern and Southeastern Europe. A lesser known fact in the history of immigration is that while immigration become much more restrictive on paper in 1924, an underground network of smuggling illegal immigrants into the United States continued to thrive after its passage. See Libby Garland, "Not-quite-closed Gates: Jewish Alien Smuggling in the Post Quota Years," *AJH* 94 (September 2008), 197-224.

46 "Puncturing the Protocols," from the *Weekly Review*, 1921, in File: Jews 1922-28, Commerce Papers, HHPL; Brown to Hoover, 9 December 1920, "American Committee on Rights of Religious Minorities in Europe, 1920-21," Pre Commerce Subject Files, HHPL; and Herter to Brown, 18 December 1920, "American Committee on Rights of Religious Minorities in Europe, 1920-21," Pre Commerce Subject Files, HHPL

47 Strauss, "Herbert C. Hoover and the Jews of Eastern Europe," 759.

48 Herbert Hoover, *Memoirs - Volume II: The Cabinet and the Presidency, 1920-1933* (New York: MacMillan, 1952), 33-34; Kendrick A. Clements, *The Life of Herbert Hoover: Imperfect Visionary, 1918-1928* (New York: Palgrave Macmillan, 2010), 68, 395-396.

49 "Hoover Must Appeal to the Jewish People" (advertisement), NP, 26 October 1928; "Vote for Hoover and Ottinger" (advertisement), NP, 2 November 1928, 146,

50 Dekel-Chen, *Farming the Red Land*, 89-90. However, by 1936 even the JDC's tune changed, when the editor proposed to ignore Hoover's endorsement of the Agro-Joint because the former president was no longer "a political force of first magnitude." Instead, the editor proposed to solicit Franklin D. Roosevelt's endorsement. Cited in Dekel-Chen, *Farming the Red Land,* 177; also see Rosenstock, *Louis Marshall*, 54-56; Cohen, *Not Free to Desist*, 30-31; and Marshall to Strauss, 26 July 1928, File: "Louis Marshall," LLS.

51 Marshall to Strauss, 26 July 1928, File: "Louis Marshall," LLS.

52 Warburg to Cohn, 23 August 1928, File: "Campaign of 1928, Felix M. Warburg," LLS.

53 Radio speech by Felix M. Warburg, 30 October 1928, File: "Campaign of 1928. Felix M. Warburg," LLS; Radio speech by Felix M. Warburg, 30 October 1929, File: "Politics," FMW; Warburg to Strauss, 24 August 1928, File: "Campaign of 1928," FMW.

54 Three hundred Southern women residents of New York adopted a resolution, condemning the campaign of religious bigotry against Governor Smith and criticizing Hoover for his silence on the matter. See Elesha Coffman, "The 'Religious Issue' in Presidential Politics," *American Catholic Studies* 119 (Winter 2008), 1-20; Michael J. Hostetler, "Gov. Al Smith Confronts the Catholic Question: The Rhetorical Legacy of the 1928 Campaign," *Communication Quarterly* 46 (Winter 1998), 12-24; "Bigotry Condemned by Southern Women," *New York Times* [hereafter NYT], 14 October 1928, 1; Mrs. Willie W. Caldwell, Virginia's woman member of the Republican National Committee, wrote letter to Mrs. Clara Lyon, on the assumption that she was a party official. It was Lyon who had the letter published in the *Washington Post*; see "Hoover Reiterates His Keen Indignation Over Religious Appeal," *NYT*, 30 September 1928, 1, and "Hoover Repudiates 'Anti-Roman' Letter by Woman Leader," NYT, 29 September 1928, 1.

55 Leonard Schlup and Mary Ann Blochowiak, *Henry C. Hansbrough: Political Maverick of the Northern Plains* (Akron, OH: Midwest Press, 2007), 92-97.

56 "Hansbrough Bigoted, Smoot Declares," *NYT*, 7 September 1928, 3; "Hansbrough Hit By Hoover Bureau," *NYT*, 15 September 1928, 4.

57 "Denies Hoover Held Any Oil 'Concession'," *NYT*, 11 October 1928, 5; "Raskob Repudiates Attack on Hoover," NYT, 12 October 1928, 10.

58 "Mr. Hoover States His Position In Accepting Republican Nomination," Stanford University, 11 August 1928, *Congressional Digest* Vol. VII (January 1928 to December 1928) (Washington, D.C: Alice Gram Robinson, 1929), 234; Baruch to Marshall, Hoover et al, 16 October 1928, File: "Intolerance," Campaign and Transition Papers, HHPL.

59 Hoover to Baruch, 19 October 1928, File: "Intolerance," Campaign and Transition Papers, HHPL. Clements (*Imperfect Visionary,* 419) argues that Hoover's somewhat "half-hearted" response to his critics and his insistence that the Smith camp had been leveling unfair charges against him showed little empathy on Hoover's part and a certain narcissism that prevented him from acknowledging mistakes.

60 Burstein to Richey, 6 August 1929, File: "Bursc-Burst, 1929-32," Presidential Papers, Secretary's File, HHPL; Rosenwald to Hoover, 16 February 1928, File: "Jewish Matters," Commerce Papers, HHPL.

61 Interestingly, Rosenman, who was a political adviser to Al Smith and a member of the executive committee of the American Jewish Committee (later FDR's chief legal counselor and important presidential speech writer), unsuccessfully urged the AJC to adopt a resolution condemning ethnic-based voting as "contrary to American democracy." ("Twenty-first Annual Report of the AJC," *American Jewish Year Book* 30 [1928-29]: 62, 287-80.) Felix Warburg, although a staunch Republican, made a large anonymous contribution to the campaign fund for the Independent Citizens Committee for Roosevelt and Lehman, the Democratic candidates for governor and lieutenant governor. Herbert H. Lehman was a personal friend of Warburg's. (Survey, Election of 1928, File: "Campaign of 1928. Voting Behavior New York State," LLS.)

The difficulty of definitively determining Jewish voting patterns is illustrated by the varying estimates of prominent political scientists regarding 1928. Focusing on the results from different, but all heavily Jewish, precincts in that year's presidential election, John M. Allswang (*The Political Behavior of Chicago's Ethnic Groups, 1918-1932*, [North Stratford, NH: Ayer Company, 1980], 50) found that 60% of Chicago's Jews voted for Smith, while Lawrence Fuchs (*The Political Behavior of American Jews* [Glencoe, Ill: The Free Press, 1956], 66) calculated a figure of 74.5%. On the other hand, whereas Rosenman estimated that 72% of Jews in New York voted for Smith, Fuchs (ibid., 67) found somewhat lower numbers in four heavily Jewish districts: 66% in a Brooklyn district, 67 and 69% in two Bronx districts, and 71% in Manhattan. Regarding Boston, see Gerald H. Gamm, *The Making of New Deal Democrats: Voting Behavior and Realignment in Boston* (Chicago: University of Chicago Press, 1986), Chapter 2; for Philadelphia, see John L. Shover, "The Emergence of a Two-Party System in Republican Philadelphia, 1924-1936," *Journal of American History* 60 (March 1974), 985-1002. Also see Edgar Litt, "Status, Ethnicity, and Patterns of Jewish Voting Behavior in Baltimore," *Jewish Social Studies* 22 (July 1960), 159-164, and David G. Dalin, "Louis Marshall, the Jewish Vote, and the Republican Party," *Jewish Political Studies Review* 4 (Spring 1992), 55-84.

62 Henry L. Feingold, *A Time for Searching: Entering the Mainstream, 1920-1945* (Baltimore: Johns Hopkins University Press, 1993), 198; Plesur, *Jewish Life*, 84-85; Christopher M. Finan, *Alfred E. Smith: The Happy Warrior* (New York: Hill and Wang, 2002), 66-67, 85-91, 189-190.

63 Hoover, *The Memoirs of Herbert Hoover - Volume III: The Great Depression, 1929-1941* (New York: Macmillan, 1952), 218; Doak to Richey, 28 July 1932, File: "Edward Rosenblum 1932," E. French Strother Papers, HHPL.

64 Pfau, 1-10.

65 Hoover, *Memoirs - Volume I*, 425.

66 "Telegram from Colonel Grove, 10 April, 1919 to American Mission, Paris," *American Relief Administration: Documents of the ARA European Operations, 1918-1919. Vol. XVIII Poland* (Stanford University, 1932), copy included in Pre-Commerce Papers, HHPL. The Westward Ho was a joint venture by the JDC and the Polish National Committee to send food shipments to Poland. The first such shipment began on 26 January 1919. Just a few weeks before the April 5 incident, Col. Grove received an excerpt from a report by H.M. Brailsford to Lord Robert Cecil, describing the brutal treatment of the civilian population by the gendarmerie at Pinsk. "His [the commandant's] whole bearing towards the people, especially Jews, was, even in my response, so brutal, that I cannot dismiss this saying as a light threat." (Excerpt from report to Lord Cecil, 21 March 1919," File: "Grove, William," Box 9, LLS.

67 The Polish Question was also tied to the Allied policy toward Russia, which was "confused and uncoordinated," and even included the possibility of a reconstituted Russian federation that was at odds with a commitment to Russia's independent border-states. See Charlotte Alston, "'The Suggested Basis for a Russian Federal Republic:' Britain, Anti-Bolshevik Russia and the Border States at the Paris Peace Conference, 1919," *History* 91 (January 2006), 24-44.

68 Oleksandr Pavliuk, "Ukranian-Polish Relations in Galicia in 1918-1919," *Journal of Ukrainian Studies* 23 (Summer 1998): 1-23; Margaret Macmillan, *Paris 1919: Six Months that Changed the World* (New York: Random House, 2002), 221ff; Mark Levene, "Britain, a British Jew, and Jewish Relations with the New Poland: The Making of the Polish Minority Treaty of 1919," *Polin* 8 (1997): 24-6.

69 Fink, *Defending the Rights of Others*, 108-111. Violence in Lwòw was "the most prolonged and extensive carnage against civilians in Eastern Europe since 1906" and it was well documented by the Jewish Rescue Committee. The locally administered committee recorded hundreds of depositions from victims and eyewitnesses in the pogrom's immediate aftermath and some of them were published in Stockholm and Vienna in early 1919. Hundreds of Jews, caught in the middle of the Ukrainian-Polish struggle over Eastern Galicia that would last for eight months, were killed. The Jews' proclamation of neutrality during the fighting freed Ukrainian forces to attack the initially outnumbered Poles, and exposed the Jews to Polish charges of opportunism and treason. An interesting look at the Lw w pogrom as a social ritual is William W. Hagen, "The Moral Economy of Popular Violence: The Pogrom in Lwow, November 1918," in Robert Blobaum, ed., *Anti-Semitism and its Opponents in Modern Poland* (Ithaca, NY: Cornell University Press, 2005), 124-147. Hagen points out that the characterization of the Jew as an outsider greatly fueled the anti-Semitic violence in Lwòw.

70 Amid economic despair and the tensions of civil war, excesses against minorities, especially against Poland's Jews did not abate. The question of the status of minorities in the new nation states of Eastern Europe became a pressing one and "represented a rather critical subtext to the peace." See Mark Levene, "Britain, a British Jew, and Jewish Relations with the New Poland: The Making of the Polish Minority Treaty of 1919," *Polin* 8 (1997): 23.

71 Report by Colonel W. R. Grove to General Kernan at the American Mission in Warsaw, February 27, 1919, File: "American Mission of Relief for Poland, 1919," Box 79 Hugh S. Gibson Papers [hereafter HSG], Hoover Institution Archives [hereafter HIA], Stanford University, Stanford, CA.

72 Bogen, *"Born A Jew"* draft manuscript, 151.

73 Ibid., 151-158.

74 Becker to Strauss, 14 March 1919, File: "Becker, James," Box 9, LLS; Becker to Strauss, 26 March 1919, File: "Becker, James," LLS.

75 Ibid.,

76 Bogen, *Born a Jew*, 156-57.

77 Ibid.

78 Bogen, *Born a Jew*, 139.

79 Becker to Strauss, 26 March 1919, File: "Becker, James," Box 9, LLS.

80 Bliss to Wilson, 18 April 1919, in Arthur S. Link, ed. *The Papers of Woodrow Wilson* [hereafter PWW] - Volume 57 (Princeton, NJ: Princeton University Press, 1978), 464; Hankey's and Mantoux's Notes of a Meeting of the Council of Four, 21 April 1919, *PWW* Vol. 57, 549.

81 Lansing to Sharp, 2 December 1918, *Foreign Relations of the United States - Volume 2* (1919) [hereafter FRUS 1919], (Washington, D.C.: U.S. Government Printing Office, 1919), 746. When the war ended in November 1918, Poland had two potential governments, one in Paris, the other in Warsaw. Roman Dmowski's National Polish Committee in Paris was supported by the French, yet the British and the Americans urged Dmowski to build a coalition with Jozef Pilsudski in Warsaw. In the end, the great Polish pianist Ignace Paderewski, who also happened to be an old friend of Woodrow Wilson and fairly well acquainted with Hoover, managed to bring the forces of Dmowski and Pilsudski together by accepting the position of Prime Minister at the head of a coalition government. Yet despite Paderewski's popularity, the competing visions of a strong Poland either along federalist or incorporationist lines, would lead to serious tensions between the forces of Dmowski and Pilsudski. (Macmillan, *Paris 1919*, 210-213; Wandycz, *Soviet-Polish Relations, 1917-1921*, 120.)

82 Sharp to Polk, 6 December 1918, *FRUS* 1919, 746. Dmowski was the head of the Polish National Committee and leader of the nationalist Endejca party, who had been one of the chief exponents of the economic boycott against Polish Jews.

83 Pinsk was a town of 26,000 people with a large Jewish population. The town was left devastated, with no infrastructure or food, as a result of German and then Bolshevik occupation. (Fink, *Defending the Rights of Others*, 174.)

84	Hoover to Heebner, 10 November 1963, Post-Presidential Personal Correspondence, HHPL. Hoover gave a slightly different account of their first meeting in *Memoirs - Volume I*, 357.
85	Strauss, "Herbert C. Hoover and the Jews of Eastern Europe," 747.
86	"In this district [Pinsk and the territory of White Russia in general], which is the scene of serious warfare against the Bolshevists, it becomes necessary," the Polish prime minister explained, "to act with considerable energy and prompt decision. It is a case of destroying the Bolshevistic disease or being destroyed by it." To further justify the army's action against so-called enemies of the state, Paderewski concluded rather insensitively, "in such warfare the application of means of securing for the army and the population becomes at times incompatible with the desire of safeguarding every individual Jew." (Paderewski to Hoover, 12 April 1919, File: "Correspondence Herbert Hoover," LLS.)
87	In *Defending the Rights of Others*, Carol Fink pieces together conflicting reports about the Pinsk incident and describes that the meeting did not take place in a synagogue but rather at the city's Zionist headquarters in order to organize the distribution of matzo flour. She concludes that the April 5th Pinsk incident was misnamed a pogrom, but that news about the shootings nonetheless reverberated at the peace conference due to prior incidents of violence against Poland's Jews and that it arrived at a particularly tense moment of peace negotiations with implications for Poland's future. The public outcry over Polish mistreatment of Jews would pressure Poland to sign the minority protection treaty. Fink, *Defending the Rights of Others*, 171-208.
88	Hoover to Paderewski, Paris, 15 April 1919, File: "Correspondence Herbert Hoover," LLS. Years later, Hoover revealed in his memoirs that negative reports about Poland in the American press "began to threaten our relief work." Hoover, *Memoirs - Volume I*, 358.
89	Hoover to Paderewski, 12 April 1919, File: "Correspondence Herbert Hoover," LLS; *Documents of the American Relief Administration, European Operations, 1918-22*, Vol. XVIII. Poland. (Stanford University Press: Stanford, CA, 1932). Strauss, *Men and Decisions*, 24-25. Also see the cryptic notes on the back of Colonel Grove's telegram, indicating that Hoover acted immediately. (Grove to Hoover, 10 April, 1919, File: "Herbert Hoover," LLS.)
90	Gibson letter to his mother, 1 May 1919, File: "Diaries, 1919 May," Box 69, HSG.
91	The Morgenthau Report as printed in *The Jews in Poland* (National Polish Committee of America, 1920), in File: "Poland Report, Jews in Poland," ARA-European Unit, Box 609, HIA.
92	"Call on Nations to Protect Jews: Massacres in Poland Stir Madison Square Garden Meeting in Earnest Protest," *NYT*, 22 May, 1919, 1.
93	Polk to Gibson, 23 May 1919, FRUS 1919, 749.
94	"Call on Nations to Protect Jews: Massacres in Poland Stir Madison Square Garden Meeting in Earnest Protest," *NYT*, 22 May, 1919, 1.
95	Marshall to Wilson, 23 May 1919, *PWW*, Vol. 59, 445-46.
96	Strauss, "Herbert Hoover and the Jews of Eastern Europe," 747.
97	Paderewski to Wilson, 31 May 1919, *PWW*, Vol. 59, 638.
98	"Denies that Poland is Slaying Jews," NYT, 23 May 1929, 2.
99	Andrzej Kapiszewski, "Polish-Jewish Conflict in America during the Paris Peace Conference: Milwaukee as a Case Study," *Polish American Studies* 49 (1992), 5-18.
100	Hoover to Wilson, 2 June 1919, *PWW*, Vol. 60, 39.
101	Ibid. Hoover wrote years later after the Pinsk incident that the American investigative mission sent to Poland "quieted both the persecutions and the exaggerated reports." Hoover, *The Ordeal of Woodrow Wilson*, 141.
102	Hoover, *Memoirs - Volume I*, 301, 355, 475; Hoover, *American Individualism* (New York: Doubleday, Page & Co., 1922). Hoover even endorsed economic aid to the Bolsheviks themselves. Relief to the Bolshevists was the only way to bring about a change of government or "at least a period of rest along the frontiers of Europe" and "some hope of stabilization." (Hoover to Wilson, 28 March 1919, *PWW* Vol. 56, 378.)

103 Henry Morgenthau III, *Mostly Morgenthaus: A Family History* (New York: Ticknor & Fields, 1991), 197. It is interesting to note that the three key members of the commission did not have any familiarity with either Polish or Yiddish, and hence conducted all hearings with the help of interpreters. (Morgenthau, *Mostly Morgenthaus*, 198.)

104 James Becker to his parents, 13 July 1919, File: "Correspondence 1917-1920," Box 1, JHB.

105 Fink, *Defending the Rights of Others,* 171-208.

106 Marshall to Frank, 3 June 1921, File: "Jews in Poland," Commerce Papers, HHPL. Morton Rosenstock, *Louis Marshall: Defender of Jewish Rights* (Detroit: Wayne State University Press, 1965), 53. Frank's letter led Marshall to believe that Hoover's objections to the minority treaties centered on the use of public funds for parochial schools. An argument that Marshall rejected, since Poland did not have a public school system and most of the schools were parochial ones. The treaty clause would simply guarantee that funds would be appropriated fairly regardless of the school's religious affiliation.

107 Gibson to Phillips, 6 July 1919, File: "The Jewish Question, Poland, Reports by Hugh Gibson," Box 92, HSG.

108 Clipping from *Rozwoj*, June 1919, File 425: "Poland," Box 15, LLS.

109 Translation of article "Accusative State" from *Rozwoj*, 5 July, 1919, File: "American Relief Administration," Box 8, LLS.

110 Translation of article "A Provocative Commission," from *Rozwoj*, 12 July 1919, File: "American Relief Administration," Box 8, LLS.

111 Strauss to Warburg, 9 June 1919, File: "Correspondence," Folder 6, Box 12, LLS.

112 Polk to Gibson, 23 June, 1919, File: " The Jewish Question, Poland, Reports by Hugh Gibson," Box 92, HSG. Excesses against the Jews were often minimized by Gibson. On one occasion he wrote to his mother: "I am blessed if I think it is worth the time as our Jewish friends come dashing in and tell us every time they hear of anybody who made a face at a Jew..." Quoted in Martin Weil, *A Pretty Good Club: The Founding Fathers of the U.S. Foreign Service* (New York: W.W. Norton & Company, 1978), 42.

113 Gibson to Phillips, 6 July 1919, File: " The Jewish Question, Poland, Reports by Hugh Gibson," Box 92, HSG.

114 Gibson to Harrison, 7 July 1919, File: "Correspondence Leland Harrison, 1919-1929," Box 43, HSG.

115 Gibson to Harrison, 8 July 1919, File: "Correspondence Leland Harrison, 1919-1929," Box 43, HSG.

116 Gibson to Secretary of State, 10 November 1922, File: "Diplomatic Posts, Correspondence with the Secretary of State, 1919-23," Box 100, HSG.

117 "The Facts about Pogroms in Poland," Herman Bernstein review of Arthur L. Goodheart's book *Poland and Minority Races*, NYT, 12 December 1920, BR4.

118 Ibid. Gibson observed that Morgenthau had a good rapport with General Jadwin, since both of them even started attending synagogue together on a regular basis. When Jadwin jokingly remarked that if this ever got out, he would lose his standing as a Presbyterian, Gibson retorted that he had nothing on him as he was "known as Jugh Gibson." Considering Gibson's tensions with American Jews, the American minister's nickname, most likely given to him by the Poles, reveals a certain self-assuredness about being the point man for Jewish affairs—at least from the Polish perspective. However, Gibson did not intimate whether his nickname implied sympathy for the Jews or simply reflected his active role in managing the pogrom crisis. (Hugh Gibson to Mary Gibson, July 1919, File: "Correspondence Mary Gibson," Box 36, HSG.

119 "Doughboy" was a nickname for American soldiers who served in the American Expeditionary Force (AEF) during World War I. .

120 Hoover, *Memoirs - Volume I*, 359.

121 Entry for August 12-14, 1919, in Galpin, Perrin C., ed. *Hugh Gibson 1883-1954: Extracts from His Letters and Anecdotes from His Friends* (New York: Belgian American Educational Foundation, 1956), 70-71; Hugh Gibson to Mary Gibson, 14 August 1919, File: "Correspondence Mary Gibson," Box 36, HSG; Hoover, *Memoirs - Volume I*, 360-61.

122 Hoover, *Memoirs - Volume I,* 358-59.
123 Hugh Gibson to Mary Gibson, 15 August 1919, File: "Correspondence Mary Gibson," Box 36, HSG.
124 Morgenthau to Gibson, 14 January 1920, File: "Correspondence, Henry Morgenthau, 1919-23," Box 54, HSG. See Jadwin and Johnson Report as printed by the National Polish Committee of America, The Jews in Poland, 1920," General Office File, Poland Report, Jews in Poland," ARA - European Unit, Box 609, HIA.
125 See Jadwin and Johnson Report as printed by The National Polish Committee of America, *The Jews in Poland*, 1920, "General Office File, Poland Report, Jews in Poland, " ARA-European Unit, Box 609, HIA.
126 Gibson to Polk, 2 June 1919, *FRUS*, Vol. II (1919), 758.
127 The Morgenthau Report as printed by the National Polish Committee of America, *The Jews in Poland, 1920*, General Office File: "Poland Report, Jews in Poland," ARA - European Unit, Box 609, HIA.
128 Jadwin and Johnson Report as printed by the National Polish Committee of America, *The Jews in Poland, 1920*, General Office File: "Poland Report, Jews in Poland," ARA - European Unit, Box 609, HIA.
129 Strauss, *Men and Decisions*, 25; Oscar Handlin, *A Continuing Task: The American Jewish Joint Distribution Committee, 1914-1964* (New York: Random House, 1964).
130 Strauss, "Herbert C. Hoover and the Jews of Eastern Europe," 747.
131 Hoover Speech, 11 April 1920, "Correspondence Herbert Hoover," LLS.
132 Frank to Billikopf, 14 February 1921, File: "Jews in Poland," Commerce Papers, HHPL.
133 Marshall to Frank, 3 June 1921, File: "Jews in Poland," Commerce Papers, HHPL.
134 Hoover to Frank, 24 June 1921, File: "Jews in Poland," Commerce Papers, HHPL; Marshall to Hoover, 27 June 1921, File: "Jews in Poland," Commerce Papers, HHPL. Marshall, evidently a bit embarrassed, quickly expressed his confidence in Hoover and his "thorough understanding of the situation of the Jews in Poland." Marshall reiterated, "I have always been grateful for the sympathy which you manifested at a time when it was most important."
135 Hoover, *An American Epic,* Vol. 2, 214-223; Hoover to Strauss, 16 September 1919, File: "Correspondence Herbert Hoover," LLS.
136 According to the American Jewish Joint Distribution Committee Report, more than $6-million was sent to Poland, Lithuania, and the Kurland region of Latvia in 1919, which amounted to almost six times the aid going to the next highest funded country, Austria (including Galicia). Poland still received the largest amount, four times more than Palestine and four times more than Russia and Ukraine combined. Statistics included in File: "American Jewish Joint Distribution Committee Reports, 1914-1936," Box 817, American Relief Administration [hereafter ARA]-European Unit, HIA.
137 Sims to ARA, 24 March 1919, File: "Correspondence Herbert Hoover," LLS; Lowenstein to Hoover, 30 July 1919, File: "American Fund for Jewish War Sufferers 1919," Pre-Commerce Subjects, HHPL.
138 Timothy Snyder, *The Reconstruction of Nations: Poland, Ukraine, Lithuania, Belarus, 1569-1989* (New Haven: Yale University Press, 2003), 137; Ukraine's demographics at the end of the Russian empire broke down as follows: 32,893,000 Ukrainians (67.71%); 5,400,000 Russians (11.11%), and 4,288,000 Jews (8.82%). (See Burakovskiy, "Key Characteristics and Transformation of Jewish-Ukrainian Relations during the Period of Ukraine's Independence: 1991-2008," 111.)
139 The French and the Americans were clearly pro-Polish. The British seemed more divided, especially within the Political Intelligence Department of the Foreign Office, where some supported the Ukrainian position. Mark Baker focuses on the influence of Lewis Namier and the problem of Eastern Galicia, but comes to the conclusion that while the latter's efforts certainly influenced the British position, "they were not sufficient to avert Allied recognition of the Polish occupation of Eastern Galicia." Mark Baker, "Lewis Namier and the Problem of Eastern Galicia," *Journal of Ukrainian Studies* 23 (1998), 91. Namier's pro-Ukrainian stance was all the more remarkable since his own family and their estate fell victim to an attack by forces of the UHA in the summer of 1919. See also Alan Sharp, "Some Relevant Historians—the Political Intelligence Department of the Foreign Office, 1918-1920," *The Australian Journal of Politics and History* 34 (1988), 359-368.

140 Commission to Negotiate Peace to Secretary of State, 17 October 1919, *FRUS 1919* (Russia), 779; Commission to Negotiate Peace to Secretary of State, 26 October 1919, *FRUS 1919* (Russia), 781; "Secretary of State to the Commission to Negotiate Peace, 29 October 1919," *FRUS 1919* (Russia), 783-84

141 Commission to Negotiate Peace to Lansing, 26 October 1919, *FRUS 1919* (Russia), 782; JDC Weekly Newsletter, 12 July 1920, File: "Poland," Box 13, LLS.

142 Lou Hoover to Dyer, 17 February 1920, Lou Henry Hoover Papers, Box 2, "Personal Correspondence, 1872-1920, D Miscellaneous," cited in Clements, *The Life of Herbert Hoover: Imperfect Visionary*, 78.

143 Clements, *The Life of Herbert Hoover: Imperfect Visionary*, 76.

144 Isaac F. Marcosson, "American Relief--And After: An Interview with Herbert Hoover," *Saturday Evening Post*, 30 April 1921, 36, as quoted in Clements, *The Life of Herbert Hoover: Imperfect Visionary*, 1918-28, 85.

145 Clements, *The Life of Herbert Hoover: Imperfect Visionary*, 74-79.

146 Hoover to Wilson, 28 March 1919, PWW Vol. 56, 378, and Hoover to Wilson, 21 April 1919, PWW Vol. 57, 565. The enclosure that discusses Hoover's rationale for humanitarian aid to Eastern Europe including Russia is printed as part of letter from Wilson to Hoover, 23 April 1919, PWW Vol. 58, 41-42. In an exchange with Justice Louis D. Brandeis, Hoover agreed with the latter's assertion that Bolshevism "can not be killed except by kindness." Economic reconstruction rather than political or military intervention was needed to gradually bring about a "more stable government" and return Russia to the family of nations. An interview with Justice Louis D. Brandeis on United States policy with Russia, dated 15 November 1918, may be found in "Documents of the American Relief Administration, European Operations, 1918-1922, Vol. 14 (Stanford University, 1932)," Pre-Commerce Papers, HHPL. For a detailed discussion of Hoover's rationale, planning, and implementation of relief to Russia, see Bertrande M. Patenaude, *The Big Show in Bololand: The American Relief Expedition to Soviet Russia in the Famine of 1921* (Stanford: Stanford University Press, 2002), 30-60, passim.

147 Clements, *Imperfect Visionary*, 149-156.

148 Patenaude, 350, 362, 601-2. On May 11, 1922, Colonel W. N. Haskell, Director of ARA relief operations in Moscow, felt compelled to send a confidential letter to Walter I. Brown, head of ARA Europe, in London, strongly advising against the employment of additional Jewish personnel. After receiving a request from Colonel William Grove, who found that the employment of Jewish personnel was not detrimental to the relief in Russia but quite the opposite, Haskell quickly reminded his colleagues that maintaining control of operations was key to the ARA's success: "On general principles, I would say that New York not be encouraged to increase the number of Jews on this work until after we have turned over the Ukraine to them [...] I believe that if the bars are let down by the ARA that we will be flooded and that there will be no check on it if we give our general approval of the use of these men. It is now limited and I believe it would be a good thing to keep it limited." (Haskell to Brown, 11 May 1922, "New York Office, Personnel, Jews," ARA Russian Operations, Box 71, HIA.)

149 Rosenberg to Fletcher, 26 October 1922, File: "European Children's Fund - American Jewish Joint Distribution Committee," Box 636, ARA European Unit, HIA.

150 Rickard to Child Fund, 20 October 1920, General Office File, Folder 15, Jews - Cables January 1920, February 1920," ARA European Unit, Box 510, HIA. In late January 1920, accusations were leveled against ARA stations in Hungary that they were discriminating against Jewish children, and a month later Jewish newspapers reported about similar discriminatory practices in Vilna, Lithuania.

151 Extract from *The Jewish Journal*, 18 August 1922, translated by International Jewish Press Bureau, Inc., New York, "European Children's Fund Austria, Anti-Semitism," Box 657, ARA European Unit, HIA; Richardson to Brown, 31 August 1922, "European Children's Fund Austria, Anti-Semitism," ARA European Unit, Box 657, HIA; Kahn to Richardson, 31 August 1922, "European Children's Fund Austria, Anti-Semitism," ARA European Unit, Box 657, HIA.

152 International Jewish Press Bureau, "Press File, Folder 8," ARA-Russian Unit, Box 464, HIA.

153 *Die Naye Velt*, 18 February 1922, in "Press File, Folder 6, clippings, summaries, abstract, Jewish," ARA-Russian Unit, Box 464, HIA.

154 Baker to Cahan, 16 June 1922, "Press File, Folder, *Jewish Daily Forward, clippings*," ARA Russian operations, Box 465, HIA.

155 Hoover to Quinn, 21 December 1922, "New York Office, Relief Organization, JDC Letters 1921-22, " ARA-Russian Unit, Box 89, HSG; Rosenberg to Hoover, 17 February 1922, "Washington Office. Subject File. James N. Rosenberg," ARA Russian Operations, Box 347, Folder 16, HSG; International Jewish Press Bureau, "Press File, Folder 8," ARA-Russian Unit, Box 464, HSG.

156 Entries for 27 August 1929 (p.274) and 3 September 1929 (p.282), *William R. Castle Diaries, 1927-30*, HHPL. Castle later emerged as an ardent isolationist and headed the Washington, D.C. chapter of the extremist America First movement. (See Alfred L. Castle, *Diplomatic Realism: William R. Castle, Jr., and American Foreign Policy, 1919-1953* [Honolulu: Samuel N. and Mary Castle Foundation, 1998], 112-113.)

157 Minutes of the American Jewish Committee Executive Committee, 15 September 1929, Folder 4, Box 2, LLS.

158 Ibid. Hoover's successor, Franklin D. Roosevelt, would choose a different site in Thurmont, Maryland, called Shangri'La, the future Camp David, later renamed by President Eisenhower for his grandson David.

159 *Palestine: A Study of Jewish, Arab, and British Policies*. Published for the Esco Foundation for Palestine, Inc. Vol. 2 (New Haven: Yale University Press, 1949), 597-98. Segev, *One Palestine, Complete*, 298-301. A widely circulated rumor in the Arab community was that of an alleged Jewish conspiracy to destroy the two mosques in order to rebuild the Jewish Temple. (Kolinsky, *Law, Order and Riots in Mandatory Palestine, 1928-35*, 31-35; Segev, *One Palestine*, 296-97.)

160 The U.S. Vice Consul in Jerusalem, J. Thayer Gilman, reported in detail about the Western Wall incident. While expressing sympathy for Jewish religious sensibilities, Gilman claimed in his report that Jewish protests and demonstrations over the incident had been exaggerated and served the deliberate purpose to strengthen the Jewish claim to the wall. "It can not help but be felt that the majority of the exaggerated demonstrations which followed was timely propaganda for the acquisition of a site, the outright ownership of which has long been coveted by the Jews." (J. Thayer Gilman, vice consul, Jerusalem, to Secretary of State, 28 September 1928, 867n.404/21, Record Group 59, Records of the State Department [hereafter RSD], National Archives, College Park, MD.)

161 Martin Kolinsky argues that the Supreme Muslim Council, under the leadership of Mufti, perceived the issue of the Western Wall as a "significant means of stimulating the fervor of the Arab community, both urban and rural." As a matter of fact, Kolinsky explains, "the Mufti did not want a negotiated settlement nor an international inquiry [which could have regulated Arab and Jewish claims as well as rights] because compromises would have had to be made and the Jews might establish their rights." (Kolinsky, *Law, Order and Riots in Mandatory Palestine, 1928-35*, 38.)

162 Kolinsky, *Law, Order and Riots in Mandatory Palestine, 1928-35*, 17-30, 79. Kolinsky argues that British concerns over administrative costs and a lack of violent confrontations during the twenties in Palestine let to a policy of disarmament and ultimately to a dangerous neglect of security needs. The Zionist Executive protested against financial reductions but Jewish concerns over security went unheeded.

163 Knabenshue to Stimson, 24 August 1929, 25 August 1929, and 26 August 1929, 867n.404-Wailing Wall/5, Record Group 59, RDS; Vincent Sheean, *Personal History* (Garden City, New York: Country Life Press, 1935), 368. For a detailed analysis of the response of the State Department and American Jewish community to the 1929 riots and their aftermath, see Naomi W. Cohen, *The Year After the Riots: American Responses to the Palestine Crisis of 1929-30)* (Detroit; Wayne State University Press, 1988).

164 Sheean, 333, 337, 367-368.

165 Knabenshue to Stimson, 25 August 1929, 867n.404 – Wailing Wall/7, Record Group 59, RDS; Knabenshue to Stimson, 24 August 1929, 840.1, File: "Palestine: Confidential Correspondence, 1920-35," Record Group 84, RDS.

166 Knabenshue to Stimson, 26 August 1929, 840.1, File: "Palestine: Confidential Correspondence, 1920-35," Record Group 84, RDS.

167 Knabenshue to Stimson, 27 August 1929, 840.1, File: "Palestine: Confidential Correspondence, 1920-35," Record Group 84, RDS.

168 Stimson to American embassy in London, 26 August 1929, 867n.404 – Wailing Wall/23, Record Group 59, RDS; *The Times*, 27 August 1929, article included in report by F. Lammot Belin, 30 August 1929, 867n. 404 – Wailing Wall/174, Record Group 59, RDS; Directive to American embassy in London included in telegram from Stimson to Knabenshue, 28 August 1929, 840.1, File: "Palestine: Confidential Correspondence, 1920-35," Record Group 84, RDS.

169 Celler to Stimson, 23 August 1929, 867n.404-Wailing Wall/3, Record Group 59, RDS; Dickstein to Stimson, 24 August 1929, 867n.404-Wailing Wall/9, Record Group 59, RDS.

170 Ibid.

171 Rabbi Louis C. Gross, editor of the *Brooklyn Examiner*, to Secretary Stimson, 24 August 1929, 867n.404-Wailing Wall/10, Record Group 59, RDS.

172 Interdepartmental Memo, 23 September 1929, 867n.404—WW/255, Record Group 59, RDS.

173 Ibid.

174 Ibid.

175 Memorandum, "Anglo-American Relations," by the President of Education to the Cabinet, 16 January 1929, CAB 24/201, 4, National Archives, UK.

176 "Clash in Palestine Hits Naval Parley: 'Big Navy' Party in Britain Is Expected to Point to Value of Ships There," NYT, 26 August 1929, 1.

177 "Denies Our Navy Will Act: Stimson Sees No Need of Sending Warship to Palestine," NYT, 27 August 1929, 3. When civil war broke out in Nicaragua, which technically functioned as an American protectorate, and the lives and property of foreign nationals were threatened or in serious danger, Great Britain, after informing the Americans, dispatched a war vessel to the coast of Nicaragua in February of 1927 to protect British citizens there. See *FRUS*, 1927, Vol. 3 (Washington, D.C.: Government Printing Office, 1942), 312-15.

178 Dawes to Stimson, 28 August 1929, 867n.404-Wailing Wall/67, Record Group 59, RDS.

179 Ibid.

180 Dawes to Stimson, 27 August 1929, 867n.404-Wailing Wall/37, Record Group 59, RDS.

181 Howard to Henderson, 30 August 1929, FO 371/13752/E4546, cited in Naomi W. Cohen, *The Year After the Riots*, 38.

182 *The Times*, 27 August 1929, article included in a report by F. Lammot Belin, first secretary of American embassy in London, to Secretary Stimson, 30 August 1929, 867n.404-Wailing Wall/174, Record Group 59, RDS.

183 The delegation consisted of David J. Kaliski, Acting Chairman of the Administrative Committee, Nelson Ruttenberg, Judge Bernard A. Rosenblatt, Judge Gustave Hartman, Rabbi Israel Goldstein, Herman Bernstein, Emanuel Neumann, Dr. Abram Coralnik, Jonah J. Goldstein, Mrs. Zip Szold, President of Hadassah, former Congressman Nathan D. Perlman, Bernard F. Deutsch, Max Rhoade and Charles Cowan.

184 Michael B. Oren, *Power, Faith, and Fantasy: America in the Middle East, 1776 to the Present* (New York: W.W. Norton, 2007), 90, 221, 365; "A Dangerous Movement," NYT, 28 May 1922, 28.

185 Hoover to Mosessohn, 25 August 1922, File: "Zionism," Commerce Papers, HHPL; Hoover endorsement of Jewish national home, Folder 322 Box 10, Herman Bernstein Papers [hereafter HBP], AJHS; Herman Bernstein, "Political Relations," *The New Palestine* [hereafter NP], 23 August 1929, 553; "Sokolow Meets Hoover: Discusses Palestine Rebuilding Work: President of Zionist Executive Also Sees Vice-President," NP, 24 May 1929, 449.

186 "Stimson Receives Protest By Zionists: Letter to British Will Be Held for Recouching in More Diplomatic Language," NYT, 28 August 1929, 1.

187 "The Entire World Protests Against the Arab Atrocities in Palestine," NP, 6 Sept. 1929," NP, 6 September 1929, 137. Hoover's message was originally sent to the Zionist Organization of America on 29 August 1929. (Hoover to Zionist Organization of America, 29 August 1929, File: "Countries - Palestine, 1929-31," Presidential Papers, Foreign Affairs Series, HHPL.

188 Bernstein to Hoover, 30 August 1929, "Countries-Palestine 1929-31," Presidential Papers, Foreign Affairs Series, HHPL.

189 Samuel Untermeyer, "We Rededicate Ourselves," *The New Palestine* [hereafter NP], 6 September 1929, 147; Resolution Adopted at the Madison Square Garden Meeting," NP, 6 September 1929, 157.

190 Reference to Bernstein interview included in letter by American Jewish Committee to members of its Executive Committee, 29 August 1929, Box 2, Folder 4, LLS.

191 Waldman to members of Executive Committee, 29 August 1929, File: "American Jewish Committee," LLS.

192 Minutes of the American Jewish Committee Executive Committee, 15 September 1929, Folder 4 , Box 2, LLS.

193 Waldman to members of Executive Committee, 30 August 1929, File: "American Jewish Committee," LLS.

194 "The Entire World Protests Against the Arab Atrocities in Palestine," NP, 6 Sept. 1929, 157.

195 Syro-Palestinian Congress to Hoover, 30 August 1929, File: "Countries-Palestine, 1929-31," Foreign Affairs Series, Presidential Papers, HHPL; American Consul of Damascus to Secretary Stimson, 3 September 1929, 867n.404-WW/152, Record Group 59, RDS.

196 Rubinstein to Stimson, 31 August 1929, 867n.404-WW/169, Record Group 59, RDS. American Jews in Jerusalem complained that Consul Knabenshue was less than helpful in preparing his offices as a place of refuge for the victims of the riots. Many were forced to sleep on the floor of the American consulate, whereas other embassies did more to accommodate people's needs.

197 William R. Castle Diaries, 1927-30, 3 September 1929, 282, HHPL; Randolph to Stimson, 7 September 1929, Confidential U.S. Diplomatic Post Records, Middle East, 1925-41, Iraq, 800-Anti-Zionist Demonstration in Baghdad. (University Publications of America, Frederick, Maryland).

198 Knabenshue to Stimson, 1 September 1929, 867n. 404-Wailing /139, Record Group 59, RDS: Segev, *One Palestine, Complete*, 327; "Palestine Emergency. Narrative of Operations between August 24th and September 12th 1929," British Colonial Office, Palestine Correspondence, 1927-30, C.O. 733/175, Public Record Office [hereafter PRO], London; Randolph to Stimson, 7 September 1929, op.cit.

199 B. J. C. McKercher, *Esme Howard: A Diplomatic Biography* (New York: Cambridge University Press, 1989), 343-45. The MacDonald government decided to slightly modify the belligerent-rights subcommittee proposals concerning Britain's American policy. Britain decided not to conclude a new arbitration treaty with the United States but to rely on the League of Nations in matters of arbitration. Also, both sides agreed in principle to make compromises over the positions the two governments had held in Geneva in 1927. Both were determined to avoid any deterioration in relations. The differences concerned 25,000 tons out of an aggregate tonnage of both nations of 2.4-million tons.

200 Dawes, *Journal as Ambassador to Great Britain*, 68.

201 Weizmann to Warburg, 24 September 1929 and 30 September 1929, Folder 5, Box 252, FMW; Weizmann to Warburg, 24 September 1929, Folder 7, Box 252, FMW.

202 Knabenshue to Stimson, 19 September 1929, 867n.404-WW/229, Record Group 59, RDS.

203 Knabenshue to Stimson, 16 October 1929, 840.1, Record Group 84, RDS; Warburg to Goldstein, 16 October 1929, Folder 10, Box 251, FMW. Warburg was perturbed by the allegation, but he also advised the latter to let the incident die. He seemed especially concerned that Goldstein was keeping the story alive by trying to clear his name. By contacting the High Commissioner and the State Department, Goldstein was being a nuisance and casting a bad light on Jewish efforts in Palestine. Warburg implored his friend to "not trouble [the] State Department" anymore. In a letter to Judah Magnes, Warburg acknowledged

that the Goldsteins were probably not the best choice to work on behalf of Jewish interests. It had been a matter of time and availability that the Goldsteins were sent to Palestine, he explained, but if they had been "recognized as useful people" they might not have "blown themselves up unnecessarily." (Warburg to Magnes, 9 October 1929, Folder 3, Box 251, FMW.)

204 Richard Law, "Why Mr. Ramsay MacDonald want to pay a personal call on Mr Hoover," *Philadelphia Public Ledger*, in File: MacDonald, Prime Minister Correspondence and cables, September to October 1929, Post Presidential Files [hereafter PPF], HHPL.

205 Hoover to Stimson, 17 September 1929, File: Disarmament Correspondence-September 1929, Presidential Papers, Foreign Affairs Series, HHPL.

206 David Carlton, *MacDonald versus Henderson*, 115-17. Carlton writes that President Hoover took the initiative on every issue and MacDonald often made off-the-cuff statements that London later denied. It seems the Prime Minister was more concerned with appearance and the reaction to his visit than with the specifics of the negotiations. The talks were supposed to address the remaining gap between London and Washington with regard to cruisers. But since MacDonald had not brought a naval consultant, Hoover could not pin him down on specifics. The president wanted to address the subject of food ships and the freedom of the seas in spite of earlier agreement that it should not be tied to any talks on naval disarmament. Hoover hoped a British willingness to treat food ships as hospital ships would bring the freedom of the seas controversy to an end. (Carlton, *MacDonald versus Henderson*, 115-17.) At one point, Hoover even offered to purchase Bermuda, Trinidad, and British Honduras as part of a debt settlement. The president later noted in his memoirs that MacDonald was not interested in the offer at all. "He did not rise to the idea at all...I had a hunch he did not take the payment of the debt very seriously." (Hoover, *Memoirs: The Cabinet and the Presidency*, 346.) Many commentators noted with great satisfaction that despite the spirit of Anglo-American understanding, the joint declaration faced the differences in the American and British positions. While Hoover made clear that Americans would never consent to become entangled in European diplomacy, MacDonald said Britain would pursue a policy of cooperation with European neighbors. "It shows that, for all limitless zeal to work for peace, we are still mindful of the advice of George Washington against entangling alliances...Neither the President nor the Prime Minister could have said anything more appealing to American idealism or more satisfactory to American common sense." (Walter Lippmann, "Mr. MacDonald In Washington," *New York World*, 11 October 1929, and Richard Y. Oulahan, "Hoover and MacDonald Join in Saying War Between US Is Now 'Unthinkable;' Confident of 5 Power Naval Agreement," NYT, 10 October 1929, 1," in File: Ramsay MacDonald, Prime Minister, Clippings 1929, October 6-20, PPF; Raymond G. O'Connor, *Perilous Equilibrium: The United States and the London Naval Conference of 1930* [Lawrence: University of Kansas Press, 1962], 49.)

207 Walter Lippmann, "Mr. MacDonald in Washington," *New York World*, in File: "GB Correspondence, 1929 September to October," Presidential Papers, Foreign Affairs Series, HHPL. In fact, British Cabinet papers reveal that Lippmann played no insignificant role in facilitating this Anglo-American rapprochement. ("Memorandum on Anglo-American Relations by the President of Education to the Cabinet, 16 January 1929, CAB 24/201, 4, National Archives, UK.) The best *modus vivendi* suggested by Mr. Lippmann recently to Sir Esme Howard, i.d. mutual agreement between ourselves and the United States not to exceed our existing programmes of naval construction..If however this proposal is to be put forward ti must be put forward by the United States. It would be fatal for us to take the initiative of making any proposal for limitation by programmes, partly because the Big Navy Party in the United States would immediately accuse us of trying to buck the question of parity, and partly because American opinion is traditionally suspicious of proposals by foreign Powers directly limiting the right of Congress to legislate. Our best course, therefore, would be to approach the new Administration privately before the next meeting of the Preparatory Commission with a view to arranging, if possible, that a proposal on these lines should come from the United States Government."

208 Minutes of Meeting between Prime Minister MacDonald and Jewish Deputation, 11 October 1929, Folder 2, Box 248, FMW.

209 Address to the Prime Minister by the American Jewish Deputation, Folder 3, Box 248, FMW.

210 "MacDonald Gives Jews Assurances," *New York World*, 12 Oct 1929, in File: MacDonald, Prime Minister, Clippings, October 6-20, 1929, PPF, HHPL; Kutnick, *Non-Zionist Leadership: Felix M. Warburg, 1929-37*, 220.

211 Warburg to Weizmann, 11 October 1929, Folder 5, Box 252, FMW. Even the Zionist periodical *New Palestine* reported favorably on MacDonald's visit. See NP, 11 October -18 October 1929.

212 Bernard Wasserstein, "The Arab-Jewish Dilemma," in *Like all the Nations? The Life and Legacy of Judah L. Magnes*, ed. William Brinner and Moses Rischin (New York: State University of New York Press, 1987), 188-89; "Memorandum on the activities of Dr, Magnes," Folder 2, Box 248, FMW; Menahem Kaufman, *The Magnes-Philby Negotiations, 1929: The Historical Record* (Jerusalem: Magnes Press, 1998), 14-18; "Confidential Report by Colonel Kisch to Members of the Zionist Executive, London, 10 November 1929," Folder 4, Box 248, FMW; and Warburg to Weizmann, 4 November 1929, Folder 5, Box 252, FMW. Weizmann especially took issue with Magnes's proposal to give up the Balfour Declaration and the Mandate in order to establish peace with the Arabs: "I am of the opinion that if we do give it up we can just as well clear out of Palestine: not only will the Arabs feel that they have driven us out of the country and of our right, but not a single Jew will ever give us a penny and will think that we have betrayed the trust reposed in us." In the current situation, Weizmann implied, Arabs considered such gestures a sign of weakness. There was no other choice, he explained, but to "show a bold front if you want to negotiate with your adversary." Violence should not be rewarded with negotiations for a political settlement. On the contrary, "they [the Arabs] must be made to feel that acts of violence will be of no service to them and [that] they are weakening their position by perpetrating them." (Weizmann to Warburg, 13 November 1929, Folder 7, Box 252, FMW; Deutsch to Warburg, 22 November 1929, Folder 6, Box 247, FMW; "American Jewish Congress repudiates Magnes for conduct and utterances; sees united Jewish front broken," NYT, 23 November 1929, 9. "Magnes criticized by Jewish leaders," NYT, 25 November 1929, 10.)

213 Knabenshue to Shaw, 6 November 1929, 840.1, Record Group [hereafter RG] 84, Records of the Department of State [hereafter RDS], National Archives, College Park, MD.

214 Knabenshue to Stimson, 12 January 1930, 840.1/800, RG 84, RDS.

215 Cohen, op.cit., 33.

216 Knabenshue to Stimson, 23 November 1929, 867n.00/76, Record Group 59, RDS; Knabenshue to Stimson, 16 November 1929, 867n.404-Wailing Wall/ 273, Record Group 59, RDS; Knabenshue to Stimson, 12 January 1930, 840.1/800, Record Group 84, RDS.

217 Louis D. Brandeis, "The Will to a Jewish Palestine," NP, 29 November 1929, 454-55.

218 Shaw's deliberations also included a meeting at the request of Congressman Hamilton Fish, accompanied by ZOA lobbyist Max Rhoade. In that interview, Fish insisted the U.S. government had no need to give consideration to Britain's obligations under the Mandate, since the 1922 pro-Zionist congressional resolution spoke for itself and that the Hoover administration "should respect it." Memorandum of Conversation with Major Hopkin, Labor Member of Parliament, U.S. Congressman Hamilton Fish, and Max Rhoade by Wallace Murray, 18 January 1930, 867n.00/81, Record Group 59, RDS.

219 Great Britain, *Report of the Commission on the Palestine Disturbances of August 1929*, Cmd. 3530 (London: 1930).

220 Knabenshue to Stimson, 11 January 1930, 867n.00/82, Record Group 59, RDS.

221 Knabenshue to Murray, 15 April 1930, 801.01/Palestine Mandate, Record Group 84, RDS.

222 Knabenshue to Murray,13 April 1930, 801.01/Palestine mandate, Record Group 84, RDS; Solicitor of State Department to Murray, 15 April 1930, 867n.01/526, Record Group 59, RDS. Knabenshue reasoned: "If a preamble could be considered to be part of a convention and binding on the signatories of the convention, in this instance it would follow that the obligations of the convention, in this instance it would follow that the obligations of the mandate would be binding upon the United States. This, of course, is ridiculous for it is thoroughly well known that this Government did not care to take upon itself any mandate obligation...Therefore, it is apparent that the presence of the Balfour Declaration in the preamble to the convention as a preamble to the mandate and as referred to in Article 2 of the Mandate, can

have no effect upon this Government to bind it in any way to take action in favor of the National Home for Jews in Palestine." Murray made precisely the same argument in the aftermath of the 1936 riots in Palestine. On May 7, 1937, Murray explained that an internal study established beyond any doubt that the United States "has no right nor responsibility to question the administration of the Palestine Mandate except for the purpose of protecting American interests in that area." (Murray to Secretary of State, 7 May 1937, 867n.01/744, Record Group 59, RDS.)

223 *"Es genuegt, Ihnen zu sagen, dass wir den Eindruck bekamen, dass die Regierung nicht alle Ansichten des Shaw-Berichtes teilt und bereit ist, verschiedene dort aufgeworfene wesentliche Fragen nochmals gruendlich und wissenschaftlich zu pruefen."* Meeting of the Administrative Committee of the Jewish Agency in Berlin, 29 August 1930, Folder 2, Box 258, FMW.

224 Meeting of the Administrative Committee of the Jewish Agency, 29 August 1930, Folder 2, Box 258, FMW.

225 Raymond G. O'Connor argues that the treaty helped lessen the hostility among Great Britain, the United States, and Japan that had developed from the naval rivalry. "It did nothing, however, to temper the motives behind this rivalry; so it alleviated the symptom but accomplished no cure." O'Connor, *Perilous Equilibrium*, 127. The final agreement worked out between the United States and Great Britain was based on the American offer of 4 February 1930. Under its provisions the United States was allowed eighteen 18-inch-gun cruisers, Great Britain fifteen, and Japan twelve. The cruiser dispute was resolved by splitting the difference at 323,500 tons. The crucial concession in order to resolve the cruiser dispute was made by the United States in accepting eighteen eight-inch-gun cruisers instead of the twenty-one that had been considered a minimum required initially. (O'Connor, *Perilous Equilibrium*, 69-75.)

226 Members of the Navy Board urged the rejection of the treaty on the ground that it left the United States with an insufficient preponderance of naval strength to enforce the open door in the Far East in the face of Japanese opposition. London Naval Treaty. Hearings before the Committee on Naval Affairs, United States Senate, 71st Congress (Washington, D.C.: Government Printing Office, 1930).

227 *Congressional Record*, 70th Congress, House, 17 June 1930 (Washington, D.C,: Government Printing Office, 1929), 11029.

228 Secretary Stimson to President Hoover, 25 June 1930, "Foreign Affairs Series. Countries—Palestine 1929-31," Presidential Papers, HHPL.

229 Memorandum 24 June 1930, "Foreign Affairs Series. Countries—Palestine 1929-30," Presidential Papers, HHPL.

230 It is unclear how seriously British officials took the rumor about Zionist political pressure on the U.S. government. Confidential Foreign Office reports on the United States noted that the U.S. government was most unwilling to intervene in Zionist matters. Although Jewish pressure might be difficult to resist, the report went on, "it should be recollected that a large number of influential American Jews are anti-Zionist." (Annual Reports on the United States, 1930, *British Documents on Foreign Affairs: Reports and Papers from the Foreign Office Confidential Print*, Part II, Series C, Vol. 20, 194. Warburg Memorandum of conversation with Judge Mack, 3 June 1930, Folder 1, Box 259, FMW.)

231 The British Foreign Office evaluated the ratification process as a Hoover success that had not come easy. The President had to enlist the sympathies of the ardent pacifists, while at the same time refraining from making such sweeping concessions that would enrage big navy men. He also had to make sure not to offend the isolationists by even the appearance of involving the country in foreign entanglements. In the end the Naval Treaty was approved by an overwhelming majority—58 to 9—although both navy men and pacifists expressed themselves as highly skeptical. The nine senators who opposed the treaty had basically resorted to a filibuster in the hope to postpone the debate and raise up feeling against the treaty during the congressional election campaign in the fall. See Annual Report on the United States for 1930, *British Documents on Foreign Affairs: Reports and Papers from the Foreign Office Confidential Print*, Part II, Series C, North America (1919-39), Vol. 20, Annual Reports (1928-32), 190-92; MacDonald to Hoover, 25 July 1930, File: "MacDonald, Prime Minister Ramsay Correspondence and Cables November 1929 to 1933," PPF, HHPL; Hoover, *The Memoirs of Herbert Hoover: The Cabinet and the Presidency, 1920-33*, 352.

232 *Palestine: A Study of Jewish, Arab, and British Policies*, published for the Esco Foundation for Palestine, Inc., Volume 2 (New Haven: Yale University Press, 1947), 636-48.

233 Warburg to Kahn, 30 October 1930, Folder 2, Box 259, FMW; "Statement of Mr. Felix M. Warburg, Chairman of the Administrative Committee of the Jewish Agency for Palestine," 21 October 1930, Folder 1, Box 258, FMW; Sirovich to Hoover, 22 October 1930, 867n.01/536, RDS; Murray to Borkon, 28 October 1930, 867n.01/538, RDS: Doctors, Nurses, Teachers, Rabbis, and Students to Hoover, 22 October 1930, 867n.01/53, RDS; Gross to Hoover, 22 October 1930, 867n.01/535, RDS; Celler to Stimson, 22 October 1930, 867n.01/534, RDS; Murray to Borkon, 28 October 1930, 867n.01/538, RDS; Knabenshue to Stimson, 22 October 1930, 867n.01/533, RDS; Murray to Stimson, 23 October 1930, 867n.01/540, RDS; "Protest regarding British Policy in Palestine," 20 October 1930, RDSP, 867n.01/5391/2, RDS.

234 Hoover to Stimson, 28 October 1930, 867n.01/588, RDS.

235 *The Diaries of Henry L. Stimson*, Reel 2, Volume 11 (State Department, Important Statements and Letters, March 28, 1929 – December 10, 1931), 104.

236 *The Diaries of Henry L. Stimson*, Reel 2, Volume 11, 117-18. According to Stimson, Brandeis described the Palestine situation as a reprise of what had happened in Massachusetts 300 years earlier, when white settlers ran the Indians out of the country and took their land. Later on, when the secretary told Justice Holmes about his conversation with Brandeis, they both appeared somewhat amused at the comparison. Stimson assured his friend, however, that he did remind Brandeis that the old colonial model did not fit the terms of the Palestine mandate since it was intended for both Arabs and Jews, living side by side.

237 Hoover to Hopkins, 28 June 1930, "Messages to Jewish Religious Organizations and Leaders, 1930," PPF, HHPL. Hoover actually sent two telegrams. The first one was very short and did not include a reference to the recent developments. Hoover asked to ignore the first one, however, and sent a second telegram that specifically addressed the 1929 riots and the hope that Jewish aspirations would go forward.

238 Delegates of the 33rd Zionist Convention of America to Hoover, 1 July 1930, "Messages to Jewish Religious Organizations and Leaders to 1930," PPF, HHPL. The American Zionist movement needed all the well wishes it could get. At the Cleveland ZOA meeting the delegates were disappointed that Justice Brandeis, the most prominent American Jew, turned down the opportunity to assume the official responsibility of leadership in the ZOA. Citing his age and his obligations as justice, Brandeis opted for the more limited role of advising from time to time. (Brandeis to Delegates to the ZOA Convention, 28 June 1930, *Letters of Louis D. Brandeis* Vol. V [1921-41], 429-30; Neumann to Hoover, 7 January 1932, "Jewish Religious Organizations and Leaders-Messages 1932-33," PPF, HHPL; President Hoover to Emanuel Neumann, 11 January 1932, "Jewish Religious Organizations and Leaders-Messages 1932-33," PPF, HHPL.)

239 Rhoade to Wise, 19 November 1932, File: Zionism, Box 74, SSW-AJHS.

240 Remarks of Felix Frankfurter at Madison Square Garden Meeting, 2 November 1930, 867n.01/587, RDS. Frankfurter also forwarded the text of his speech to Secretary Stimson and stressed that the important part was information on the effect of Jewish development in Palestine upon the Arab. Felix Frankfurter to Secretary Stimson, 10 November 1930, 867n.01/587, RDS. Mayor Jimmy Walker was introduced by Frankfurter as the mayor of the "biggest Jewish city in the world." Police Commissioner Mulrooney was impressed with the orderly nature of the mass meeting. See "40,000 Here Protest on Palestine Policy, Charging 'Betrayal': 25,000 Fill Madison Square Garden—Others, Turned Away, Hold Meeting in Street," NYT, 3 November 1930, 3.

241 Knabenshue to Murray, 5 November 1930, Records of the Department of State relating to Internal Affairs of Palestine, 1930-44, 867n.01/577, RDS.

242 Jonah Goldstein to President Hoover, 26 November 1930, 867n.01/575, RDS. (The Zionists held a Maccabean Festival on 13 December at Madison Square Garden in order to commemorate the victory of Judas Maccabeus over the foreign invaders of Palestine. The object of the festival was a demonstration of Zionist sentiment and solidarity with the up-building of the Jewish national home.) Also see Cotton to Strother, 5 December 1930, "Churches, Jewish, 1929 August to December," Pres. Subject File, HHPL; and Murray to Cotton, 4 December 1930, 867n.01/575, RDS.

243 Cited in Emanuel Neuman, *In the Arena* (New York: The Herzl Press, 1976), 114.

244 Annual Report on the United States for 1930, *British Documents on Foreign Affairs: Reports and Papers from the Foreign Office Confidential Print*, Part II, Series C, Vol. 20, 194.

245 Justice Brandeis provided the classic synthesis of Americanism and Zionism: "Let no American imagine that Zionism is inconsistent with patriotism. Multiple loyalties are objectionable only if they are inconsistent. A man is a better citizen of the United States for being also a loyal citizen of his state and of his city; for being loyal to his family, and to his profession or trade; for being loyal to his college or his lodge. Every Irish American who contributed towards advancing home rule was a better man and a better American for the sacrifice he made. Every American Jew who aids in advancing the Jewish settlement in Palestine, though he feels that neither he nor his descendants will live there, will likewise be a better man and a better American for doing so...Indeed, loyalty to America demands rather that each American Jew become a Zionist. For only through the ennobling effect of its[Zionism's] strivings can we develop the best that is in us and give to this country the full benefit of our great inheritance." (Louis D. Brandeis, "The Jewish Problem: How To Solve It," *Maccabean* 26 [June 1915]: 109, reprinted in *Brandeis on Zionism: A Collection of Addresses and Statements by Louis D. Brandeis* [Washington, D.C.: Zionist Organization of America, 1942], 28-29.)

246 Mack to Strauss, 8 March 1920, Folder 12/13-Julian Mack, LLS.

247 Bisgyer to Strauss, 16 September 1932, File: "Campaign of 1932, Jewish Voters," LLS; Richey to West, 19 October 1932, File: "Churches, Jewish, 1932-33," Presidential Papers, HHPL; Felix Warburg, 28 September 1932, File: "Campaign of 1932, Jewish Voters," LLS; Strauss to Strother, 26 October 1932, File: "Campaign of 1932," LLS.

248 Entry for May 25, 1939, Diary of J. Pierrepont Moffat, Houghton Library, Harvard University.

249 Wise to Mack, 8 March 1933, in Carl Hermann Voss, ed. *Servant of the People: Stephen S. Wise - Selected Letters* (Philadelphia: Jewish Publication Society of America, 1969), 180; Strauss to Richey, 23 March 1933, File: Correspondence with Lewis Strauss, 1933-June 1934, PPI, HHPL; Strauss to Hoover, 29 June 1933, and Hoover to Strauss, 5 July 1933, Correspondence with Herbert Hoover, January-July 1933, Strauss Papers, HHPL; William E. Dodd, Jr. and Martha Dodd, eds. *Ambassador Dodd's Diary, 1933-1938* (New York: Harcourt Brace and Company, 1941), 5.

250 Wise to Mack, 8 March 1933, in Carl Hermann Voss. ed., *Stephen S. Wise: Servant of the People - Selected Letters* (Philadelphia: Jewish Publication Society of America, 1970),, 180; Wise to Mack, 18 October 1933, in Voss, 195.

251 "Anti-Nazi Protest March Through New York Voted by American Jewish Congress," *Jewish Telegraphic Agency Daily Bulletin* (hereafter JTA), 21 April 1933, 1; Dodd, 3.

252 Richard Breitman and Alan M. Kraut, *American Refugee Policy and European Jewry, 1933-1945* (Bloomington and Indianapolis: Indiana University Press, 1987), 18; Laurel Leff and Rafael Medoff, "New Documents Shed More Light on FDR's Holocaust Failure," *American Jewish World*, 30 April 2004, 5.

253 David S. Wyman, *Paper Walls: America and the Refugee Crisis 1938-1941* (Amherst, MA: University of Massachusetts Press, 1968), 44.

254 Adler to Dickstein, 28 March 1933, reprinted in Michael N. Dobkowski, ed., *The Politics of Indifference: A Documentary History of Holocaust Victims in America* (Washington, D.C.: University Press of America, 1982), 316.

255 Stember, 53-55, 84-85, 121-128, 131-133; Lloyd P. Gartner, "The Two Continuities of Antisemitism in the United States," in Shmuel Almog, ed., *Antisemitism through the Ages* (New York: Oxford University Press, 1998), 317-318; Charles H. Stember et al, *Jews in the Mind of America* (New York: Basic Books, 1966), 8, 210, 215; David S. Wyman and Rafael Medoff, *A Race Against Death: Peter Bergson, America, and the Holocaust* (New York: The New Press, 2002), 5-6. At his peak, Coughlin displayed a frightening amount of political influence. In 1935, he played a key role in mobilizing the public outcry that blocked the Roosevelt administration's proposal for U.S. participation in the World Court (Coughlin regarded it as an attempt by "international bankers"—those with Jewish surnames were always highlighted in

his speeches and literature—to rule the world.) Congressional candidates in Ohio and Michigan whom Coughlin targeted in 1936 were defeated due to a torrent of votes "directed to their opponents by Father Coughlin," according to the *New York Times*, and candidates associated with, or endorsed by, Coughlin did surprisingly well. "Senate Beats World Court, 52-36, 7 Less Than 2/3 Vote; Defeat for the President," NYT, 30 January 1935, 1; "Taft Captures 47 Seats, Borah 5; 15 Coughlin Candidates Win in Ohio," NYT, 14 May 1936, 1.

256 Morris D. Waldman, *Nor By Power* (New York: International Universities Press, 1953), 55-56; Cohen, op.cit., 174-175; and Geismar, Maxwell, ed. *Unfinished Business: James N. Rosenberg Papers* (Mamaroneck, NY: Vincent Marasia Press, 1967), 102-103; Haim Genizi, "James G. McDonald: High Commissioner for Refugees, 1933-1935," *Wiener Library Bulletin* XXX (1977), New Series Nos. 43/44, 40-52; Richard Breitman, Barbara McDonald Stewart, and Severin Hochberg, eds. *Advocate for the Doomed: The Diaries and Papers of James G. McDonald 1932-1935* (Bloomington and Indianapolis: Indiana University Press, 2007), 88-89, 110-111, 122-123.

257 "Hoover Mentioned to Aid Reich Exiles," NYT, 29 September 1933, 11; Breitman et al, 126-128, 133-135.

258 Stephen H. Norwood, *The Third Reich in the Ivory Tower: Complicity and Conflict on American Campuses* (New York: Cambridge University Press, 2009), 38, 112.

259 Wise to Brandeis, 6 October 1936, File: Brandeis, Louis D., SSW-AJHS.

260 Anne O'Hare McCormick, "Hitler Seeks Jobs for All Germans," NYT, 10 July 1933, 1.

261 Guido Enderis, "Highland Retreat Sees History Made," NYT, 18 September 1938, 4:5.

262 John Lukacs, "Herbert Hoover Meets Adolf Hitler," *The American Scholar*, Spring 1993, 235-238; Smith, 253-255; "Hoover Blunt to Hitler on Nazism; Says Progress Demands Liberty," NYT, 9 March 1938, 1; "Hoover Reaffirms Faith in Freedom," NYT, 10 March 1938, 15; "Hoover Arrives Here," NYT, 29 March 1938, 10.

263 G.E.R. Gedye, "Nazi Terrorism in Austria Bared; Vienna Arrests Are Put at 34,000," NYT, 3 April 1938, 1.

264 "Foreign Polices for America - New York City, March 31, 1938," in Herbert C. Hoover, *Addresses Upon the American Road* (Stanford, CA: Stanford University Press, 1951), 308-334. In a second address a week later, in San Francisco ("Challenge to Liberty, 1938 - San Francisco, California, April 8, 1938," ibid.), Hoover repeated his condemnation of the "upsurge of abhorrent brutality from which the Jews are helpless victims."

265 V. O. Key Jr., *Public Opinion and American Democracy* (New York: Alfred A. Knopf, 1961), 277; "Washington Sees Similarity Between Lindbergh's and Berlin's Anti-Jewish Propaganda," JTA, 14 September 1941, 1; "Hoover Sees Peril of 'Five Horsemen'," NYT, 24 February 1939, 1; "Text of Hoover Speech Opposing Convoying Ships to Britain," NYT, 12 May 1941, 4; "Hoover Says Wait Till Hitler Loses," NYT, 17 September 1941, 1; Melvin I. Urofsky, *A Voice That Spoke for Justice: The Life and Times of Stephen S. Wise*. (Albany, NY: State University of New York Press, 1982), 308-311.

266 "Peace Rally Hears Attack on Clergy," NYT, 5 April 1938, 11; "Cardinal Hayes Prays for Franco," *Montreal Gazette*, 24 March 1938, 1; Norwood, 208; Wise to Korn, 1 September 1939, in Voss, 234; Urofsky, 308-311; Travis Jacobs and Beatrice Berle, eds., *Navigating the Rapids: The Diaries of Adolf Berle* (New York: Houghton Mifflin, 1973), 342.

267 "U.S. 'Hands-Off' Policy in Internal Affairs of Other Nations Stressed by Welles," JTA, 25 May 1938, 4. State Department officials attributed the pressure to what they called "certain Congressmen with metropolitan constituencies." See Wyman, *Paper Walls*, 44.

268 Wyman, *Paper Walls*, 50.

269 Henry L. Feingold, *The Politics of Rescue: The Roosevelt Administration and the Holocaust 1938-1945* (New Brunswick, NJ: Rutgers University Press, 1979), 121.

270 Roosevelt to Ickes, 18 December 1940, President's Official File 3186, Franklin D. Roosevelt Library, Hyde Park, NY (hereafter FDRL); "Alaska Colonization Essential for National Defense, Ickes Tells Senate

Group," JTA, 14 May 1940, 1-2; Harold L. Ickes, *The Secret Diary of Harold L. Ickes, Volume 3: The Lowering Clouds 1939-1941* (New York: Simon and Schuster, 1954), 56-57; Henry L. Feingold, "Roosevelt and the Resettlement Question," in *Rescue Attempts During the Holocaust: Proceedings of the Second Yad Vashem International Historical Conference*, April 1974 (Jerusalem: Yad Vashem, 1977), 123-181.

Prior to the onset of the Holocaust, some American Zionist leaders were likewise skeptical about the ability of German Jewish refugees to build a new life in some of the proposed havens. "Must a human being, because he is a Jew, be the guinea pig of each experiment in colonization?," Zionist Organization of America president Solomon Goldman asked in his address to the October 1939 Hadassah national convention. "I ask, must a Jew who has a standard of living, a family attachment, a cultural heritage, a religious tradition, a cultivated taste for the museum, the theater, the opera, must he, solely because he is a Jew, abandon it all for strips of sand and swamp in Africa and South America which the natives in those parts of the world, have thus far shunned?" (Proceedings: 25th Annual Convention of Hadassah, The Women's Zionist Organization - October 24 to 29, 1939, Hotel Astor, New York City," 14, Hadassah Archives, New York City.

271 Baruch to Strauss, 31 January 1939, File: February, Box 42, LLS.

272 Herbert Hoover, "Memorandum [on Africa plan]," undated [1939], File: Hoover, Herbert, Box 67, LLS.

273 Strauss, *Men and Decisions*, 113-116; "Hoover Envisions Refuge to 10 Million," NYT, 12 February 1940, 3; Lewis Strauss, untitled memo to Hoover, 22 August 1939, File: "Strauss, Lewis," PPI, HHPL.

274 Wyman, *Paper Walls*, 73.

275 "Hoover Protests Brutality in Reich," NYT, 14 November 1938, 11; "Texts of the Protests by Leaders in U.S. Against Reich Persecution," NYT, 15 November 1938, 4; Smith, 265.

276 "Hoover Backs Bill to Waive Quota Act for Reich Children," 23 April 1939, NYT, 1; Johnson to Kenworthy, 17 May 1939, Kenworthy to Johnson, 19 May 1939, Johnson to Kenworthy, 2 June 1939, and Johnson to Inglis, 20 June 1939 and 27 July 1939, all in Folder 4: "Winthrop Johnson - Los Angeles California," Box 1, Marion E. Kenworthy Papers (hereafter MEK), AJHS.

277 Minutes of the Fourteenth Meeting of the President's Advisory Committee on Political Refugees - Friday, December 23, 1938, at 12:30 P.M.," American Jewish Committee Papers, YIVO Institute, New York City; Richard Breitman, Barbara McDonald Stewart, and Severin Hochberg, eds., *Refugees and Rescue: The Diaries and Papers of James G. McDonald 1935-1945* (Bloomington and Indianapolis: Indiana University Press, 2009), 160.

278 Jon Meacham, *Franklin and Winston: An Intimate Portrait of an Epic Friendship* (New York: Random House, 2003), 32.

279 Feingold, 50; Wyman, *Paper Walls*, 97; Judith Tydor Baumel, *Unfulfilled Promise: Rescue and Resettlement of Jewish Refugee Children in the United States, 1934–1945* (Juneau, AK: The Deli Press, 1990), 145.

280 William R. Perl, *The Four-Front War* (New York: Crown, 1978), 236-240. Perl was a central figure, along with Ben-Horin, in the refugee-smuggling network that organized the voyage of the *Parita* and other ships during 1937-1940, bringing an estimated 20,000 European Jews to Palestine in defiance of the British.

281 "Nazis Machine-Gun All Jews on Town Near Warsaw, Refugees Report," JTA, 8 December 1939, 1; "Nazis Machine-Gun 400 Jews in Polish Town on Sniping Charge" JTA, 14 December 1939, 1; "Thousands of Jews in a New Exodus from Vienna to Poland," *San Francisco Chronicle,* 3 November 1939, 7.

282 Smith, 295-298. The dispute between Hoover and the White House regarding food shipments continued throughout the war. See, for example, "White House Denies Aiding Hoover Drive," *PM,* 8 February 1944, 5.

283 "Thousands of Bukovina Jews Evacuated Into Soviet Interior," JTA, 8 July 1941, 1; "Thousands of Jews Killed by Nazi Bands in Zhitomir and Berditchev," JTA, 9 July 1941, 1; "Thousands of Jews Among Civilians Killed in Nazi-Soviet War; 500 Executed in Lublin," JTA, 10 July 1941, 1; "Nazis Force Jews in Minsk District to Dig Their Own Graves," JTA, 12 August 1941, 1; Alex Grobman, "What Did They

Know? The American Jewish Press and the Holocaust, 1 September 1939-17 December 1942," AJH 68 (March 1979), 342-43. The JTA dispatch on the killings in Kiev referred to the massacre that took place in the Babi Yar ravine on September 29-30, 1941. An estimated 34,000 Jews were slaughtered on those two days, and additional thousands were killed in the ravine during subsequent months.

284 "Slaying of Jews in Galicia Depicted," NYT, 26 October 1941, 5.

285 "What Jews Must Remember" (editorial), *Congress Weekly* [hereafter CW], 1 May 1942, 3; "Accounts of Nazi Pogroms in Occupied White Russia Related at Moscow Jewish Rally," JTA, 25 May 1942, 3. The text of the June 1942 report was reprinted in Yehuda Bauer, "When Did They Know," *Midstream* 14 (April 1968), 57-58.

286 Walter Laqueur, *The Terrible Secret: Suppression of the Truth about Hitler's 'Final Solution'* (Boston: Little Brown, 1980).

287 Wise to Frankfurter, 16 September 1942, Box 109, SSW-AJHS; James McDonald, "Himmler Program Kills Polish Jews," NYT, 25 November 1942, 10.

288 Wise to Roosevelt, 2 December 1942, File: Correspondence Between FDR and Wise, 1929-1945, SSW-AJHS; Wise to Niles, 9 December 1942, Correspondence File, Stephen S. Wise Collection, American Jewish Archives [hereafter SSW-AJA], Cincinnati.

289 Adolph Held, "Report on the Visit to the President," 8 December 1942, Part 3, Section 1, #15, Jewish Labor Committee Archives, text reprinted in David S. Wyman, ed., *America and the Holocaust - Volume 2: The Struggle for Rescue Action* (New York: Garland, 1990), 72-74.

290 Cited in Wyman, *Paper Walls*, 147.

291 Minutes of the Jewish Agency executive meeting, 28 September 1944, 10, Central Zionist Archives, Jerusalem [hereafter CZA].

292 David S. Wyman, *The Abandonment of the Jews: America and the Holocaust, 1941-1945* (New York: Pantheon, 1984), 75.

293 Reams to Atherton and Hickerson, 9 December 1942, 740.00116 European War/694, RSD.

294 Laurel Leff, *Buried by* The Times: *The Holocaust and America's Most Important Newspaper* (New York: Cambridge University Press, 2005).

295 R.W. Apple, Jr., "The Jewish Voter In New York's Poll," NYT, 6 April 1976, 5.

296 Halifax to Eden, 25 May 1943, FO 317/35035, PRO.

297 Akzin to The Presidency, 13 May 1940, File 5-gimel/4/1/, Metzudat Ze'ev (Jabotinsky Institute) [hereafter MZ], Tel Aviv; Akzin to The Presidency, 4 June 1940, File 5-gimel/4/1, MZ; Akzin to The Presidency, 5 June 1940, File 5-gimel/4/1, MZ; Akzin to Nye, 22 June 1940, File 13/4/5-gimel, MZ; Gerald P. Nye, "America, Jewry and the War," *American Jewish Chronicle*, June 1940, 5-6.

298 Hoover to Ben-Horin, 25 May 1943 and 8 June 1943, Ben-Horin, Eliahu, PPI, HHPL; Ben-Horin to Landon, 28 July 1943, 20 August 1943, and 18 September 1943, and Landon to Ben-Horin, 17 August 1943 Landon Papers, Kansas State Historical Society-Topeka; Landon to Ben-Horin, 30 July 1943, Eliahu Ben-Horin Collection [hereafter EBC], MZ; NYT, 4 October 1943, 12; Netanyahu interview, 25 June 1997.

299 "Massacred by Foe, Ignored by Friend, a People Appeals to the Conscience of America" (advertisement), NYT, 23 February 1943, 13; "Mr. Churchill, Drop the Mandate!" (advertisement), NYT, 18 May 1943, 15; Wise to Goldmann, 4 August 1943, Box 109, SSW-AJHS; Foreign Relations of the United States - Diplomatic Papers: Volume 4, 1943 (Washington, D.C.: Government Printing Office, 1969), 802-3; Murray to Hall, 16 August 1943 and 17 August 1943, and Murray to Long, 25 October 1944, 867N.01/1908, RSD; Morgenthau-Cohen-Weisgal talk, 4 August 1943, Z5/387, CZA; and Goldmann to Wise, 5 August 1943 and 8 August 1943, Z5/1216, CZA, cited in Penkower, *The Holocaust and Israel Reborn*, 159, 162, and 173 n.39.

300 Goldmann to Gruenbaum, 5 April 1943, File: z6/302, Yitzhak Gruenbaum Papers, CZA.

301 Rabinowitz to Jonah Wise, 2 July 1943, File: Emergency Committee to Save the Jewish People of Europe, First Emergency Conference to Save the Jewish People of Europe - 2/1/11-chet, Bergson Group Collections [hereafter BGC], MZ; Wyman, *Abandonment*, 115-118; "20,000 at Garden in Appeal or Jews Under Heel of Nazi," Boston Herald, 3 May 1943, 1. Berle's message is cited in Monty Noam Penkower, *The Jews Were Expendable: Free World Diplomacy and the Holocaust* (Urbana and Chicago: University of Illinois Press, 1983), 330, n37.

302 "Bermuda Conferees Agree to Another Conference," *Independent Jewish Press Service*, 30 April 1943, 3; "Failure in Bermuda" (editorial), *Opinion*, May 1943, 4; "The Mockery at Bermuda," address by Dr. Israel Goldstein, April 28, 1943, A364/235, 2, Israel Goldstein Papers [hereafter IGP], CZA; "Minutes of the Meeting of the Joint Emergency Committee for European Jewish Affairs, May 24, 1943," File: Joint Emergency Committee for European Jewish Affairs, Box 8, American Jewish Committee Papers [hereafter AJCP], YIVO Institute, New York City.

303 Wyman and Medoff, *A Race Against Death*, 74.

304 For more on the controversies that the Bergson ads often ignited, see Ben Hecht, *A Child of the Century* (New York: Scribner's, 1954), 565, and Wyman and Medoff, *A Race Against Death*, 65–69, 241, n16.

305 Murray Everett, "Inside and Out," *The New Leader*, 8 April 1944, 10; Halifax to Eden, 13 January 1943 and 15 January 1943, FO 371/35031, PRO; Wyman and Medoff, *Race Against Death*, 139.

306 *Bulletin* [of the 2 June 1943 meeting], File: Emergency Committee to Save the Jewish People of Europe - First Emergency Conference to Save the Jewish People of Europe - 2/1/11-chet, BGC, MZ.

307 Wise to Margaret Lehand, 23 September 1938, PPF 3292, FDRL; Memo, Wise to Lipsky and Shultz, 7 June 1938, File: American Jewish Congress, SSW-AJHS; Wise to Neumann, 13 October 1936, in Voss, 217; Geoffrey Wigoder and Menahem Kaufman interview of Dr. Israel Goldstein, 29 May 1977, 18, in File: Israel Goldstein, Box 1, Melvin I. Urofsky Papers, AJHS; Monty Noam Penkower, "Ben-Gurion, Silver, and the 1941 UPA National Conference for Palestine: A Turning Point in American Zionist History," AJH 69 (September 1979), 66-78.

308 Vandenberg's statement appears in an Editor's Note appended to Melvin I. Urofsky, "Stephen S. Wise in Historical Perspective," *The American Zionist* 44 (May 1974), 36; Wise to Roosevelt, 28 August 1936, PPF 3292, FDRL.

309 The list also included "Moslem leader Husseini," although it is not clear which Husseini they had in mind. There were, in the end, no Muslim speakers at the event.

310 Perlzweig to Wise, 16 June 1943, File: Emergency Committee to Save the Jewish People of Europe - First Emergency Conference to Save the Jewish People of Europe - 2/1/11-chet, BGC, MZ; Hyman to Pickett, 13 July 1943, Refugee Services File 1943, Committees and Organizations, American Jewish Joint Distribution Committee (reprinted in Wyman, *Documents*, 9); Tucker to Wise, 17 June 1943, File: Proskauer Emergency Committee 1943, AJCP; Bromfield to Taylor, 21 June 1943, Taylor to Welles, 23 June 1943, Welles to Taylor, 23 June 1943, and Taylor to Bromfield, 24 June 1943, File: Correspondence 1938-1954, Box 5, Myron C. Taylor Papers, FDRL.

311 M.J. Nurenberger interview with Hillel Kook, undated, 35-36, File: Nurenberger Interviews, Bergson Group Papers, The David S. Wyman Institute for Holocaust Studies, Washington, D.C.

312 Wyman and Medoff, *Race Against Death*, 125-126; *News from the Committee for a Jewish Army*, 21 June 1943, File: Committee for a Jewish Army - New York: Public Relations, Advertisements and Publicity, Correspondence - 9/2 - 3-chet, BGC.

313 "Emergency Conference to Save the Jews of Europe" (news release), 24 June 1943, File: Comittee for a Jewish Army - New York: Public Relations, Advertisements and Publicity, Correspondence - 9/2 - 3-chet, BGC, MZ; "5 Senators Sign Statement Urging Aid to Jews," Independent Jewish Press Service, 16 July 1943, 2; "Plans Offered to Save 4 Million Jews," *PM*, 21 July 1943, 3.

314 "Plans Offered to Save 4 Million Jews," *PM*, 21 July 1943, 5; "Save Jews Now, Conference Demands," *New York Post* [hereafter NYP], 21 July 1943, 7; "Quick Aid is Asked for Europe's Jews," NYT, 21 July 1943, 8; "Allied Agency To Save Jews in Europe Urged," *New York Herald Tribune* [hereafter NYHT], 21 July 1943, 7.

315 "Jews' Rescue Seen in Red Cross Help," NYT 22, July 1943, 11; "Reprisal Warning Drafted To Save Jews in Europe," *PM*, 22 July 1943, 10.

316 "Jews' Rescue Seen in Red Cross Help," NYT 22, July 1943, 11; "Plan is Outlined for Feeding Jews," NYT, 23 July 1943, 14.

317 Draft resolution, File: Panel on Public Opinion, Emergency Conference to Save the Jewish People of Europe, F25/651, CZA; "Roosevelt's Aid Asked to Save Jews in Europe," NYHT, 22 July 1943, 8; "Christian Churches Get Appeal to Save Jews," NYHT, 24 July 1943, 5; "Ships Seen Ample for Rescuing Jews," NYT, 24 July 1943, 13.

318 Hull to Lerner, 22 July 1943, OF 76-C, FDRL; Roosevelt to Lerner, 22 July 1943, OF 76-C, FDRL.

319 "The Emergency Conference" (internal memo, possibly authored by Eri Jabotinsky), 27 July 1943, File: First Emergency Conference to Save the Jewish People of Europe, 2/1/11-chet, BGC; President Pledges Aid to Save Jews," NYT, 26 July 1943, 19; "Hoover Urges Central African Jewish Refuge," NYT, 26 July 1943, 13; "Hoover Asks Haven For Jews," NYP, 26 July 1943, 7.

320 Samuel Grafton, "I'd Rather Be Right," NYP, 22 July 1943, 26.

321 Wise to Weizmann, 23 July 1943, Box 109, SSW-AJHS; Wise to Frankfurter, 14 October 1942, Box 109, SSW-AJHS; "U.S. Urges England to Bar Discussions on Palestine for the Duration, Pearson Reports," JTA, 10 August 1943, 1; "Celler Sees Palestine Hopes Dashed," PM, 13 August 1943, 8; "State Dept. Tries to Keep Jews Out of Palestine, Celler Charges," PM, 19 August 1943, 1; "Roosevelt Asked to Consult with Curchill in Quebec on the Palestine Question," JTA, 20 August 1943, 1; "Shape of Things to Come" (editorial), IJPS, 20 August 1943, 1-A; Baruch Rabinowitz, Unpublished Autobiography, 121-122, DSWIHS; Ben-Ami to Bergson, 13 August 1943, File: Committee for a Jewish Army - New York: Formation of a Free Palestine Committee and American League for a Free Palestine, Sept. 1943-1944," 21/3/3, BGC; Monty N. Penkower, "The 1943 Joint Anglo-American Statement on Palestine," in Melvin I. Urofsky, ed., Herzl Year Book VIII - Essays in American Zionism (New York: Herzl Press, 1978) 212-241.

322 Wise to Rosenman, 24 August 1943, File: Wise, Stephen S., Box 4, Samuel Rosenman Papers, AJHS.

323 "Conference Hears Allies Accused of Stalling on Jews," *PM*, 31 August 1943, 10; "United Nations Delay On Aid Upsets Jews," *PM*, 3 September 1943, 9; "Jews Pay Tribute to Hitler's Victims; Impressive Ceremony Held at Opening of National Gathering," NYT, 30 August, 1943, 6; "Rescue at Once of Europe's Jews Demanded at Conference Here," NYT, 31 August, 1943, 1; "Jewish Conferees Assail Rival Plan, Meeting here Call Statement," NYT, 1 September 1943, 12; "Opening of Palestine as Homeland Demanded by Jewish Conference," NYT, 2 September 1943, 1; "Immediate Rescue of Jews is Urged, Conference Asks That as Many as Possible Be Assisted From Nazi Territory," NYT, 3 September 1943, 13; "Refugees and the Future," NYT, 4 September 1943, 2-E.

324 Barbour to Bergson, 13 October 1943, File: First Emergency Committee to Save the Jewish People of Europe - Jabotinsky, Eri, Correspondence - 8/10/11-chet, BGC; "Joint Action of U.S. Political Organizations," Circular Letter #210 - 14 September 1943, File: First Emergency Committee to Save the Jewish People of Europe - Jabotinsky, Eri, Correspondence - 8/10/11-chet, BGC; "Democratic and Republican Parties Urge Congress to Admit European Jews," JTA, 12 September 1943, 1; "Asylum in America" (editorial), CW, 24 September 1943, 4."Senate Immigration Committee to Study Proposal to Admit Religious Refugees, JTA," 17 October, 1943, 3; "Revival of Conscience" (editorial), JF, November 1943, 3; "It Can Be Done!" (advertisement), NYT, 2 October 1943, 18.

325 Sheldon M. Neuringer, "American Jewry and United States Immigration Policy, 1881–1953" (Ph.D. dissertation, University of Wisconsin, 1969), 246-247; *Morgenthau Diaries*, 15 January 1944, 694/88-90, 94-97.

326 See "Establishment of a Commission to Effectuate the Rescue of the Jewish People of Europe," in *Problems of World War II and Its Aftermath - Part 2: The Palestine Question, Problems of Postwar Europe* (Washington, D.C.: Government Printing Office, 1976), 15-249 (La Guardia's testimony is pp. 147-156; Wise's is pp. 217-243); Rogers to Goldstein, Monsky, and Wise, 8 February 1944, A364/1954, IGP.

327 *Problems of World War II*, 171; Frederick R. Barkley, "580,000 Refugees Admitted to United States in Decade," NYT, 11 December 1943, 1; "Statement by the Commission on Rescue of the American Jewish Conference," 27 December 1943, 364/152, IGP; Wyman, *The Abandonment of the Jews*, 197-98.

328 Cited in Wyman, *The Abandonment of the Jews*, 99.

329 Rafael Medoff, *Blowing the Whistle on Genocide: Josiah E. DuBois, Jr. and the Struggle for a U.S. Response to the Holocaust* (West Lafayette, IN: Purdue University Press, 2009), chapters 3 and 4.

330 *Congressional Record - Senate*, 78th Congress, 1st Session, 9305.

331 Stephen S. Wise, "As I See It: 'The Jewish Vote'," *Opinion*, November 1932, 15; "Urges Synagogue to Reunite Jews," NYT, 24 June 1933, 6; "Jewish Vote Held Myth," NYT, 8 August 1937, 25.

332 *Morgenthau Diaries*, 19 December 1943, 688II, 106-130, FDRL.

333 Eri Jabotinsky, untitled memorandum, 9 December 1943, File: Emergency Committee to Save the Jewish People of Europe, Serial-Jabotinsky, Eri, 1943-1945, 8/10/11, BGC. The data from the "census" to which Jabotinsky referred does not appear to have survived.

334 Ibid.

335 "Zivyon," *Forverts*, 16 October 1943, 6.

336 B.Z. Goldberg, "Does the Roosevelt Administration Have the Jews in its Vest Pocket?," translated in *The Answer*, January 1944, 17-18.

337 "Minutes of Meeting held Tuesday, August 10, 1943, at 3:00 P.M., at the Congress Offices," File: Joint Emergency Committee for European Jewish Affairs, Box 8, AJCA.

338 Nahum Goldmann, untitled report on meetings with Sol Bloom (11 October 1943), and Felix Frankfurter, Emanuel Celler, Samuel Rosenman, and Peter Bergson (12 October 1943), Z5/666, CZA.

339 Celler to McIntyre, undated "Confidential" memo, File: Israel (Palestine) Correspondence, 1930-1946, Emanuel Celler Papers, Library of Congress. The memo itself is not dated but almost certainly was composed in early October 1943. It includes a reference to the Republican leadership's Makinac Island conference, which was held 23-25 September 1943; in addition, Nahum Goldmann's untitled report (op.cit.), in an entry for 12 October 1943, mentions that Celler recently with Hull.

340 *Morgenthau Diaries*, 15 January 1944, 694/88-90, 94-97, FDRL.

341 John L. Blum, *The Price of Vision: The Diaries of Henry A. Wallace, 1942-1946* (Boston: Houghton Mifflin 1973), 211.

342 Blum, 265; "Message from Wendell L. Willkie to Balfour Meeting, Carnegie Hall, November 1, 1943," A364/235, IGP.

343 Medoff, *Blowing the Whistle on Genocide*, 53-64; Executive Order 9417, *Federal Register 9*, 26 January 1944, 935-36; Fred L. Israel, ed., *The War Diary of Breckinridge Long* (Lincoln, NE: University of Nebraska Press, 1966), 336-337.

344 *Morgenthau Diaries* 696/183-192, FDRL.

345 Samuel Grafton, "I'd Rather Be Right," NYP, 22 July 1943, 26.

346 Wyman, *The Abandonment of the Jews*, 66, 285. The Washington, D.C. correspondent for the Independent Jewish Press Service had a somewhat similar take on the implications of the president's action: "The President's order creating the War Refugee Board showed that the President did not share Mr. Long's opinion on the [issue of rescue]," he contended. (Arnold Levin, "Heard in the Lobbies: Capitol Line," IJPS, 19 May 1944, 2F)

347 "The Task of Rescue" (editorial), *Congress Weekly* 11:5 (11 February 1944), 3; "Jewish Organizations Acclaim Roosevelt's Establishment of a Refugee Board," JTA, 24 January 1944, 3.

348 "Why State Dept. Holds Up Repeal of Nuremberg Laws," *PM*, 18 January 1943, 18; "Jewish Groups Charge Nazi Laws Stay in North Africa," *Los Angeles Times*, 15 February 1943, 9; "Jewish Committee, Locked Out of Bermuda Parley, Offers 12-Point Program For Rescue of Europe's Enslaved Jews; Suggests British Open Up Palestine," *PM*, 19 April 1943, 14-15; Alexander H. Uhl, "Jews Disappointed In

Refugee Parley," 16 April 1943, 6; "Hadassah President Hopes Bermuda Conference 'Will Not Turn Out to be a Mockery,'" JTA, 13 April 1943, 3; Israel Goldstein, "Bermuda Failure," CW 10 (7 May 1943), 9; "To 5,000,000 Jews in the Nazi Death-Trap Bermuda Was a 'Cruel Mockery'" (advertisement), NYT, 4 May 1943, 17; "Bermuda Conferees Agree To Another Conference," *Baltimore Jewish Times* [hereafter BJT], 7 May 1943, 9; "Celler Sees Palestine Hopes Dashed," PM, 13 August 1943, 8

349 "Shipping For Refugees" (editorial), BJT, 14 May 1943, 3; "How to Continue Our Traditional Foreign Policy: Radio Address to be Delivered by Congressman Samuel Dickstein - April 17, 1944, 11:30 P.M., Station WOL, Washington, D.C.," F39/54, p.4, CZA; "The Bermuda Affair" (editorial), in the World Jewish Congress's "Jewish Comment" section of *Congress Weekly*, CW 10 (14 May 1943), 13; "Is President Roosevelt Pricked by His Conscience?," *The Jewish Forum* (editorial), July 1943, 105; "Last Chance for Rescue" (editorial), *Jewish Frontier*, August 1944, 4; "Horthy Promises Leniency" (editorial), *National Jewish Ledger* [hereafter NJL], 28 July 1944, 6.

350 "Congress Must Act On the Palestine Resolution!" (advertisement), *The New Republic* [hereafter TNR] 110 (27 March 1944), 408-409; "The Bogey of 'Military Expediency' Exposed" (advertisement), NYP, 14 March 1944, 39.

351 Blum, 313.

352 Raphael, 100-101; Herbert Parzen, "The Roosevelt Palestine Policy, 1943-1945," AJA 25 (April 1974), 43-45; Blum, 313.

353 "Where Rescue Is Yet Possible" (editorial), CW, 31 March 1944, 5-6.

354 "Free Immigration of Jews into Palestine Demanded by 20,000 at Madison Square Garden Rally," JTA, 22 March 1944, 1; "Two Meetings Hear Pleas For Aid to Jews Abroad," P.M., 8 April 1944, 12; "Procession to City Hall, Work Stoppage Mark Anniversary of Warsaw Ghetto Battle," JTA, 20 April 1944, 2; "Abstract of Address by Dr. Abba Hillel Silver, of Cleveland, Ohio, delivered at the meeting of the United Jewish Appeal, Tuesday, June 20, 1944," File: F39/54, 2-3, American Zionist Emergency Council Papers [hereafter AZEC], CZA.

355 "Opposition of War Dept. to Palestine Resolution Not Due to Protests of Arab States," JTA, 8 March 1944, 2; "This too is Dunkirk...Mr. Winston Churchill" (advertisement), TNR 110 (24 April 1944), 546; "Forget Politics--Open the Doors of Palestine!," TNR 110 (10 April 1944), 512; "In the Name of Justice and Humanity" (advertisement), *Los Angeles Daily News*, 8 May 1944, 20; "25 Square Miles--or 2,000,000 Lives...Which Shall It Be?" (advertisement), NYP, 15 May 1944, 18-19; "Americans Answer a Call for Life and Liberation" (advertisement), TNR 110 (19 June 1944), 812-813; Arnold Levin, "Heard in the Lobbies: Rumors About Willkie," IJPS, 19 May 1944, 1-E; Text of remarks by Clare Booth Luce, Hotel Commodore, New York City, 23 April 1944, File 16-gimel/6, New Zionist Organization of America Papers [hereafter NZOA], MZ; "Clare Booth Luce Supports Free Ports," IJPS, 12 May 1944, 1; "Roosevelt Receives First Report on Activities of War Refugee Board in Rescuing Jews," JTA, 12 May 1944, 2.

356 "The Shutting of a Door"(editorial), PM, 31 March 1944, 3; "United States Charged with Failure to Fulfill Promise to Aid Jews in Europe," JTA, 27 April 1944; "Scores Diplomats' Stand on Refugees," IJPS May 22, 10; "F.D.R. Supports Palestine Partition, Mowrer Charges," IJPS, May 22, 8; "Urges Public Pressure to Have F.D.R. Act on Rescue Camps Here," IJPS, 9 June 1944, 2.

357 Joseph Levy, "Jews in Hungary Fear Annihilation," NYT, 10 May 1944, 5; Joseph Levy, "Savage Bows Hit Jews in Hungary," NYT, 18 May 1944, 5; "Admission of 1,000 Refugees to United States is Not Enough, House is Told," JTA, 12 June 1944, 2; Marie Syrkin, "Free Port," *Jewish Frontier* 7 (July 1944), 6-8; "What They Are Saying: 'Token Rescue'," IJPS, 23 June 1944, 1-G; "Polish-Jewish Relations" (editorial), NJL, 23 June 1944, 6; "Hungary Plans Jewish Extermination," in the World Jewish Congress's "Jewish Comment" section of CW 11:20 (26 May 1944), 10; "Six Trains Carry Deported Jews from Hungary to Extermination Camp in Poland," JTA, 20 June 1944, 1; "100,000 Hungarian Jews Have Been Executed in Polish Death Camp, Underground Reports." JTA, 26 June 1944, 1.

358 The "vote catcher" remark is cited in Monty Noam Penkower, *Decision on Palestine Deferred: America, Britain and Wartime Diplomacy 1939-1945* (London: Frank Cass, 2002), 281.

359 "Republican Palestine Plank," *NZOA Bulletin* No. 2 (6 July 1944), 16-gimel/1, NZOA, MZ; Netanyahu to Klinger, 26 July 1944, 16-gimel/4, BGC, MZ; Mendelsohn telegram to Mirelman, 16-gimel/11, BGC, MZ; Netanyahu to Taft, 22 June 1944, 16-gimel/3, NZOA, MZ; Netanyahu to Klinger, 26 July 1944, 16-gimel/4, NZOA, MZ; Netanyahu to Sokolsky, 21 June 1944, 6/16-gimel, NZOA, MZ; Netanyahu interview with Rafael Medoff, 25 June 1997.

360 See, for example, Clare Boothe Luce, "Memorandum re Peace," 2 July 1943, File: Roosevelt, F.D., Box 599, 5, Clare Boothe Luce Papers [hereafter CBL], Library of Congress [hereafter LOC], Washington, D.C..

361 Willis Birchman, "Faces and Facts: Clare Boothe Luce or beauty goes to Washington," *New Haven Register*, 30 May 1943, 5. FDR made the remark in a private conversation with Vice President Henry Wallace and others on October 15, 1942; Wallace noted it in his diary. See Blum, 122.

362 Undated and untitled speech beginning, "Some weeks ago I was introduced to Pierre van Paassen...," File: Palestine, Box 599, 1, CBL.

363 Clare Boothe Luce, "Negro: Answers to Questions," undated (apparently 1944), File: Statements - 1944, Box 593, CBL, LOC, 3-4.

364 Pierre van Paassen, *The Forgotten Ally* (New York: Dial Press, 1943); "Massacred by Foe, Ignored by Friend, a People Appeals to the Conscience of America" (advertisement), NYT, 23 February 1943, 13; Clare Boothe Luce, "Under a National Flag," *Zionews* IV: 31-32 (September-October 1943), 12; Clare Boothe Luce, untitled speech (23 April 1944), File: 16-gimel/6, NZOA, MZ. In a tragically ironic twist, Mrs. Luce's only daughter, Ann, was killed in an automobile accident with a German Jewish refugee in California in January 1944. See Andrew R. Heinze, "Clare Boothe Luce and the Jews: A Chapter from the Catholic-Jewish Disputation of Postwar America," AJH 88 (September 200o), 372-373.

365 Netanyahu to Luce, 25 April 1944, File: 16-gimel/6, MZ; Mendelsohn to Luce, 26 April 1944, File: 16-gimel/6, NZOA, MZ.

366 Hoover to Luce, 19 June 1944 and 8 November 1944, File: Herbert Hoover, Box 425, CBL, LOC; Morano (for Luce) to Mendelsohn, 27 April 1944, File: 16-gimel/6, NZOA MZ; Hess (for Netanyahu) to Luce, 9 May 1944, File: 16-gimel/6, NZOA MZ; Netanyahu interview with Rafael Medoff, 25 June 1997.

367 Netanyahu to Sokolsky, 21 June 1944, File: 6/16-gimel, NZOA, MZ.

368 Zvi Ganin, "Activism versus Moderation: The Conflict between Abba Hillel Silver and Stephen Wise during the 1940s," *Studies in Zionism* 5:1 (Spring 1984), 76-77; Marc Lee Raphael, *Abba Hillel Silver: A Profile in American Judaism* (New York: Homes & Meier, 1989), 98-101; Samuel Halperin, *The Political World of American Zionism* (Detroit: Wayne State University Press, 1961), 271. Silver and his camp also believed that securing pro-Zionist planks in the two parties' platforms would, in turn, help bring about passage of the Taft resolution. (Feuer to Silver, 24 March 1944, File F39/24, AZEC, CZA.)

369 Marc Lee Raphael, *Abba Hillel Silver: A Profile in American Judaism* (New York: Homes & Meier, 1989), 112; Ganin, 77-78; Netanyahu interview, 25 June 1997; "Republican Palestine Plank," *NZOA Bulletin* II (6 July 1944) 1; Brewster to Mendelsohn, 11 July 1944, File: 16-gimel/3, MZ; Landon to Mendelsohn, 21 August 1944, File: 16-gimel/3, MZ; Wise to The President, 28 June 1944, File: Correspondence between FDR and Wise, 1929-1945, SSW-AJHS; "The Voice of America" (editorial), *Zionews* 2 (July 1944), 6.

370 "Republican Platform Calls for Opening Eretz Yisrael to Refugees" (Yiddish), *Morgen Zhurnal*, 28 June 1944, 1; "Republicans Adopt Platform" (Yiddish), *Forverts*, 28 June 1944, 1; "Dewey for President; Republicans for Eretz Yisrael; Candidates Make it Clear" (editorials, Yiddish), *Morgen Zhurnal*, 29 June 1944, 4; "Palestine Plank of Republicans Lauded by Silver; Hopes Democrats Will Follow Suit, 28 June 1944, JTA; "Zionist Emergency Council Issues Statements on Republican Plank on Palestine," 11 July 1944, JTA; "Republicans Endorse Jewish Commonwealth, Some Jewish Leaders Irked by Criticism of F.D.R.," 30 June 1944, IJPS; "Reports State Department 'Unhappy' Over Republicans' Plank," 3 July 1944, IJPS, 1; "Arabs 'Upset' By Palestine Plank," 3 July 1944, 2; "Celler Urges Democrats Adopt Strong Palestine, Rescue Resolutions," 3 July 1944, IJPS, 1-2; Arnold Levin, "Heard in the Lobbies: Palestine Plank," 21 July 1944, IJPS, 1-E.

371 Wise to the President, telegram, 7 July 1944, File 3292 - Stephen Wise, Personal Files, FDRL; Norman M. Littell, *My Roosevelt Years* (Seattle and Lond: University of Washington Press, 1987), 268-269 ; "The Democratic Party—Yours is the Responsibility!" (advertisement), *Chicago Daily News*, 18 July 1944, 17; "Spokesman for Zionism," *NZOA Bulletin*, 20 July 1944, I, 16-gimel/1, NZOA, MZ; Melvin I. Urofsky interview with Israel Goldstein, 9 December 1973, 30-31, in File: Israel Goldstein, Melvin I. Urofsky Papers, AJHS.

372 Wise to Roosevelt, 16 September 1944, File: Correspondence Between FDR and Wise, 1929-1945, SSW-AJHS; Wise to Rosenman, 26 September 1944, File: Rosenman, Samuel, SSW-AJHS; *Foreign Relations of the United States - Vol. V: 1944* (Washington, D.C.: U.S. Government Printing Office, 1965), 615; Penkower, *Decision on Palestine*, 314-315.

373 "An Insult to America" (editorial), CW 11 (3 November 1944), 3; Sharon R. Lowenstein, *Token Refuge: The Story of the Jewish Refugee Shelter at Oswego, 1944-1946* (Bloomington: Indiana University Press, 1986), 111-112; "Anti-Semitism in the Recent Election Campaign" (editorial), *The Reconstructionist* 10 (1 December 1944), 5.

374 Thomas remarks in the *Congressional Record*, 28 August 1944, 22.

375 Carl Hermann Voss, "The American Christian Palestine Committee," in Melvin I. Urofsky, ed. *Herzl Year Book - Volume VIII: Essays in American Zionism* (New York: Herzl Press, 1978), 242-262. Founded in 1932 as the American Palestine Committee, the group added "Christian" to its name after merging, in 1942, with the likeminded Christian Council for Palestine.

376 "Indignation Sweeps America," JTA, 14 November 1938, 3; Kenworthy to Winthrop, 16 June 1939, Box 1, Folder 4: "Winthrop Johnson—Los Angeles California," Marion E. Kenworthy Papers, AJHS; Gerald S. Berman, "Reaction to the Resettlement of World War II Refugees in Alaska," *Jewish Social Studies* 44 (Summer-Fall 1982), 271-282; Orlando W. Miller, "Jewish Refugees for Alaska 1933-1945," Western States Jewish History [hereafter WSJH] 36 (Fall 2003), 43-64; Idem., "Jewish Refugees for Alaska 1933-1945—Part II," WSJH 36 (Summer 2004), 338-352; Sharon Kay Smith, "Elbert D. Thomas and America's Response to the Holocaust," Ph.D. dissertation, Brigham Young University, 1992; Rabinowitz to Thomas, 26 July 1944, Folder: J-3 Jewish Literature, Box 80, Elbert Thomas Papers , Utah State Historical Society; Caitlin Carenen, "The American Christian Palestine Committee, the Holocaust, and Mainstream Protestant Zionism, 1938-1948," *Holocaust and Genocide Studies* 24 (Fall 2010), 273-296.

377 Ian J. Bickerton, "President Truman's Recognition of Israel," AJHQ 58 (December 1968), 188-189; Urofsky, *We Are One! American Jewry and Israel* (Garden City, NY: Doubleday, 1978), 62.

378 Van Paassen to Silver, 6 January 1945, A123/103, AZEC, CZA.

379 Foreign Office Minutes, 10 September 1945, FO 226/277, PRO.

380 Rosenman to Truman, 23 October 1945, cited in Michael J. Cohen, *Truman and Israel* (Berkeley, CA: University of California Press, 1990), 124; Michael J. Cohen, "The Genesis of the Anglo-American Committee on Palestine, November 1945: A Case Study in the Assertion of American Hegemony," *Historical Journal* 22 (1979), 186-207; Bevin to Halifax, 12 October 1945, FO 371/45381, PRO; Halifax to Foreign Office, 27 October 1945, FO 371/45382, PRO; Bartley Crum, *Behind the Silken Curtain: A Personal Account of Anglo-American Diplomacy in Palestine and the Middle East* (London: Victor Gollancz Ltd., 1947), 16.

381 Cited in Cohen, *Truman*, 54-55; Hague to Hannegan, 26 November 1945, Office File-Misc. 204, Harry S. Truman Papers [hereafter HSTP], Harry S. Truman Presidential Library, Independence, MO, cited in Bickerton, 191.

382 William A. Eddy, *FDR Meets Ibn Saud* (New York: American Friends of the Middle East, 1954), 37.

383 Ben-Horin to Hoover, 21 November 1945 with enclosure, Post Presidential Subjects [hereafter PPS]-Jewish-Zionist, HHH; "Hoover Suggests Sending Palestinian Arabs to Iraq" (Yiddish), *Der Tog*, 20 November 1945, 1; "Hoover's Plan for the Arab Problem" (editorial, Yiddish), *Morgen Zhurnal*, 21 November 1945, 8. Three years later, Israeli leaders tried to persuade Hoover to head a committee to promote the resettlement in Arab countries of the hundreds of thousands of Palestinian Arabs who fled

from newborn Israel during its 1948 War of Independence. But the former president, now 74 and preoccupied with his duties as chairman of the Truman administration's Commission on the Organization of the Executive Branch of the Government, had no appetite for diving into the labyrinth of Middle East policy and politics. For the full story of Hoover's Palestine initiative, see Rafael Medoff, "Herbert Hoover's Plan for Palestine: A Forgotten Episode in U.S. Middle East Diplomacy," AJH 79 (Summer 1990), 449-476.

384 Ruth Hershman, ed., *The American Jewish Conference: Proceedings of the Third Session: February 17-19, 1946 - Cleveland, Ohio* (New York: American Jewish Conference, 1946), 136, 138, 143, 233; "President Truman Joins With Britain in Blocking Jewish Freedom" (advertisement), NYP, 11 December 1945, 29; "Our Government is Following Britain in the Betrayal of the Jews" (advertisement), NYP, 15 May 1946, 39.

385 "The Proof of the Grand Mufti's War Crime" and "Confirm Mufti's Part in 'Kill All Jews' Plot," NYP, 11 February 1946, 38; "The Grand Mufti and His Nazi Pals," NYP, 11 April 1946, 30; Arthur Hurwich, "Documents Prove Mufti a War Criminal," 20 April 1946, 2; Edgar Ansel Mowrer, "What Was Mufti's Secret Power That Let Him Escape Trial?," NYP, 2 June 1946, 32; Id., "The Rise of Another Mass Murderer--Mufti's Career Rivals Hitler's," NYP, 3 June 1946, 2; Id., "Iraqi Revolt Led by Mufti Nearly Won the War for Hitler," NYP, 4 June 1946, 2; Id., "Hitler Built Up Mufti To Ready Arab Offensive," NYP 5, June 1946, 18; Id., "Allies Soft-Pedaled Mufti's Aid to Nazis to Appease Arabs," NYP, 6 June 1946, 32; Id., "Evidence Shows Mufti Inspired Jews' Murder," NYP, 8 June 1946, 5; Id., "Mufti Recruited Moslem SS To Help Nazis Beat Russia," NYP, 10 June 1946, 17; Id., "Evidence Shows Mufti Inspired Jews' Murder," NYP, 11 June 1946, 5; Id., "Nazis in Mideast Working With Arabs and Local Germans," NYP, 12 June 1946, 2; Id., "Official Documents Convict Mufti Of Complicity in 6,000,000 Murders," NYP, 13 June 1946, 2; "Allies Won't Try Mufti Now—Jackson," NYP, 18 June 1946, 2; Alexander Uhl, "Did Mufti Collaborate With Hitler? Here's the Proof," PM, 28 June 1946, 3; Eliahu Epstein, "Middle Eastern Munich," *The Nation* 162:10 (9 March 1946), 287-288; I.F. Stone, "The Case of the Mufti," *The Nation* 162:18 (4 May 1946), 526-527.

386 Wise to Byrnes, 13 December 1945 and "Memorandum Submitted to the Secretary of State by the American Zionist Emergency Council - December 12, 1945," 740.00116EW/12-1345, NA; "Will War Criminals Determine Palestine's Destiny?" (advertisement), NYT, 21 March 1946, 18.

387 Harold Callender, "Mufti Disappears; British Prod Paris," NYT, 11 June 1946, 1; "American Zionist Leaders Say Mufti's 'Escape' Will Promote Pogroms in Palestine," JTA, 12 June 1946, 1; "U.S. Zionist Leaders Charge Bevin with Anti-Semitism at Huge Protest Demonstration," JTA, 13 June 1946, 1; "The Mufti Must Be Brought to Trial! We Demand Congressional Action!" (advertisement), NYP, 1 June 1946, 37.

388 Celler to Connelly, 28 June 1946, cited in Cohen, *Truman,* 132.

389 Cohen, *Truman,* 137; Flynn to Truman, 30 July 1946, cited in Cohen, *Truman,* 142. In a diary entry on February 12, 1943, Wallace wrote: "Flynn is very much prejudiced against the Jews and urged me to read a book by Hilaire Belloc about the Jews. [Probably Belloc's *The Jews*, published by Houghton Mifflin in 1922.] He bemoaned the fact that the Jews had control of all phrases of the amusement business, movies, radios, song writers, theater, etc. He said the trouble with their having control is that in this way they consciously or unconsciously impose on all the people in the United States their own ideals of what culture really is." (Blum, 189-190)

390 Blum, 606-607; Cohen, *Truman,* 8, 9, 13; Rebecca Dana and Peter Carlson, "Harry Truman's Forgotten Diary," *Washington Post,* 11 July 2003, 10; Truman to Thomas, 19 November 1947, Correspondence between Truman and Thomas, HSTP.

391 Bruce J. Evensen, *Truman, Palestine, and the Press: Shaping Conventional Wisdom at the Beginning of the Cold War* (New York: Greenwood Press, 1992), 142.

392 Cohen, *Truman,* 136.

393 Inverchapel to Foreign Office, 31 July 1946, FO 371/52548, PRO.

394 Wise to Frankfurter, 31 October 1946, Box 109, SSW-AJHS.

395 Truman to Bess, 15 September 1946, in Robert H. Ferrell, ed. *Dear Bess: The Letters from Harry to Bess Truman 1910-1959* (New York: W.W. Norton, 1983), 537; Cohen, *Truman,* 143; Inverchapel to

Foreign Office, 14 August 1946, FO 371/57693, PRO; Inverchapel to Foreign Office, 19 August 1946, CO 733/467/76021/48/3, PRO; Notes of the Acheson-Inverchapel conversation, 3 October 1946, 867N.01/10-346, NA; Inverchapel to Bevin, 22 November 1946, FO 371/52571, PRO; Ben-Gurion to Silver, 9 October 1946, Weizmann Archives, Rehovot, Israel; Truman to Bess, 15 September 1946, *Dear Bess*, 537; Bickerton, 193, 197.

396   "Let the U.S. Speak Out!" (editorial), *Boston Jewish Advocate*, 1 May 1947, 2; "The Palestine Executions" (editorial), *Kansas City Jewish Chronicle*, 25 April 1947, 2; Harry S. Truman, *Memoirs - Volume 2: Years of Trial and Hope 1946-1952* (Garden City, NY: Doubleday, 1956), 158.

397   Truman, *Memoirs*, 158; Niles notes, 13 May 1947, File: "Foreign-Palestine," Box 184, HSTP; Cohen, *Truman*, 156.

398   Clifford memo to Truman, 19 November 1947, cited in Cohen, *Truman*, 60; Cohen, *Truman*, 151, 156, 158-159; Walter Millis, ed. *The Forrestal Diaries* (New York: Viking Press, 1951), 344.

399   Cohen, *Truman*, 174-75; "Silver Warns of Greater Bloodshed in Palestine if U.S. Embargo on Arms is Not Lifted," JTA, 8 February 1948, 1.

400   "To the United States and the United Nations" (advertisement), 19 January 1948, *New York Herald Tribune*, 11; Celler, Murray et al to Lovett, 10 March 1948, and Lovett to Celler, 27 March 1948, File: "Israel (Palestine) Correspondence 1948," Emanuel Celler Papers [hereafter ECP], Library of Congress; "Truman Urged to Lift Embargo On Arms to Jews in Palestine," *New York Herald Tribune* [hereafter NYHT], 19 January 1948, 1; "J.W.V. Appeals to Government to Lift Embargo on Arms to Middle East," JTA, 16 January 1948, 2; "House Hears Plea for Lifting of State Department Embargo on Palestine Arms," JTA, 23 January 1948, 3; "Jewish Federations Parley Asks U.S. to Lift Embargo on Shipment of Arms to Palestine," 27 January 1948, 1; "State Department Does Not Intend to Modify Arms Embargo to Palestine, Marshall Says," JTA, 29 January 1948, 1; "Senate Hears Criticism of U.S. Policy on Palestine; Lifting of Embargo is Asked," JTA, 5 February 1948, 2; "U.S. Govt. Giving 'Aid and Comfort' to Arabs, Lehman Charges in Washinton Address," JTA, 18 March 1948, 1; "100,0000-Signature Petition for Lifting Palestine Arms Embargo Submitted to State Dept.," JTA, 31 March 1948, 2.

401   Myers to Truman, 4 March 1948, cited in Cohen, *Truman*, 181.

402   Evensen, 153-154; Bickerton, 218-219.

403   Cohen, *Truman*, 210-211; Henderson to Lovett, 22 April 1948, in *Foreign Relations of the United States - 1948, Volume V: The Near East, South Asia, and Africa* [hereafter *FRUS 1948*] (Washington, D.C.: U.S. Government Printing Office, 1976), 841.

404   Memorandum by Robert McClintock, 12 May 1948, *FRUS - 1948*, 972-976; Cohen, *Truman*, 212-213.

405   Cohen, *Truman*, 215-216.

406   Henderson to Rusk, 20 November 1977, cited in Cohen, *Truman*, 90.

407   Leon I. Feuer, "Abba Hillel Silver: A Personal Memoir," AJA 19 (November 1967), 107-127.

408   Harold L. Ickes, "Man to Man," NYP, 24 May 1948, 23; Celler to Jewish Telegraphic Agency, 9 July 1948, Subject File: Israel (Palestine) Correspondence 1948, ECP; Robert J. Donovan, "Platform Stand On Israel Stirs Up a New Fight," NYHT, 13 July 1948, 1.

409   Memo, Wise to Lipsky and Shultz, 7 June 1938, File: American Jewish Congress, SSW-AJHS; Wise to Neumann, 13 October 1936, in Voss, 217.

410   Many popular accounts assert that Eisenhower received as much as 40% of the Jewish vote in 1956. One of many examples is the popular textbook *Jews in American Politics*, edited by L. Sandy Maisel (New York: Rowman & Littlefield, 2001), which on p.153 cites the 40% figure and gives as its source Stephen D. Isaacs, *Jews and American Politics* (Garden City, NY: Doubleday, 1974). The figure appears on p. 152 of Isaacs's book, but has no source note to support it. For evidence that the Jewish vote for Eisenhower in 1956 actually was approximately 25%, see Moses Rischin, "Our Own Kind": Voting by Race, Creed, or National Origin (Santa Barbara, CA: Fund for the Republic, 1960), 4, 11, 23, 28; Lawrence H. Fuchs, "American Jews and the Presidential Vote," *American Political Science Review*, 49 (June 1955), 388; Maurice

G. Guysenir, "Jewish Vote in Chicago," *Jewish Social Studies* 20 (October 1958), 198, 200, 202; and "Jewish Vote Triples for Nixon; Jewish Majority Goes for McGovern," JTA, 9 November 1972.

411   There were approximately 2 million Jews in New York City in 1976, of whom an estimated two-thirds, or about 1.3 million, were of voting age. Given the typical turnout rate among Jews of 75% in presidential elections, it may be estimated that about 975,000 Jewish voters went to the polls in the city. The 70-30 split of the Jewish vote in favor of Carter means that Carter won 682,000, and Ford 293,000. But a 52-48 split would have meant 536,000 Jewish votes for Carter, and 439,000 for Ford. Carter's loss of 146,000 Jewish votes, and Ford's gain of 146,000, would have been enough for Ford to overcome Carter's statewide margin of victory of 289,000.

412   Philip Slomovitz, "White House Refutes Fears That Carter, if Re-elected, Could Resort to Pressuring Israel," JTA, 15 August 1980, 1; and Joseph Polakoff, "Focus on Issues : Three Candidates Woo Jewish Voters," JTA, 10 September 1980, 3.

Index

Acheson, Dean, 151, 152
Achilles, Theodore, 77
Adams, John, 47
Adams, John Quincy, 47
Adler, Stella, 87
Akzin, Benjamin, 89
Alaska refugee settlement proposal, 75, 138
Alfange, Dean, 105, 155
Allen, Henry J., 18
Allied Declaration on Nazi mass murder, 85, 119
America First movement, 72, 195 n156
American Committee on the Rights of Religious Minorities, 14
The American Hebrew, 14
American Jewish Committee, 13, 27, 50, 67, 189 n61
American Jewish Conference, 103-104, 118
American Jewish Congress, 6, 64, 113, 118, 124-125
American Jewish Joint Distribution Committee, 9-11, 14-15, 24-25, 31, 36, 37, 40, 83, 96, 186 n38, 188 n50, 189 n66, 193 n136
American League for a Free Palestine, see Bergson Group
American Legion, 78
American Palestine Committee, 60, 138

American Relief Administration, 5, 10-11, 23, 25-27, 30, 31, 33, 36, 38-40, 196 n148, 196 n150
American Zionist Emergency Council, 122, 134, 145, 147, 148-149, 154
Anderson, John, 163
Anglo-American Committee of Inquiry on Palestine, 143, 149, 151
Anglo-American Convention on Palestine, 54-55, 57
Arvey, Jacob, 157
Austin, Warren, 156
Ayers, Eben, 156

Baker, George C., 40
Baldwin, Joseph, 105
Baldwin, Raymond, 155
Balfour Declaration, 11, 45, 47, 49, 53, 54, 55, 57, 61, 90, 138, 199 n212
Baltimore Jewish Times, 120
Barbour, Warren, 104
Baruch, Bernard, xi, 18-19, 21, 75
Becker, James, 7, 10-12, 25, 29
Bellamy, Ralph, 104
Ben-Gurion, David, 85
Ben-Horin, Eliahu, 79-81, 86, 89, 90, 144-145
Bennet, William S., 104, 147
Bentwich, Norman, 67
Berenger, Henry, 68

Bergson, Peter, 86, 105
Bergson Group, 91, 96, 112, 125, 127
　American League for a Free
　　Palestine, 146
　Emergency Committee to Save the
　　Jewish People of Europe, 102,
　　103, 147
　Emergency Conference to Save the
　　Jewish People of Europe, 94,
　　96-102, 116, 131, 138
　lobbying on Capitol Hill, 104-105
　march by 400 rabbis in
　　Washington, 104 107, 120
　newspaper advertisements of, 93,
　　94, 104, 107, 126, 142, 147,
　　162
　opponents of, 111
　rescue resolution in Congress,
　　105-107, 111, 115, 139
　salute to Denmark and Sweden,
　　104
　supporters of, 94
Berle, Adolph, 73, 91
Bermuda Conference (1943), 90-94,
　105, 120
Bernstein, Herman, 15-16, 19, 21,
　48-49
Bevin, Ernest, 143, 151, 153
Bilbo, Theodore, 119
Billikopf, Jacob, 31
Bisgyer, Maurice, 61
Blackstone Memorial, 138
Bloom, Sol, 92, 105-106
B'nai B'rith, 61
Bogen, Boris, 11, 25-26, 31, 37
Borah, William, 58
Boston Jewish Advocate, 153
Brandeis, Mrs. Alice, 98
Brandeis, Louis, 31, 54, 58, 69, 194 n146,
　201 n236, 201 n238, 202 n245

Brewster, Owen, 133, 139, 155
Bricker, John W., 137
Bridges, Styles, 126, 129
Brooklyn Jewish Examiner, 45
Brown, Cecil, 156
Brown, Walter Lyman, 39
Burstein, Rabbi Abraham, 19
Bush, George H.W., 164
Bush, George W., 164
Byrnes, James, 143, 151

Cannon, Bishop James, 99
Caplane, Louis D., 99
Carter, Jimmy, 163, 164
Castle, William R., 41, 45-46, 50,
　195 n156
Celler, Emanuel, 45, 92, 103,
　114, 115, 120, 134, 149, 152,
　155, 159
Central Conference of American
　Rabbis, 109
Chancellor, Sir John, 43, 56
Chicago Daily News, 135
Christian Zionism, 48, 58, 60, 128,
　137-139
Churchill, Winston, 78, 90, 115-116
Clifford, Clark, 154, 157
Clinton, Bill, 164
Cohen, Ben, 115
Cohen, Rabbi Armond, 98
Committee for Polish Relief, 82
Committee for the Relief of
　Belgium, 4
Committee to Arm the Jewish
　State, 155
Committee to Feed the Small
　Democracies, 82, 99
Compton, Ranulf, 126
Congress Weekly, 124
Connally, Tom, 107

INDEX 217

Coolidge, Calvin, xi, 15
Coolidge, Grace, 77
Cotton, John, 57-58, 59
Coughlin, Father Charles, 67, 111, 202-203 n255
Council on Foreign Relations, 71, 73
Cox, James, 110
Cox, Oscar, 105, 111, 115
Curley, James, 127
Curtis, Charles, 60, 138

Daughters of the American Revolution, 78
Davis, John W., 110
Dawes, Charles G., 46, 51
Dearborn Independent, 14
Debs, Eugene, 110
Demby, Bishop Edward Thomas, 98
Democratic congressmembers sign letter against Palestine embargo, 155
Denikin, General Anton, 37
Der Tog, 112, 145
Dewey, Thomas, 114-116, 122, 133, 136, 151, 152, 159, 163
Dickstein, Samuel, 45, 66, 92, 100, 120-121, 127
Die Naye Velt, 40
Dmowski, Roman, 26, 190 n81, 190 n 82
Dodd, William E., 64
Domengeaux, John, 94
Doughty, Robert, 156-157
DuBois, Josiah E., Jr., 106-107, 115, 116-118
Dukakis, Michael, 164
Duff, Douglas, 42

Eden, Anthony, 88
Eisenhower, Dwight, 9, 163

Emergency Committee to Save the Jewish People of Europe, see Bergson Group
Enderis, Guido, 69
Epstein, Eliahu, 152
Evian Conference (1938), 73-74, 91, 121
Factory Investigating Commission, 20
Feinberg, Rabbi Abraham, 109
Feuer, Leon, 159
Ferguson, Homer, 105
Field, Henry, 74
Fink, Reuben, 13
Fischer, Judge, 37
Fish, Hamilton, 47, 55-56, 59, 199 n218
Fitzpatrick, Paul, 150, 154
Flynn, Ed, 150, 154, 156, 157, 212 n389
Fonda, Henry, 77
Ford, Henry, 14
Ford, Gerald, 164
Foreign Policy Association, 67
Forrestal, James, 151, 154
Fortune, 129
Forverts, 40, 112, 134
Franco, Francisco, 72
Frank, Anne, 63
Frank, Mrs. Edith, 63
Frank, Margot, 63
Frankfurter, Felix, 30, 31, 58, 201 n240

Galpin, Perrin, 99
Gibson, Hugh, 4-5, 27, 30-34, 126, 192 n112, 192 n118
Gillette, Guy, 105, 139
Gilman, J. Thayer, 195 n160
Gladstone, Jacob, 127
Goldberg, A.M., 39-40
Goldberg, B.Z., 112
Goldman, Solomon, 204 n270

Goldmann, Nahum, 85, 91, 114
Goldstein, Israel, 92, 135
Goldstein, Jonah, 51-52, 143
Goldwater, Barry, 163
Gone with the Wind, 87
Goodheart, Captain Arthur L., 32
Gorky, Maxim, 38
Gorski, W.O., 28
Grafton, Samuel, 102, 118
Grant, Ulysses, 138
Gray, Joseph, 69
Greater New York Jewish War Relief Fund, 35
Green, William, 97
Gross, Rabbi Louis, 45
Grove, Colonel William, 23-24, 189 n66

Hadassah, 120
Haganah, 80
Hannegan, Robert, 144, 154
Hansbrough, Henry C., 18
Harding, Warren, xi, 15, 39, 110
Harrison, Benjamin, 138
Harrison, Earl G., 142-143
Hart, Henry M., Jr., 85
Hart, Moss, 87
Hashomer Hatzair, 144
Haskell, Colonel William N., 39, 196 n148
Hawkes, Albert, 129, 155
Hayes, Helen, 77
Hayes, Patrick Cardinal, 72
Hays, Arthur Garfield, 97
Hearst, William Randolph, 97, 105
Hecht, Ben, 87-88
Held, Adolph, 84
Henderson, Alan, 44
Henderson, Loy, 159
Herzog, Chief Rabbi Yitzhak, 98

Hillquit, Morris, 109-110
Hitler, Adolf, xii, 9, 64, 73, 76, 80, 83, 91, 93, 122, 124, 128, 153
  Americans' view of, 68-69
  meets Herbert Hoover, 70-71
Hoover, Herbert
  as American Relief Administration chief, 5, 15, 23-30, 33, 36, 37-40
  awareness of the Holocaust, 82
  and Bergson Group, 94, 122, 161
  biography, 2-3, 161, 185 n10
  Central Africa refugee settlement proposal, 75-76, 144, 162
  and the Emergency Conference to Save the Jewish People of Europe, 96-97, 100-101, 116
  chairs Commission on the Organization of the Executive Branch (1947-1949), 148
  and evacuation of Americans from Europe, 3-4
  chairs Famine Emergency Committee (1946-1947), 148
  and Great Depression, 9, 59-61, 110, 119, 161
  and immigration restrictions, xii, 66-67
  interaction with American Jews, xi, 14, 47, 95, 161, 194 n146
  Iraq plan, 144-146, 162
  and isolationism, 71-73
  and post of League of Nations High Commissioner for Refugees, 67-68
  meets Adolf Hitler, 70-71
  member of the American Committee on the Rights of Religious Minorities, 14

naval negotiations with British, 46-51, 55-56, 198 n206, 198 n207, 200 n225, 200 n226, 200 n231
and Palestine plank of Republican platform, 133-134, 158-159, 162
Presidential campaign of 1920, 15
Presidential campaign of 1924, 15
Presidential campaign of 1928, 15-20, 188 n54, 188 n59
Presidential campaign of 1932, 61
relationship with Revisionist Zionists, 81
relationships with aides, 1-2, 8
and Republican national convention of 1944, 129
and Republican presidential nomination, 71, 77, 102
response to Arab riots in Palestine (1929), 41, 43, 44-51
response to the Holocaust, 92, 102, 161
response to Kristallnacht, 76
response to persecution of Jews in Germany, 64-65, 161
response to pogroms in Poland, xi, 6-7, 14-15, 23-30, 33-35
as Secretary of Commerce, 15
as United States Food Administration chief, 4-6, 10-11, 15
on Wagner-Rogers bill, 64, 77-78, 161
and *We Will Never Die*, 87
World War I relief efforts of, xi, 1-5, 8, 12, 117, 161, 185 n16, 186 n21
World War II relief efforts of, 82

Zionism, view of, 48, 49, 57-58, 59-61, 128, 138, 161
Hoover, Mrs. Lou Henry, 7, 38
Hope-Simpson Commission, 56
Hoskins, Lt.-Col. Harold, 102
Houghteling, Laura Delano, 63-64, 78
Hughes, Charles E., 28
Hughes, Langston, 98
Hull, Cordell, 82, 100, 114, 115, 124
Hurley, Brig.-Gen. Patrick, 102
Hurston, Zora Neale, 98
Husseini, Haj Ami al- (Grand Mufti), 42, 148-149
Hyman, Joseph, 96

Ibn Saud, 141
Ickes, Harold, 75, 76, 97, 159
Ihud, 144
Immigration Acts (of 1921 and 1924), 14, 63, 187 n45
Immigration of European Jews to the United States, 65-66, 99-100, 121, 126
Independent Jewish Press Service, 134, 208 n346
Innitzer, Archbishop Theodor, 72
Intergovernmental Committee on Political Refugees, 74
International Jewish Press Bureau, 39
Inverchapel, Lord, 151-152
Irgun Zvai Leumi, 86
Isacson, Leo, 156
Ives, Irving 153

Jabotinsky, Eri, 112
Jabotinsky, Vladimir Ze'ev, 80, 88, 89
Jacobson, Eddie, 158-159
Jadwin, Maj.-Gen. Edwin, 32-35, 37, 192 n103, 192 n118

Jewish Agency for Palestine, 50, 51, 55, 85, 152
Jewish Forum, 121
Jewish Frontier, 92, 121, 127
Jewish Telegraphic Agency, 45, 81, 134
Jewish Tribune, 19
Jewish Vote
    for Al Smith (1928), 16-17, 19-21, 110, 189 n61
    for Barry Goldwater, 163
    for Dwight Eisenhower, in 1952, 163
    for Dwight Eisenhower, in 1956, 163, 213 n410
    for Eugene Debs (1920), 110
    for Franklin Roosevelt, in 1932, 61, 110, 111
    for Franklin Roosevelt, in 1936, 111
    for Franklin Roosevelt, in 1940, 111
    for Franklin Roosevelt, in 1944, 115, 116, 132-137, 163, 165
    for George McGovern, 163
    for Gerald Ford, 214 n411
    for Harry Truman, 1948, 160, 165
    for Herbert Hoover, in 1928, xii, 15-21
    for Herbert Hoover, in 1932, 61, 110
    for James Cox (1920), 110
    for Jimmy Carter, 163, 165, 214 n411
    for John Anderson, 163
    for John W. Davis (1924), 110
    for Republicans in the 1940s, 102, 111, 112, 114, 116, 119, 128, 133-135, 162
    for Richard Nixon, in 1960, 163
    for Richard Nixon, in 1968, 163
    for Richard Nixon, in 1972, 163
    for Robert La Follette, (1924), 110
    for Ronald Reagan, 163
    for Thomas Dewey, in 1944, 163
    for Thomas Dewey, in 1948, 160
    for Warren Harding (1920), 110
    in 1945 New York City mayoral election, 143, 151
    in 1946 congressional elections, 144, 146, 149-152
    in 1948 congressional election in the Bronx, 155-156
    in 1948 presidential election, 152, 154-159
    Jewish opposition to the idea of, 16, 109
Jewish War Veterans, 155
Joint Emergency Committee for European Jewish Affairs, 91, 92-93
Johnson, Edwin, 98
Johnson, Homer, 32, 34-35, 190 n103

Kansas City Jewish Chronicle, 153
Kennedy, John A., 157
Kerry, John, 164
King, William H., 138-139
Klein, Arthur, 156
Knabenshue, Paul, 43-44, 46, 50-57, 59, 197 n196, 199-200 n222
Knox, Frank, 77
Kook, Chief Rabbi Abraham Isaac, 86
Kook Hillel, see Bergson, Peter
Ku Klux Klan, 67

La Follette, Robert, 110
La Guardia, Fiorello, 105
Landman, Rabbi Isaac, 109
Landon, Alf, 76, 77, 90, 129, 133

INDEX

Langer, William, 89
Lansing, Robert, 26, 37
Lehman, Herbert, 89, 155, 157, 189 n61
Lehman, Irving, 65, 153
Lerner, Max, 96, 99
Life, 129
Lincoln, Abraham, 34, 47
Lindbergh, Charles, 72, 119
Lippmann, Walter, 52
Littell, Norman, 134
Lodge, Henry Cabot, 47, 89
Lodge-Fish resolution, 47
London, Meyer, 110
London Times, 45, 47
Long, Breckinridge, 99, 105-106, 116, 120, 208 n346
Lovett, Robert, 157
Lowenstein, Harriet, 31
Lowenthal, Max, 157
Luce, Clare Boothe, 89, 96
   biography, 129
   fights for rights of women and African-Americans, 130-131
   foreign policy views of, 129
   keynote address at 1944 GOP convention, 131\
   and Palestine plank of Republican convention, 129, 133, 162
   political career, 130
   supports Bergson Group, 131
   supports Revisionist Zionists, 126, 130, 131-132
Luce, Henry, 129

MacDonald, Malcolm, 76, 114
MacDonald, Ramsay, 47, 49, 51-54, 56, 58, 59, 60
Mack, Julian, 61
Magnes, Judah, 53, 144, 199 n212

Madariaga, Salvador de, 67
Marshall, Gen. George C., 122-123, 157-158
Marshall, Louis, xi, 7, 12-14, 15, 16, 28, 29, 30, 35, 51, 60, 80-81, 187 n42, 187 n43, 193 n134
Martin, Edward, 126, 147
Mavrogordato, Arthur, 43
McCormick, Anne O'Hare, 69
McGovern, George, 163
McGrath, J. Howard, 154
McDonald, James G., 67-68, 77, 84-85, 127
McIntyre, Marvin, 114, 115
Mead, James, 153
Moffat, Jay Pierrepoint, 63
Moore, Herbert, 99
Morgen Zhurnal, 127, 134, 145
Morgenthau, Henry, Jr., 65, 98, 105-107, 111, 115-117
Morgenthau, Henry, Sr., 29-30, 32-35, 37, 192 n103, 192 n118
Morrison-Grady plan, 144, 149-151
Mowrer, Edgar Ansel, 127
Murray, James, 155
Murray, Wallace, 57-58, 59
Mussolini, Benito, 76
Mufti, see Husseini, Haj Ami al-
Muni, Paul, 87
Murray, Philip, 97
Myers, Francis, 156

Nansen, Fridtjof, 145
Nash, George, 6
The Nation, 127, 148
National Democratic Club, 104
National Jewish Ledger, 121, 127
National Polish Relief Committee, 25
National Republican Club, 104
Nelson, Donald M., 88

Netanyahu, Benzion, 89, 123, 126, 128-129, 133, 142, 146-148, 162
The New Leader, 94
The New Palestine, 15, 48, 50
The New Republic, 123
New York Herald Tribune, 155
New York Post, 102, 118, 126, 127, 148
New York Sun, 132
New York Times, 46, 47, 69, 70, 71, 77, 82, 83, 86, 104, 109, 116, 126, 131, 149, 152
New York Tribune, 38
New York World, 52
New Zionist Organization of America (U.S. Revisionists), 89-90, 122, 123, 131, 135, 147-148
Niles, David, 84, 152, 153
Nixon, Richard, 163
North American Newspaper Alliance, 43
North China Star, 132
Norwegian Journal of Commerce and Shipping, 99
Nye, Gerald, 89

Obama, Barack, 164
O'Dwyer, William, 143, 154

Paderewski, Ignace, 26-28, 33, 35, 190 n81, 191 n86
Passfield White Paper, 56, 58, 60
Pearson, Drew, 103, 120, 151
Pehle, John, 117-118
Peliura, Simon, 37
Pets Magazine, 78
Philadelphia Public Ledger, 52
Pilsudski, Jozef, 190 n81
Pine, Max, 37
PM, 96, 104, 120, 126, 148, 156
Polish Information Bureau, 28

Polish National Committee, 14, 189 n66
Pope Pius XII, 85-86
Pro-Palestine Committee, 58
President's Advisory Committee on Political Refugees, 74, 77, 84, 121, 127
Propper, Karl, 155-156
The Protocols of the Elders of Zion, 14

Rainey, Henry T., 138
Rankin, John, 119
Randolph, John, 50
Raskob, John J., 18
Reagan, Ronald, 163
Republican congressmembers
  sign pro-Zionist letter to Truman in 1945, 146
  sign pro-Zionist statement in 1945, 146
  support American League for a Free Palestine, 146
  support Political Action Comittee for Palestine, 146
Republican National Committee, 61, 97
Rescue Resolution, see Bergson Group
Reston, James, 152
Revisionist Zionists in America, see New Zionist Organization of America
Rhoade, Max, 58, 199 n218
Riegner, Gerhart, 83
Robinson, Edward G., 87
Rogers, Edith, 77
Rogers, Will, Jr., 93, 98, 105, 139
Rokeach, Israel, 155
Roosevelt, Eleanor, 88, 94, 96, 98
Roosevelt, Franklin, xi, 61, 71, 89, 141

and Palestine issue, 102-103, 120, 122-124, 126, 136
policy in liberated North Africa, 120
relationship with American Jews, 95, 103-104, 112-114, 119, 123-125, 132-133, 136, 162
relationship with Herbert Hoover, 68, 77, 117
response to the Holocaust, 84, 88, 90, 100, 127, 161
response to persecution of Jews in Germany, 64-65, 69, 73-74, 76, 85, 161
on Wagner-Rogers bill, 63, 78, 161
Roosevelt, Theodore, 47
Rose, Billy, 87-88
Rosen, Joseph, 40
Rosenberg, James, 40
Rosenblum, Edward, 21
Rosenman, Samuel, 19-20, 90, 103, 114, 115, 135, 143, 189 n61
Rosenwald, Julius, 6, 16, 19, 59
Roswoj, 30
Rothenberg, Morris, 113-114
Russian Information Bureau, 10

Sack, Leo, 154
Sackett, Frederic, 64
San Francisco Chronicle, 70, 81
Scarface, 87
Schiff, Frieda, 9
Schiff, Jacob, 9, 29, 187 n42
Scott, Hugh, 103
Sergio, Lisa, 99
Shaw Commission, 54-56
Sheean, Vincent, 43-44
Sherman, Karl 154
Shultz, Lillie, 113-114
Sidney, Sylvia, 87

Silver, Rabbi Abba Hillel, 95, 103, 122-124, 126, 132-134, 141-142, 145, 147, 151-152, 154- 155, 162
Smith, Al, 16-21, 105, 110, 188 n54, 188 n59, 189 n61
Smith, Harold D., 87
Smith Independent Organization, 18
Smith, Paul, 70
Smoot, Reed, 18
Social Justice, 67
Sokolow, Nahum, 48
Sokolsky, George, 129, 132, 133
Spangler, Harrison, 97
Stimson, Henry, 44, 46, 47-48, 52, 57-58, 117, 201 n236
Stirling, Rear Admiral Yates, Jr., 99
Stone, Harlan, 60, 96, 138
Stone, I.F., 118, 127
Strauss, Lewis, xi, 6, 11, 12, 14, 41-48, 57, 64
biography, 1, 8-9
Central Africa refugee settlement proposal, 75-76
Presidential campaign by Hoover (1928), 15, 16, 19-21
relationship with Herbert Hoover, 7-8, 186 n29
response to Arab riots in Palestine (1929), 49
response to pogroms in Poland, 23-30, 35
Zionism, view of, 60-61, 80-81
Sulzberger, Arthur Hays, 86
Synagogue Council of America, 92, 135
Syrkin, Marie, 127

Taft, Martha, 89
Taft, Robert, 89, 105, 122, 124, 125, 128, 129, 133, 143, 162

Taylor, Myron, 96
Thomas, Elbert, 107, 138-139, 151
Thomas, Lowell, 94
Thompson, Dorothy, 73
Time, 129
Tobey, Charles, 139, 155
Truman, Bess, 152
Truman, Harry, xi, 141
    antisemitic remarks by, 150-151
    embargo on weapons to Palestine, 154-156, 159-160
    and Jewish vote, 141, 144, 149, 152-154, 157-160
    Palestine policy of, 142-144, 147, 150, 153-158
Tucker, Bishop Henry St. George, 96-97, 99
Tully, Grace, 117

United Hebrew Resistance, 142
United Jewish Appeal, 126, 152
United Nations Special Committee on Palestine, 153
United States Food Administration, 1-2, 4, 10
Untermeyer, Samuel, 49
Utley, Clifton, 156

Van Kleeck, Mary, 94
Van Paassen, Pierre, 130-131, 142
Vandenberg, Arthur, 95, 155
Vanity Fair, 129
Vassar Review, 69
Virgin Islands refugee settlement proposal, 75
Vogue, 129

Wagner, Robert, 59, 77, 136, 143, 155
Wagner-Rogers bill, xii, 63, 77-78, 105, 138, 161

Waldman, Morris, 67
Walker, Jimmy, 59, 201 n240
Wallace, Henry, 104, 116, 123, 141, 150, 151, 156, 212 n389
Wallenberg, Raoul, 118
War Industries Board, 19
War Refugee Board, 116-119, 121, 125, 127, 136, 162, 165
Warburg, Felix, xi, 7, 9-11, 12, 13, 16, 17, 21, 31, 49, 50, 51-53, 56-57, 59, 60, 61, 80-81, 189 n61, 197 n203
Warburg, Paul, 9
Warburg, Max, 9
Watson, Edwin "Pa," 85
We Will Never Die, 87-88, 94
Weizmann, Chaim, 49, 51, 55, 56-57, 60, 132, 155, 199 n212
Welles, Orson, 104
Welles, Sumner, 73, 83, 91, 94, 96
Wheeler, Burton, 89
White, William Allen, 97
White Paper (1939), 114, 122-123, 125, 126
William, Maurice, 98
Willkie, Wendell, 96, 98, 105, 112, 116, 117, 122
Wilson, Hugh, 68, 70
Wilson, Woodrow, 2, 3, 4, 26, 28, 29, 30, 33, 37-38, 47, 75, 138, 147, 154, 190 n81
Wise, Rabbi Stephen S., 6, 73, 147
    awareness of the Holocaust, 83-85
    and Bergson Group, 96-97
    criticism of Bermuda Conference, 92
    and Franklin Roosevelt, 64-65, 69, 89, 90, 95, 102-103, 114, 162
    criticism of Herbert Hoover, 72, 77

and Jewish vote issue, 109, 134-136, 152
and Mufti issue, 149
and Palestine issue, 122-125, 141, 151
and Palestine plank of Democratic convention, 134
and Palestine plank of Republican convention, 134
testimony on congressional rescue resolution, 105

World Jewish Congress, 64, 83, 85, 91, 114, 121
World Zionist Congress (1929), 50
World Zionist Executive, 48
World Zionist Organization, 49, 132

Zangwill, Israel, 16
Zion, Sidney, 87
Zionews, 131, 133
Zionist Organization of America, 47, 48, 58, 204 n270

CPSIA information can be obtained
at www.ICGtesting.com
Printed in the USA
LVHW080846300920
667489LV00017B/2337